The Common Good

First published in 2004 by Polity Press Ltd
Polity Press

Reprinted 2006, 2007

Polity Press
65 Bridge Street
Cambridge CB2 1UR, UK

Polity Press
350 Main Street
Malden, MA 02148, USA

A catalogue record for this book is available from the British Library.

Library of Congress Cataloging-in-Publication Data
Etzioni, Amitai.
    The common good / Amitai Etzioni.
        p. cm.
Includes bibliographical references and index.
    ISBN: 978-0-7456-3266-7
    ISBN: 978-0-7456-3267-4 (pb)
    1. Common good. 2. Communitarianism. 3. Social values. I. Title.

JC330.15.E866 2004
320'.011–dc22

                                                                2003019620

Typeset in 10.5 on 12 pt Times New Roman
by Kolam Information Services Pvt. Ltd, Pondicherry, India

For further information on Polity, visit our website: www.polity.co.uk

Contents

Acknowledgments

I am indebted to Marjorie Heins, Peter Swire, Orin Kerr, Andrew Volmert, Jason Marsh, Shlomo Avineri, Henry Nau, Joel Rosenthal, Simon Serfati, Nancy Willard, and Eugene Volokh for critical reading of one or more chapters of this book. I am greatly indebted to Mackenzie Baris for extensive research assistance and editorial suggestions, as well as to Elizabeth Jarvis, Deirdre Mead, and Amanda Roberts. Emily Pryor prepared the book for publication.

"Are Particular Obligations Justified?" was published in *The Review of Politics* 64, no. 4 (Fall 2002): 573–98.

"Privacy as an Obligation" has not been previously published.

"Children and Free Speech" is forthcoming in the *Chicago-Kent Law Review* 79, no. 1 (Fall 2003).

"Privacy and Safety in Electronic Communications" was published in *The Harvard Journal of Law and Technology* 15, no. 2 (Spring 2002): 258–90.

"DNA Testing and Individual Rights" is forthcoming in David Lazer, ed., *The Technology of Justice: DNA and the Criminal Justice System* (Cambridge, MA: MIT Press, 2005).

"What is Political?" was published in "Der Begriff des Politischen," *The Social World* (special edition) eds. Armin Nassehi and Markus Schroer (Baden-Baden: Nomos, 2003).

"On Ending Nationalism" was published in *International Politics and Society*, no. 2 (2001): 144–53.

"Cyberspace and Democracy" was published in Henry Jenkins and David Thorburn, eds., *Democracy and New Media* (Cambridge, MA: MIT Press, 2003).

Introduction

For people not conversant with political theory or libertarian ideology, the common good (or the public interest) is a self-evident concept. It connotes those goods that serve all of us and the institutions we share and cherish – for instance, national defense or a healthy environment. The common good is much more than an aggregation of all private or personal goods. It includes things that serve no one in particular, like preserving our national monuments, and it serves members of generations not yet born, as for instance does basic research. Contributions to the common good often offer no immediate benefits, and frequently it is impossible to predict on whom such benefits will fall in the long run. Still, we invest in it not because it will necessarily or even likely benefit us, or even our children, but because we consider it a good to be nourished. In plain English, we consider it the right thing to do, by itself, for itself – which surprises only those who claim that we always have an ulterior motive.

Why would anybody be troubled by a concept such as the common good, rather than recognizing its importance, celebrating its value? Libertarians, and a fair number of those who adhere to the contemporary version of liberal political theory, hold that individuals should decide for themselves what is good, and that shared goods will arise out of the aggregation of such choices, not out of communal moral dialogues that lead to collective decisions with public policies based on them. They also fear that once there are shared formulations of the good, governments will be tempted to coerce people to serve these formulations, thereby diminishing people's liberty and autonomy, which libertarians and many liberals consider to be the goods that trump all others. It should be noted, though, that even neoclassical economics, a social science that is ideologically compatible with libertarian philosophy, recognizes that there are some goods that the market fails to provide, and therefore it is kosher to serve them collectively – basic research for instance. Economists are keen merely to keep the list of such goods as short as possible. Communitarians, who recognize liberty as merely one very important value among others such as caring and sharing, have a longer list of common goods.

Still other liberals fear that even if there is no reason to be concerned that shared formulating concepts of the common good will open the door to government enforcement, doing so will still lead to moral judgmentalism. People will chide, socially pressure, and stigmatize those who do not do their share to serve the common good – those who do not voluntarily recycle, make donations to a good cause, and so on. These fears reflect a misunderstanding of the way societies work. Societies cannot rely on people to automatically do of their own free will all that must be done, without their being encouraged by their fellow men and women. Indeed, it is these informal social forces that carry a good part of the work that must be done in society. If these forces slacken, often the government must step in. The social undergirding of the common good is the best way to limit government; to undermine the common good, in effect, fosters government intervention and expansion.

One should not, however, confuse moral judgment with judgmentalism, with the pious, self-righteous waving of fist or finger in the faces of those who do not share our moral convictions. There is nothing inherent in the concept of the common good, or the sociological insight that it is best promoted by informal communal processes, that requires it to be enforced through harsh or obnoxious means. Indeed, informal social controls work best when they are subtle, individually tailored, and inviting rather than condemning.

No society can flourish without some shared formulation of the common good. It provides criteria to draw on when the interests and values of the various groups that compose the society pull them in conflicting directions. It provides a rationale for the sacrifices members of every society have to make sooner or later for their children, for the less endowed, and for the future, among other causes. It provides a vision that guides our collective effort, as the vision of a better Europe guides those who are thickening and expanding the European Union.

The common good needs to be seen "within history." Its standing differs greatly from age to age and from one society to another.

Some societies, especially those that are totalitarian and authoritarian, use their view of the common good to demand that citizens set aside their preferences, agree to severe limitations on their autonomy, for the greater whole. They demand that their citizens find satisfaction first and foremost from doing service for whatever causes the state promotes. In such societies, one needs to curtail the demands advanced in the name of the common good and make room for greater recognition of individual expression, preferences, and choices – in short for individual rights and liberty. Most societies in earlier periods, and many today, erred on this authoritarian side of the delicate balance between the common good and autonomy that, in the judgment of this communitarian, makes for a good society.[1]

Societies can and do lose their balance in the opposite direction. As Robert Bellah and his associates showed in a widely known book *Habits of the Heart*,[2] American society has suffered from excessive individualism, a grand loss of commitment to the common good. In the 1960s, expressive individualism spread, which encouraged people to walk away from their societal obligations in order to "find themselves," to develop their identities and heed their innermost desires. In the 1980s instrumental individualism added insult to injury as Reagan, like Thatcher, made a virtue out of watching out for oneself. On top of these two waves of individualism came an explosion of a sense of entitlement and litigiousness, in the name of what was due to the individual, with precious little concern for the effects on others and the common good. In this society it was necessary to rein in excessive individualism and to shore up the common good.

As of 1990 a reaction set in, led by a group of new communitarians who should not be confused either with Asian communitarians, who are in effect authoritarian, or with the academic communitarians of the 1980s. The new communitarians included Robert Bellah, William Galston, Mary Ann Glendon, and myself, among many others.[3] The main thesis of this group was that strong individual rights presume respect for strong obligations to the common good. Since then literally thousands of groups have amended their statements of purpose to include not only rights they bestowed on members, but also responsibilities they expect their members to embrace.[4] One exception: despite concerted efforts, the United Nations Universal Declaration of Human Rights has still not been amended to include a declaration of responsibilities. Also, since the 1990s, similar themes have been embraced by other societies, especially Anglo-Saxon societies, which feared that they were leaning too far in the individualistic direction. For instance, community, and the slogan "responsibility for all, responsibility from all" played a key role in Tony Blair's first election.[5] Many Canadians found the approach attractive as their commitment to public order has strong communitarian overtones.

In this book, I assume that the reader has some basic sympathy for the notion of the common good, and focus instead on the many issues raised once its basic merit is recognized. The first chapter concerns the scope of the common good, the question of to whom we have moral obligations. There is a strong human tendency to include only the members of one's community, be it defined as family, village, or nation. However, justice may compel us to treat all human beings equally. Can particularistic obligations be justified in the face of such universal claims?

In chapter 2, the deliberations turn to a specific common good, one almost never examined: privacy. In law, social mores, and common parlance, privacy is treated as a right rather than a good or obligation. However, the conception of the common good held in nearly all cultures leads us to believe that certain activities ought to be attended to out of sight and hearing of others.[6] Over the last decades in the West, however, the notion of privacy as a social and legal obligation has declined. For instance, breast-feeding – once considered something one ought to do in the privacy of one's home – is now generally accepted in public spaces. However, does that mean that relieving oneself or sexual intercourse in public will soon be viewed similarly? We do redefine the common good, but where should new lines be drawn? On what grounds?

The third chapter is concerned with a very highly regarded common good: the well-being of children. The same libertarians and select liberals who fear the common good are also opposed to limiting the free speech of minors. Here the issue regards the consumption, rather than the production, of speech. The issue is not whether a 17-year-old student should be prevented from making a political statement, but whether children in kindergarten should be exposed to all the violent and vile materials that flood the internet, the media, and video games. Oddly, this is a matter not clearly legislated in Europe, while in the US much attention is paid to pornography, but not to the depiction of gratuitous violence, which is much more damaging to the common good and to children.

Chapters 4 and 5 deal with public safety, a common good few challenge, although most agree that it can be accorded too much weight. The issue is often framed in terms of where to draw the line between national security and individual rights. For Americans, the answer to this question was significantly altered after September 11, 2001; however, the question of where to redraw the line between safety and liberty remains. With an eye toward answering the basic question in a principled manner, I here undertake an examination of six specific measures. The often asked question of what should be tolerated or banned in the name of safety gives way to the true heart of the matter, the question of proper accountability.

I examine DNA tests in the context of fighting crime rather than enhancing national security and find that many of the criticisms leveled at DNA tests are unfounded. Indeed, if one accepts the liberal idea that it is better to let a thousand criminals walk free than to jail one innocent person, the use of DNA evidence should be embraced, celebrated, cheered, and fostered – especially by those who now criticize it, those who see liberty as *the* common good to be promoted even at the expense of other goods.

The final three chapters deal with the polity. There is a tendency to reduce society to the state. The state, to many, seems to be a clearly defined entity. It includes the head of state, the cabinet, the civil servants (or "administration,") the legislature and the court, the police and tax authorities, and so on. In contrast, society has no address, organizational chart, nor any other clearly delineated features. No wonder there are those who argue that it is a fiction. However, if we consider society as composed of families, communities, national bonds of affection, identity, and shared values, we realize the importance of society in general, especially for the formulation and informal promotion of the good. Indeed, because society is the basis for the moral deliberations from which shared formulations of the good arise – the place where the polity's claim for legitimacy is recognized or rejected – it is not merely important in its own right, but also important for the polity.

For centuries, millions of people all over the world have associated their well-being and the common good with the well-being of their nation. Indeed, nations evoke strong loyalties that often trump most, if not all, others. One tends to forget that nation-states are a relatively recent social construction, neither natural nor divine. Indeed, a strong case can be made that, in this day and age, the more we separate community from state, the more peaceful the world may become. However, for such a separation to occur, one's identity and concerns about the common good, which now involve the state, must be invested somewhere else.

Lastly, in cyberspace we now face issues that have challenged us at least since the ancient Greeks. Critics argue that our growing involvement in cyberspace undermines our communal bonds – our ability to deliberate as persons and as groups, to formulate the common good, and to govern ourselves democratically. These are the questions I explore in the closing chapter of this book.

1

Are Particularistic Obligations Justified?

If three children go hungry in a community, the members of many such communities are more distressed than if thousands starve in some faraway country.[1] Moreover, people not only care more about members of their own communities, but maintain that they are justified in doing so, that one has a higher level of obligation to one's "own kind" than to all others. Are such particularistic obligations[2] justified, and on what grounds?

This question has been the subject of an immense amount of deliberation, which is not reviewed here. This exploration is limited to an examination of communitarian justifications for particularistic obligations, and only to those in a societal rather than in a political context. That is, it concerns the obligations of members of communities, not those of citizens of states.

Introduction

Special import to communitarians

Addressing this question is of particular importance to communitarians. Those who center their social philosophy around the concept of individual rights need not recognize that collectivities (social groups, communities) have any rights or can elicit any special obligations. Indeed, Bentham argues that the very notion of the existence of a society, as distinct from an aggregate of individuals, is a fiction.[3]

In contrast, because communitarians consider shared formulations of the good essential, these formulations *ipso facto* entail particularistic moral obligations to and for the members of the communities involved. For instance, to hold that one ought to cherish one's ethnic heritage entails "do's" and "don'ts" for and to members, but not for others.

The argument could be made that given that liberals are concerned with universal rights, which the state is obligated to honor, and that communitarians deal with particularistic obligations within communities (and the society, as a community of communities),[4] there is not necessarily a conflict between these two philosophies. Indeed, one might suggest that there is no reason for liberals to object if members of communities abide by some particularistic commitments in the private realm. Such a liberal, however, may still be concerned that private commitments, if widely endorsed, will lead to state enforcement.[5] For instance, if most members of a community agree that abortion is immoral, they might well seek to use the state to ban it. The particularistic position of a community thus would become a law that might well violate one or more universal rights. Hence a liberal may well prefer not to open the door to particularistic obligations, not necessarily because they are objectionable in themselves, but in terms of what they may lead to.

Also, many liberals hold that social pressure by communities on their members to abide by particularistic obligations amounts to coercion.[6] For instance, they not only oppose laws that mandate HIV testing and disclosure of the results to one's sexual partners, but also social pressure to do so on the ground that it is coercive. Given that communities are the source of coercive social pressure, some deride them as "Salems,"[7] as places they would rather do without – one more reason they do not brook particularistic obligations.

Indeed, the basic vocabulary and paradigm of those political theories that are centered around rights, as well as those moral philosophies that are centered around universal principles and individual autonomy, do not include the concept of particularistic obligations. ("Basic" is used to remind us that there are numerous different liberal positions and that the preceding point may not fully apply to some liberals.) Even when liberals do not explicitly object to particularistic obligations, they as a rule do not examine the grounds on which these obligations may be justified. In contrast, communitarians, whose paradigm is centered around the common good as conceived by particular social entities such as communities and societies, must deal with the question of whether special commitments to these entities by their members are morally appropriate.

Communities, not state or families

The following exploration of the issue concerns only the particularistic obligations members of communities have to one another and to the common good of their communities – not obligations to the state or members of one's family. The concepts of state and society are often conflated, but the state commands special duties and can coerce compliance, raising a host of moral issues that communities do not face. These issues are explored often enough. Families, though in some sense small, intense, immediate communities, lay moral claims on their members that are readily apparent and do not apply to more extensive communities. Here, the focus is on the distinct particularistic obligations of members to their communities and to one another.

Universal AND particularistic

In many discussions that compare the liberal and communitarian positions, it is stated, or at least implied, that one has *either* particularistic obligations *or* universal ones. The two approaches seem, on the face of it, oppositional: one either respects all persons equally or holds that some individuals command higher regard than others. For instance, one holds that either all individuals are entitled to the same basic rights, say to purchase a house put up for sale, or one discriminates between members and non-members of a community, according members only the right of first refusal.

The same assumption is implied in many of the discussions comparing partiality to impartiality.[8] Although these concepts do not precisely parallel those of particularistic versus universal obligations, there are strong similarities. In both cases, it is often assumed that it is impossible both to approach all people as deserving equal regard and sometimes to hold particular people as commanding special privileges. Lawrence Blum articulates this assumption when he writes of the "unexamined presumption of traditional moral theories, especially of a Kantian or utilitarian stripe, that the impersonal demands of morality ought always and automatically to take precedence over personal pursuits."[9] Marcia Baron argues that the charge that impartialists do not allow room for partiality is incorrect, since many are not so extreme in their views.[10] This may be true for moral philosophers, but it is not the case in political theory. Indeed, one of the "hottest" current positions is that immigrants and citizens should be treated alike; or, ideally, all people of the world should be. This claim includes not only basic rights such as healthcare and employment, but *all* rights, for example voting.[11]

As I see it, the dichotomous opposition between partiality and impartiality, or between particularistic and universal obligations, holds only if we assume that one's position on this matter must be all-encompassing. But there is no logical requirement to assume such comprehensiveness, and in social reality people often combine the two orientations. The well-known concept of hyphenated Americans is centered around the notion that one has some particularistic obligations to one's ethnic community, and at the same time respects the laws of the land, including of course the Bill of Rights. Similarly, one may honor one's obligations to the nation – commonly defined as a community invested in a state, hence the reference to a member and not citizen – of which one is a member and still respect the UN Universal Declaration of Human Rights.

The observation that one can combine particularistic and universal obligations, partial and impartial considerations, is not to suggest that these orientations never come into conflict. However, this is not a reason to abandon either, and there are procedures to work out these differences and find a point of balance between the two. Here, the focus of attention is on what justifies particularistic obligations in the first place.

One may argue that such a combination may hold only as long as one limits universal rights to negative liberty rights that impose only duties of non-interference. According to this objection, if positive liberty rights are included (e.g., a right to an education), these impose a duty to provide whatever is needed to satisfy this right for all. My point, however, is that even if we owe certain obligations to provide a minimum level of well-being to all, we still may be obligated to give more to members of our own community. But this is not permissible if one's impartial morality is not rights-based but, say, some form of maximizing utilitarianism. In this case, one must ensure that the good of all, impartially considered, is an aim.[12]

This may indeed be the case, but this argument merely serves to highlight my point that one can define the opposition between the two moral orientations such that they will become mutually exclusive. However, there is no necessary reason to embrace this particular form of utilitarianism when dealing with partiality and impartiality. For the sake of the discussion that follows, I assume that there is no principled reason that a person cannot fully respect some universal rights (e.g., to free speech, to a given level of education) as well as some particularistic obligations to members of his or her community (e.g., to help a particular school). The issue explored here is not whether one ought to respect particularistic obligations *instead* of universal ones, but whether one is on justifiable moral grounds when one assumes *any obligations to members of one's community that are not extended to everyone.*

Critics fear that people will get "stuck" at a particularistic stage of development and not come to acquire universal commitments as well – thus leading to tribalism.[13] It is undoubtedly true that children acquire particularistic obligations first, especially with regards to their family members, though they are reported to display a sense of fairness, which is not particularistic, early in life. However, there is no indication that children are hindered by their early moral commitments when it comes to acquiring universal commitments such as justice and human rights. In fact, some argue that it is by first appreciating a particular person that children can acquire a sense of abstract obligations; loving a human being precedes loving humankind, and only the most dangerous zealots love humanity but not particular persons. As far as adults are concerned, in all but preliterate small tribes or isolated villages, there is no evidence that having particularistic obligations hinders the acquisition of universal obligations.

A rather different matter is to ask which obligations will take precedence when the particularistic and universal come into conflict. This is an issue often faced when communities are parts of larger entities, as in when ethnic communities are part of a larger pluralistic nation. First of all, the fact that there are different levels of obligation, while it does not speak to the issue of which takes precedence in a conflict, does show that having one kind of obligation does not prevent a person from developing the other kind. Second, it is morally preferable for universal to trump particularistic obligations – for rights to take precedence over communal bonds and values. Thus a good society does not tolerate honor killing, forced marriages, or racial discrimination simply because such practices are part of the moral culture of a particular community. On all matters not governed by universal rights, however, particularistic obligations hold sway. Critics may well find that the line between universal rights and communal bonds is not always clearly drawn, and they may even find some instances in which bonds should take precedence over rights. However, none of this undermines the claim that people can – and commonly do – respect both particularistic and universal obligations. They are not mutually exclusive, which is all that I seek to establish at this point.

Outline of the discussion

The discussion that follows first illustrates the issue at hand with a brief report about a case in which a ruling was made against parents who sought to provide special support for the particular public school their children were attending, above and beyond what they provided, through the tax system, to all children in the citywide school system. I then examine the reasons provided by those who favor particularistic obligations on empirical grounds. Next, the concepts of reciprocity and mutuality are examined to determine whether they can be drawn upon to justify particularistic obligations. This chapter closes by providing communitarian arguments that derive particularistic obligations from the roles communities have in constituting individuals, allowing them to function as full human beings, and in enabling human betterment. These arguments share elements of phenomenological, existentialist, and Aristotelian essentialist thought; however, because these designations imply many complex meanings to different people, the argument at hand follows a line of thought we will deem "constitutive communitarian arguments." Membership and participation in community is at once fundamental to human functioning and essential for the development of identity and character and human flourishing, from which emanates a moral obligation to nurture and sustain community and the particularistic obligations without which it cannot exist.

Our School vs. Schools: An Illustrative Case

In 1997, Public School 41 in Greenwich Village, part of New York City, decided to let go of a teacher for budgetary reasons. The parents reported to the school that they would raise the $46,000 needed to keep the teacher. However, Rudy Crew, New York's Schools Chancellor, ruled that such donations were unacceptable; he preferred to delve into his limited uncommitted funds to pay for the teacher rather than allow the parents to make voluntary contributions. Crew's decision reportedly avoided "opening the door to widespread efforts by parents to raise money" for their children's schools.[14] (Indeed, there were indications that parents at other New York schools were about to follow the example of those in the Village.[15]) Crew reasoned that such donations would create inequities between schools in poor and in rich districts.[16] Another reason was that such donations would undermine the willingness to support taxes (either at the current level or future increases) used to pay for the total school system, and that if parents wanted to make donations, they should make them to the total school system and not to "their" schools.

Note that the issue is not whether Village residents should have neglected their universal duties and been allowed merely to attend to their particular ones; the parents paid taxes dedicated to the total school system. The opposite question is raised: whether they should have been allowed to respond to moral claims made by their community to contribute additional funds to their particular school. Those objecting to the contributions were challenging the moral legitimacy of the claim of obligation placed on parents by the community to help their particular community's school, above and beyond what they were required to do for the whole school system.

It should be noted in passing that in this case, as in many other, the demand was not actually to make donations only to a truly universal category, say to schools in general, but merely to a larger community, in this case New York City. But the claims are made in universal terms: the parents seek to favor *their* children over "children," their affluent neighborhood over poor ones.[17]

Whether one takes the side of the parents or the Chancellor in the case at hand, it provides a vivid introduction to the question explored here in a realistic rather than hypothetical context.

Empirical, "Human Nature," Pragmatic Justifications

An often repeated argument against denying the moral appropriateness of particularistic obligations (in order to ensure commitment to universal ones) is that to do so flies in the face of human nature. I realize that many social scientists object to the use of the term "human nature" on the grounds that we have no way of studying it because all we encounter are people who are socially and culturally constructed. However, most social scientists do not raise similar objections if one points to behavioral attributes that are found widely among the members of most, if not all, societies, such as the quest (or "need") for profound affective attachments.[18] I use human nature here in this sense.

The specific ways the argument from human nature may be made differ, but the conclusion is the same: *people are unable to abide by sheer universal dictates*. For instance, J. L. Mackie writes:

> To put forward as a morality in the broad sense something which, even if it were admirable, would be an utterly impossible ideal is likely to do more harm than good. But why, it may be asked, are such moralities of universal concern impracticable? Primarily because a large element of selfishness is a quite ineradicable part of human nature.[19]

That is, at least in consequentialist terms, a position that does more harm than good is unethical.

A seemingly obvious example,[20] although, like all such, not an uncontested one,[21] is that if a person were forced to choose between saving the life of a loved one and that of a stranger, one "naturally" would choose the loved one. Thus it is imprudent to ask people to treat those to whom they have a particularistic bond as if they were the same as others.[22]

This argument takes two major forms. One is a didactic, educational argument. If you train children to jump, you should not ask them to clear a bar a yard higher than the one they currently clear, because they will soon find themselves unable to live up to your urgings and will ignore your exhortations altogether. Such excessive demands may backfire, causing resentment and detachment. Instead, you should ask children merely to jump, say, an inch higher. The assumption here is that certain demands should not be made because of the way people are. (Theoretically, children simply could do their best whether you asked for an inch or a yard.)

The same is said for the moral equivalent of stretching people too far, *a moral didactic argument*. An ethic that laid excessive requirements would lose whatever guidance it might provide to make human life more moral. Sometimes the term "heroic" is used to suggest that one should not demand that ordinary people act in ways only heroes or saints might.[23]

A different version of the same argument is implied by the body of literature dealing with supererogation. It focuses on the distinction between moral duties and acts that are praiseworthy – but not mandatory – because they are above and beyond what one can reasonably expect from human beings. The classic example is the soldier who throws himself on a grenade in order to save the lives of those around him.[24] This action is commendable, but, so the argument goes, beyond what we can reasonably expect a person to do. Though there is a universal moral obligation to save lives, normal human instincts for self-preservation are perfectly understandable – and in some sense expected – given the situation. The sacrificial act is extra-ordinary, and one cannot be faulted for not performing it.[25]

The action of the soldier who throws himself on to a live hand grenade in order to save the lives of those around him is said to be morally praiseworthy. There is, however, no such moral duty that one can lay on all soldiers.[26] Why not consider this act a duty? One can argue that one ought to cherish one's own life more than that of a group of others on some moral ground – but if this is the case, why declare such an act of sacrificial morality praiseworthy rather than morally defective? The line, in this and many other cases found in the literature on supererogation, is the same: it would be a good act, but it is "too much" to demand that it be regularly undertaken.

The soldier and the hand grenade example does not concern parti-cularistic obligations and merely illustrates the line between that which is demanded and that which is merely praised (I am not ad-dressing the legitimacy of this distinction here, and discuss super-erogation arguments only insofar as they rely on human nature for their justification); the next example can be adapted to involve parti-cularistic obligations. If a person is going to see a movie and he is asked instead to make a donation for the poor, he may do so, but it is not morally required according to supererogation scholars.[27] For those who (this author included) may not immediately see the point, the example is extended: presume the same person is asked to make such a donation every time he is on his way to see a movie.[28] (True, the cases at hand deal with self-interest; to make them communitar-ian, presume that the person is planning to buy movie tickets for her friends.) One can extend the example still further and ask – given the great number of the poor – what if the person is asked to donate the funds he sets aside for any diversion? Clearly, it is argued, that would be "asking too much," would ignore human nature. David Heyd summarizes five grounds for the distinction between " 'basic rule' (duty) and 'the higher flights of morality' (supererogation)." One is "the incapacity of ordinary men to go beyond basic duty."[29] The incapacity referred to is not an educational or training or some other such correctable lack, but a more profound one – that ordin-ary people are presumed to be inherently unable to reach a higher level of moral accomplishment; their nature hobbles them. (I am not exploring the other grounds given, because my only purpose here is to show that ethicists have used human nature as an argument to explain why one cannot expect a person to assume only universal obligations, which thus leaves room for particularistic ones.)

A colleague wrote in response to an earlier draft of this chapter that at issue here is not a concession to human fallibilities, but that:

> the general claim that a moral code is too demanding may amount to a "moral" criticism of that code. Demanding too much of people may result in them doing less than they would have done if asked to do less. Imagine I insist that nothing less than a donation of $100 to charity is morally acceptable when you are capable – psychologically or for whatever reason – only of giving $50, with the result that you give nothing. But you would have given up to $50 if I had said that you ought to give what you can. Thus the more demanding claim yields less money for charity than would have a less demanding one.

Even if one accepts this strictly consequentialist reasoning, one still must account for the reason that one is not "capable" of doing more. It seems to be a sense of congenital limitations of mortals that guides setting the moral duty at a lower level of donation rather than a higher one.

To reiterate: although not all, or even most, supererogation arguments deal with particularistic obligations or human nature, their application to the issue seems clear: abiding exclusively by comprehensive universal obligations is beyond human nature. In contrast, abiding by particularistic obligations comes naturally. Indeed, often what must be ensured is that powerful particularistic obligations do not pervert justice, fairness, the law, and much else, that obligations to one's friends, family, and community do not turn into cronyism, nepotism, and favoritism at the work place and in public office. One may argue that the fact that such obligations must be tolerated does not mean that they are morally appropriate. However, if one takes into account the human suffering and other harms that result when one strongly promotes an ethic people *cannot* adhere to, one finds here a measure of a pragmatic, consequentialist moral justification for not relying exclusively on universal obligations and hence for leaving the door open to particularistic obligations.

Reciprocity and Mutuality

Another line of argument in favor of particularistic obligations is that particularistic bonds (with friends, neighbors, co-workers) cannot be sustained without particularistic obligations. The bonds are particularistic because they entail special, favorable treatment of those encompassed compared to all those excluded. Ergo, as long as one considers the bonds at issue morally worthy, they bestow some moral justification on those obligations without which these bonds cannot be sustained.[30]

A whole school of thought, sometimes referred to as rational choice, at the heart of neoclassical economics, law-and-economics, and exchange sociology, treats particularistic bonds as based on reciprocity, which in turn is said to be based on self-interest rather than on moral obligations.[31] Their essence entails that *ego* does for *alter* what *alter* does for *ego* because both benefit. A shopkeeper pays for the delivery of goods because he needs future shipments, and the producer ships the goods because he needs a market to sell them. Initially, both sides may seek some assurances, say in the form of a deposit or a legally binding contract, but if the trade continues they will rely on the self-interest of both parties – rational choice advocates argue – to sustain the relationship.

Reciprocity, though, is a thin reed on which to rest particularistic bonds. Sociologists and anthropologists have often pointed out that even in strictly economic relations, self-interest cannot be relied upon fully, and relationships must be backed up at least by some measure of moral obligation. Reciprocity is more solidly based if it is given a moral overcoat, because reciprocal acts are never completely symmetrical, and there is typically some time gap between an act and the reciprocation. There is at least a measure of implied promise which, if not honored, undermines the relationship, but which cannot be retaliated for and hence must rest on other foundations. Moreover, the transaction costs of fully laying out all the terms of transactions and verifying that they have been abided by are prohibitive.[32] Indeed, if one of the sides finds that its self-interest is no longer served, it can often wiggle out of a contract, and the costs of enforcement may be ruinous. In short, commerce flows much more smoothly when the sides can trust each other, because there is a sense that they will abide by their mutual commitments due to their sense that obligations must be respected. As Emile Durkheim put it, contracts require some *pre*-contractual obligations.[33] (This does not mean that the parties will necessarily absorb a very large loss in order to be true to their moral obligations, but the fact that under some circumstances they might well seek to violate their moral obligations does not show that they do not have any.)[34]

If particularistic bonds that commerce draws on heavily cannot fully rely on reciprocal self-interest and require some moral

undergirding, the same holds many times over for social relationships such as those among friends, neighbors, or people who love
one another. *Here, in effect, the relationship between self-interest and
moral obligation is reversed: obligation plays a key role and self-
interest a relatively smaller one.* I refer to such a relation as one of
"mutuality."[35]

Mutuality occurs when A has a generalized (or "diffuse") relationship with B rather than a relationship involving one or more specific
exchanges.[36] Friendship, for instance, is based on open-ended commitments. A nurtures B when B is sick without keeping a registry of
time spent or thinking that if A becomes ill, he will "cash in" what
he has given, getting an equivalent number of cups of soup or bed-
side visits from B. This holds if a friend loses a loved one, needs a
loan, and so on. People care for one another because of the value
they attach to the other person and to the relationship, not primarily
because they expect to be paid back. Marriage is another relationship that is based on mutuality and not on reciprocity. It is a
common mistake to speak of marriage as a contract rather than a
covenant. The commitment is "in sickness and in health," and so on,
and not in prenuptial agreements that seek to spell out obligations
between the partners.

True, just as reciprocity contains a moral overcoat that helps sustain it, so mutuality contains an element of reciprocal self-interest
that does the same. A friendship or marriage in which the giving
flows largely one way might well gradually be undermined. However,
within very broad confines, the essence of the relationship is based
on a commitment to its value and to the other person, not to trades
and payoffs.[37] Here, particularistic obligations play a much greater
role in mutual than in reciprocal relationships. They are an integral
part of the relationship, part of its essence, even definition. Neither,
though, is sustainable without a measure of moral obligations.

One may ask whether such relationships are not sustained by affection, sympathy, and compassion rather than by either self-interest
or obligation. Indeed, there are numerous situations in which one's
affective relationships do come into conflict with self-regard. It is
then that they are sustained – to the extent that they are – by obligation. Say, for example, I have already visited my friend in the hospital many times; tonight, I would rather go to a movie, but my
sense of obligation prevails.

Communal bonds and relationships – and the particularistic obligations they entail – differ from those of commerce, friendship, and even
neighborliness, in two important ways. First, they contain a moral

commitment not merely to the other person or persons encompassed in a close relationship, but to all members of the community (including those with whom one has no personal relationship) and even future members (both children to be born to members and newcomers to join the community). Second, importantly, they contain commitment to what that particular community considers the common good, such as its environment. Here, often the element of reciprocity is especially meager and the role of obligations particularly high.

Hence, to the extent that one accepts the value of friendship, neighborliness, and communal relations and recognizes that these entail particularistic obligations, these obligations gain a considerable measure of moral endorsement. I call these "constitutive communitarian arguments." To say that if certain important, high-valued relationships cannot exist without particularistic obligations, then one ought to uphold these obligations, is like saying that if you value water, you cannot deny the value of oxygen and its bonding with hydrogen. These two elements in combination constitute water. To deny particularistic obligations is to deny the value of family, friendship, and community.

Constitutive Arguments: Obligations We Owe Our Makers

Arguably, the strongest communitarian argument in support of particularistic obligations is that they are an essential part of that which constitutes us. On closer examination, one notes that there are a couple of arguments that shade into one another but are distinct.

Community is essential for our composition

For the purpose of this book, I take for granted that particularistic relationships such as friendship, neighborliness, and love are good in themselves. (Note that I do not assume that these values trump all others, including universal obligations.) As already suggested, these valued relationships bestow a measure of moral legitimation on the obligations that these relationships entail. However, before arguing that communities also accord such legitimation to particularistic obligations, one cannot take it for granted that communities per se are good. Indeed, many liberals view them rather critically as being ascribed (membership being predetermined at birth and hence, at least initially, involuntary), authoritarian, and oppressive. Hence, the value of communities – and which kinds of communities are valuable – and the normative obligations that follow need to be carefully scrutinized. To proceed, one must first define community.[38] The definition of community here followed has two characteristics: first, a web of affect-laden relationships among a group of individuals, relationships that often crisscross and reinforce one another (as opposed to merely one-on-one or chain-like individual relationships); and second, a measure of commitment to a set of shared values, norms, and meanings, and a shared history and identity – in short, to a particular culture.

One should note that there is a strong tendency to think about communities as if they were what social scientists call a dichotomous variable rather than a continuous one, one which can vary greatly in its thickness rather than merely being present or absent. Mountains of data, recently reviewed and augmented by Robert Putnam[39] and Francis Fukuyama,[40] and long before them by Robert Bellah and his associates[41] and scores upon scores of other sociologists from Ferdinand Tönnies, Emile Durkheim, and Martin Buber on, show that when there is little or no community, people suffer physically (e.g., are more prone to have a great variety of major illnesses, including heart attacks, ulcers, and high blood pressure, as well as recover from illness more slowly[42]) and psychologically (e.g., are more prone to be depressed, have low self-esteem, or be disoriented[43]). The absence of sufficient communal bonds is also a major reason people feel detached, alienated, and powerless and either withdraw or act out in antisocial ways including joining gangs and militias (to find community) or abusing drugs and alcohol or each other.

One may object: are there not fully functional individuals who are members of no communities? The well-documented social science response is that when people are truly isolated, cut off from a fabric of bonds of affection and shared values, they are deeply diminished. Indeed, it is the mark of the modern self that its development is stunted and truncated, that it shows the ill effects of deficient connectedness as well as moral anomie. Others have noted that modern loneliness makes people neurotic, selfish, or narcissistic.[44]

In short, communities are essential for our full constitution. We can *survive* without them, but we can neither achieve nor sustain a full measure of what is considered a "fully functioning" human being without some measure of community. And thicker communities bode well for our constitution, although excessive community causes ills of its own.

Identity is particularistic

Identity is profoundly tied to communities, and thus to particularistic obligations. As Joseph de Maistre put it, "There is no such thing as *man* in the world. In the course of my life I have seen Frenchmen, Italians, Russians etc.; I know, too, thanks to Montesquieu, *that one can be a Persian*. But as for *man*, I declare that I have never met him in my life; if he exists, he is unknown to me."[45] We do not know who we are, which culture is ours, which heroes we ought to emulate, which demons we must avoid, what our origins are and much of our fate, unless we are linked up with one community or another (or with several).[46]

Michael Sandel puts it well when he writes that we cannot understand ourselves but "as the particular persons we are – as members of this family or community or nation or people, as bearers of this history, as sons and daughters of that revolution, as citizens of this republic."[47] Charles Taylor observes:

> People may see their identity as defined partly by some moral or spiritual commitment, say as a Catholic, or an anarchist. Or they may define it in part by the nation or tradition they belong to, as an Armenian, say, or a Québécois. What they are saying by this is that this provides the frame within which they can determine where they stand on questions of what is good, or worthwhile, or admirable, or of value. Put counterfactually, they are saying that were they to lose this commitment or identification, they would be at sea, as it were; they wouldn't know anymore, for an important range of questions, what the significance of things was for them.[48]

There is a tendency to collapse the contributions that community (and the particularistic obligations it entails) makes to our composition as humans with those it makes to our individual identities. The difference is that the first kind of contribution is to our existence as full-fledged human beings; the second concerns our sorting out what kind of human beings we are. The distinction is akin to the difference between learning to walk and determining which direction we shall walk. The first concerns our physical and psychological health, our general capacity to function. The second concerns which particular relationships (out of a large universe of possible ones) we will become more deeply invested in (say our ethnic group or our class, our country of origin or the one in which we currently live). It concerns how we our going to define ourselves (say, as conformist or rebellious), and which of the values that we find around us we shall particularly embrace to the point that they are going to become an integral part of our self. True, these two are connected: if our capacity to function is diminished, this will affect our ability to form and sustain our identity as well as which identity we shall be inclined to develop – and a strong identity will help nurture our ability to function. However, the fact that these two are mutually supportive does not render them a distinction without a difference.

Insofar as one's identity as a member of a community is constitutive of one's basic being as a moral agent, one has a responsibility to nurture the identity of the community itself through participation in its practices, concern for its past, present, and future members, and protection of its resources. Such responsibility may engender particularistic concern for the community above and beyond more universal obligations, and, in fact, one's understanding of universal moral obligations is itself a product of the community's role in identity formation.

To put it differently, particularistic obligations reflect a moral obligation to nurture the social environment in which people can develop, what might be called a "moral ecology." They compel us to apply to the social realm the environmental idea of stewardship toward nature, the notion that we are obligated at least not to leave the social ecology in a worse condition for future generations than it was when bequeathed to us. This argument is a specific application of a general moral position that endorses symmetry: one could not reasonably claim that we are generally entitled (as distinct from occasionally or under special conditions, e.g. when on one's deathbed) to take and not to give, to diminish the total good and not to participate in refurbishing it, within the limits of our relative ability to do so.

I cannot stress enough that the obligation of stewardship toward the moral ecology does not arise because I will be harmed if I do not nurture it. There may be sufficient stock of moral and social fortitude provided by others that the societal fabric may be sustained for a while even if I draw it down without then shoring it up (just as if I pollute a river, *I* may not be short of drinking water). Stewardship toward the social ecology arises because it is immoral to take and not to give, to diminish and not to restore (although how much I take and give depends on numerous conditions).

Although (partial) loss of community is one of the defining characteristics of modernity, there is no reason to overlook the fact that just as we can experience diminished community, we can face excessive communality. This is the case in Japan, where individuality is suppressed, rights are neglected, and autonomy is severely curbed. Community is to be considered as a good only when its social order is balanced with carefully laid protections of autonomy, when particularistic obligations are balanced with universal ones, especially to protect basic individual rights. In short, although communities and the particularistic obligations they entail are essential to our full functionality, both can be excessive.

Lawrence Blum, in commenting on this chapter, posed a pivotal question. He asked whether these arguments apply to all communities, or only to good ones. Do people have obligations to bad communities, or only to those that "realize important human goods"?[49] One possible response, Blum suggested, is to hold that "some communities will be sustaining for each individual, and particularistic obligations are being defended only in the sense that *each* individual will have *some* such obligations, not that any *specific forms* of such obligations (neighborhood, ethnic, etc.) are being defended *in general*."[50]

I could not agree more. I part way here with those who argue that antisocial communities (say gangs) may be as sustaining and constitutive as pro-social ones. Some communitarians, Michael Walzer for instance, argue that communities are the final arbiters of what is good.[51] As I see it, communities do not have the final word about what is good, and the obligations they articulate must be squared by what is otherwise justified as good. Further elaboration of this point requires a whole separate examination of how one separates true from false articulations of obligations (or good from bad ones) and whether they are universal or particularistic, an examination that cannot be undertaken here.[52] In any case, whether one values particularistic obligations per se because they are constitutive, or only those that pass some test here not articulated, one recognizes the value of this category of obligations.

Human Betterment

So far, I have made the argument that communities (and the particularistic obligations they entail) are essential for human constitution, for our ability to function as full human beings and as persons oriented by a particular identity. Next, I advance the argument that communities help make us into better people than we would be otherwise.

Particularism nurtures free agency and universalism

Communities (when thick but not excessive) help make us relatively free agents and rational beings and can help us to live up to universal obligations. As Erich Fromm put it in his *Escape from Freedom*, and as numerous studies of behavior in crowds have shown, beginning with Le Bon, isolated people tend to be irrational, impulsive, and open to demagogical appeals and totalitarian movements.[53] One could argue that these movements have risen only in societies and periods in which social integration has been greatly weakened.[54] In contrast, as Tocqueville and the enormous literature on civil society holds, people well woven into communities (including families and voluntary associations) are able to resist pressures by governments and the seductive appeal of demagogues. Moreover, community members are much more likely to have the psychological integrity and fortitude required to be able to engage in reasoned deliberations, make rational choices, act on judgment rather than on impulse, and behave as relatively free agents. (I write "relatively" because even under ideal social conditions people can only approximate the liberal ideal, and not very closely, but they certainly cannot do so in the absence of particularistic relations.)

Liberals fear that communities inherently oppress individuality, as they often did in earlier periods and still do in some parts of the world. This fear is justified in reference to excessively thick and authoritarian communities, which existed mainly in earlier periods or in non-liberal societies, although even relatively thin communities tend to restrict the individuality of their members to some extent. Nonetheless, liberalism itself is dependent on the kind of persons found in communities.

David B. Wong adds that to learn to be duty-bound and to act universally, we first must have relationships of trust with others (i.e., particularistic relations).[55] We are not born with universal obligations; they must be taught. We acquire respect for them from parents, educators, religious figures, spiritual leaders, or heads of social movements – all people with whom we have an intense particularistic involvement.

All this is especially evident when we consider our condition as children. Without those who cared for us, we would not have developed into "individuals," but would crawl on all fours and bark, inarticulate and aggressive, snarling at each other.[56] Even as mature adults, we require continued bonding with others to sustain our values in general, our universal commitments included.[57]

Communities help minimize the state (especially its application of coercion)

Communities' introduction and reinforcement of our moral commitments help make for a strong measure of a voluntary social order. There is a tendency to assume that once people are brought up properly, by strong families and good schools, possibly backed up by churches or other places of worship, they will be men and women of virtue. Actually, social science data leave little room for doubt that unless people's moral commitments are continually reinforced, they will deteriorate. The most effective way to reinforce them builds on the fact that people have a very powerful need for continuous approval by others – especially those to whom they have thick bonds of attachment. These bonds, in turn, are found most readily in communities (families and voluntary associations included).[58] Communities, then, can strengthen adherence to social norms, especially when communities endorse pro-social values.[59] Thus the role of the police and the courts can be minimized, and the state and its coercive means are less needed to maintain social order. Law and order can be largely replaced by the informal controls of communities.

Particularistic bonds humanize us

Particularistic bonds, and hence obligations, protect us from the inhumanity that has often arisen in the past from strong commitments to abstract and general ideas, leading those who believed in these ideas to fight for the betterment of humanity but to care little about their fellow human beings. Particularistic obligations stopped many children during the Nazi era from spying on their parents and some Germans from turning in their Jewish friends, thus showing that even in a severely fragmented civic environment, particularistic bonds maintain considerable moral power.[60] The history of the twentieth century – memories of the unfathomable suffering that totalitarian governments and movements inflicted on millions of people in the name of one universal cause or another (e.g. Stalinist socialism and some radical religious movements) – reminds us how crucial such particularistic tempering is.

A related but not identical point is that justice is best served when we judge people and deal with them as whole people, whose particular circumstances we are bound to take into account, rather than merely as members of one or more categories. We should treat people as unique, concrete individuals, rather than as incidents or members of abstract categories. Selznick puts this point eloquently as follows:

> [The] personal standpoint is not and cannot be embraced wholeheartedly. Judgment in the light of rule and principle has serious limitations from a moral point of view. That is so, fundamentally, because rule-centered [universal] judgment does not adequately appreciate the place of concreteness and particularity in moral experience.[61]

He adds the following telling quote: " 'There is no general doctrine,' wrote George Eliot in *Middlemarch*, 'which is not capable of eating out our morality if unchecked by the deep-seated habit of direct fellow-feeling with individual fellow-men.' " And he concludes that "the lesson is that impersonal precepts must be tempered and assessed in the light of very specific human outcomes."[62]

The merit of the obligation to take particularistic conditions into account is evident when mandatory sentences prevent judges from taking into account special circumstances, when admissions officers of colleges are expected to adhere strictly to standard guidelines, and in comparison of the Napoleonic legal and the common law traditions.

One may argue that particularistic considerations are not the same as particularistic obligations; the first deal with localized conditions, the second with moral commitments. However, note that the commitment to take into account context is, in part, a moral judgment reflecting particularism.

Human flourishing

There is an immense literature on what constitutes a good life and human flourishing. John Cottingham finds in it a ground for justifying some partiality, drawing on Aristotle. Cottingham writes:

> If I am to count as making a moral judgement I must be prepared, at least in principle, to show how my prescription contributes to the overall blueprint for the good life – how it forms part of, or connects with, my vision of how life should be lived if it is to be worthwhile... [contributing to a] fulfilled or "flourishing" life.[63]

In a very elementary sense, the connection between human flourishing and particularistic obligations is supported by the reasons already discussed: without stable and meaningful social attachments it is impossible to form and nurture fully functional human beings, individuals whose sense of self (or identity) is established, and who are able to act as reasonable, free agents. However, if one takes the term flourishing to mean a higher level of achievement, a greater realization of human potential, a life that is more virtuous than just fully functional, one finds that the relationship to particularistic obligations is a complex one, although clearly there is a connection.

A preliminary examination suggests that particularistic obligations may be compatible with, indeed highly supportive of, some forms of flourishing, but not nearly as essential, possibly even a hindrance to some extent, to some others. Cottingham writes,

> If I give no extra weight to the fact that this is *my* lover, *my* friend, *my* spouse, *my* child, if I assess these people's needs purely on their merits (in such a way as an impartial observer might do), then that special concern which constitutes the essence of love and friendship will be eliminated. Partiality to loved ones is justified because it is an essential ingredient in one of the highest human goods.[64]

But this assumes that one recognizes these particular virtues as part of the good life.

If the center of human virtue is a life of contemplation or nirvana, or other forms of self-perfection, especially if those are viewed as virtues one practices individually rather than as a member of a community, particularistic obligations will play a relatively small role. The same might hold if the good life is one that seeks to promote justice, or a world order based on the Universal Declaration of Human Rights, or on some other such universal principle.

Particularistic obligations become pivotal if one considers any of the following lives (or combinations thereof) as good: one dedicated to love and caring; tending to particular ill or poor persons (rather than to heath care or distributive justice generally); nurturing communal bonds and bonds among communities, including conflict resolution and mediation; parenting and attending to our parents; and, more generally, dedication to the betterment of family life and that of particular communities.

All this is not to suggest that particularistic obligations play no role in societies centered around self-perfection. Human flourishing of any kind takes place within a societal context. People cannot work much to improve their self unless they build or help nurture a context in which such labor is considered part of the good life. Thus, a life of learning can thrive in a Jewish *shtetl* or a Chinese *literati* society that celebrates such a life, but not in one that sees serving the poor and the ill as the main virtue. That is, whatever is considered the good society, whatever form human flourishing takes, it does not take place within a social vacuum. It thrives when it becomes the good around which a society – and the particularistic obligations it entails – is centered. Members must be committed not merely to the particular community (or society), but also to its particular vision of the good – and must be willing to absorb the costs and often the sacrifices that such visions entail. Thus for a group of *literati* to dedicate their life to philosophy, poetry, and brush painting, the other members of the far from affluent society must be willing to curtail their already meager consumption. Therefore, although some forms of human flourishing are more intimately associated with particularistic obligations than others, all draw on them and all add to their moral justification.

In Conclusion

To be full-fledged human beings, we require a certain environment, one rich in solid but not overbearing communities. These, in turn, are composed of bonds of affection, which cannot be universalized, and moral obligations to members. A measure of moral obligation to nurture the social environment in which people can develop well arises out of this understanding. That obligation is neither self-serving nor utilitarian nor consequentialist. The moral ecology particularistic obligations help sustain may well be sustained for the duration of our lifetime, or even that of our children, even if we do not abide by these obligations and draw on the existing stock of trust and affection and moral commitments as we draw them down. However, just as we are obligated to sustain the natural environment as a common good, so are we obligated to sustain the moral ecology. I call this a constitutive communitarian argument.

The same communal environment justifies our moral commitment not only because it enables people to function fully, but also because it makes us and others better than we would otherwise be. Communities provide the conditions under which people can act autonomously and curb the need for state coercion, provide for empathy that benefits not merely particularistic but also universal obligations, and contribute to human flourishing. None of these attributes – as significant and compelling as they may be – justifies ignoring our universal obligations, but they provide a strong communitarian justification for those of us who honor additional commitments to our own communities.

2

Privacy as an Obligation

In legal literature, social philosophy, and common parlance, privacy is considered a right, a point so obvious that privacy as an obligation is rarely mentioned, let alone its social importance and legal foundations recognized or the significance of its weakening in recent history discussed. This chapter suggests that for many purposes it is important to take into account privacy as both a social and legal obligation. Social, in the sense that keeping many kinds of behavior "private" is socially expected and morally prescribed; legal, in the basic sense that such an obligation is encoded in the laws of the land and enforced by them.

Because we are so conditioned to think about privacy as a right, any discussion of it as an obligation seems counterintuitive. We respect the right of a couple to privacy in the bedroom; but we also consider it wrong for them to engage in bedroom behavior in public. (Indeed, even in a blasé age, we are dismayed by those who put cameras into various rooms of their houses and broadcast the intimacies of their lives on the internet or cable TV.) People have a right to keep their private parts private; but we also demand that they do not expose them willingly. To couples who fight, we are not only enjoined from prying, but (unless we are intimate friends) we often press on them that "one should not air one's dirty linen in public." Most anything that is considered ugly or that people find distressing, from a major sore to disfigurement following a mastectomy, many in our society expect to be covered up. Dying is to occur in private. We of course have a right that prevents people from reading our mail, listening in on our phone calls, and learning our private thoughts and feelings. But we are troubled (or at least we used to be) by the kind of exhibitionism popular on some TV shows. We object strongly when employers, shopkeepers, curious teenagers, or peeping toms put cameras into our bathrooms; but we also object to people relieving themselves in public. Whatever our views about the death penalty, we have long agreed that it ought not be carried out in public. In short, if the right to privacy is defined sociologically speaking as "a legitimate claim to block visibility or audibility from others,"[1] privacy as an obligation is the mirror opposite: the requirement not to expose one's thoughts, emotions, and, above all, behavior to others.

The privacy obligation[2] appears in two main forms. I use the term "mandated privacy" to refer to the legal requirement that a person's thoughts, emotions, and, above all, behavior be kept out of the sight and earshot of others – for example, the ban on defecating in public view. And I will use the term "expected privacy" to refer to requirements backed by social mores rather than law. Either way, when privacy is considered an obligation, it falls into the category of social demands on a person; it is a responsibility, a service to the common good, rather than a personal good, entitlement, or right. As will become clear when specific cases in point are examined, these obligations are closely associated with what a society values, with what kinds of behavior and character trait it considers virtuous.

The fact that our concept of privacy as an obligation has become rather thin, as we shall see, is a reflection of our changed values. In earlier eras in our history, it was much thicker (e.g., in the colonial United States). And in some societies today it is much thicker – by prevailing Western standards much too thick in many Islamic countries, where women are not allowed to expose their hair or skin in public and are to stay out of sight when visitors come to call. This leads us to the cardinal question: has the Western conception of privacy as an obligation grown too thin, or does its thinning out merely reflect a liberation from obsolete taboos, such as breast-feeding in public? To put it differently, is the decline of the privacy obligation a cause for celebration, or is it a cause for concern – and remedial action? And if the answer to this question is the latter, what kind of remedial action is necessary?

I proceed by briefly examining the privacy obligation in societies where it is very thick, to make the point that this obligation can be excessive and oppressive. I then sketch the history of the decline of this form of privacy and the rise of privacy as a right in American society. Next, I show that currently, in the United States, privacy is so widely assumed to be a right that privacy as an obligation is often overlooked, even when it is an essential element of the issue at hand. I then explore the justifications liberal political theorists and social philosophers provide for thinning the privacy obligation. In the process, I introduce data regarding the harm inflicted on children, adults, and the society at large by thin privacy, and the ways liberals and communitarians conceptualize these effects. I close by asking whether the thinning of the privacy obligation is liberating or detrimental to the common good, tackling the questions of whether further shoring up of this privacy obligation is called for, and how a new shared understanding of what is to be kept private can be formulated.

The Privacy Obligation in a Comparative and Historical Perspective

One can see strong mandated and expected privacy in other eras and cultures, most readily in extreme and offensive forms, in societies in which rights are not respected and virtuous privacy is strenuously and even violently enforced. For instance, those Islamic societies that strictly follow the *sharia* (Islamic law) require women to conceal their hair, skin, and the contours of their body[3] – a dress code embodied in extreme form by the *burqa*. Women are not supposed to be seen by male visitors to their homes and, thus, are confined to a separate part of the house when such visitors are present.[4] Even women's voices are supposed to be kept low and used as infrequently as possible (because they are held to be seductive and therefore undermine sexual virtue).[5] Communist societies were imbued with Victorian privacy notions. During the 1940s and '50s, the Communist Party in the Soviet Union attempted to keep images and discussion of sexuality away from the public eye. In addition, the wearing of shorts was banned for both men and women in many places and discouraged nearly everywhere until the 1980s. Women who wore dresses with low necklines or without sleeves were harassed and in extreme cases fined for "denudation" or "disturbing the peace."[6]

Jeffrey Rosen points out that under medieval Jewish law, it was an offense not only to observe another's intimacies, but also to allow one's own intimacies to be seen by another. Thus, Jewish law did not provide the individual with the right to waive certain privacy protections – for example, by exposing oneself – because the effects of doing so were considered to be greater than the gains resulting from the freedom of the person.[7] As Menachem Elon writes, "one is not permitted to 'breach the fences of Israel' or act immodestly so as to cause the Divine Presence to depart from Israel."[8] Similarly, Eugene Borowitz and Frances Wienman Schwartz write that the Jewish concept of *tzeniyut*, translated loosely as "modesty," can be interpreted to mean that we ought to keep "part of ourselves to ourselves, hidden from the prying, gossip-seeking eyes of others."[9] As Anita Allen points out, these laws "define a moral tradition of thinking about privacy that is nonvoluntarist." People have an obligation to safeguard their own privacy because the "integrity of the community itself is at stake."[10]

In earlier American history, expected privacy was reflected in Puritan notions of modesty. Women in colonial New England were expected to be covered from neck to toe, to wear head coverings in public, and to refrain from unseemly activities, such as drinking and smoking, in public or among strangers.[11]

There has been a long debate among historians about whether the United States is a Lockean country whose core values are centered around individual rights (and liberty), or a nation in which the Lockean values vie with republican virtues, as is often championed by social conservatives.[12] Until 1960, this debate was largely of academic interest because American society had a very strong set of core values, while rights were often short-changed. Thus, the normative thesis of Lockean dominance served well those who fought to accord African Americans full *de jure* and *de facto* rights, those who struggled to advance women's rights, those who pushed against sexual prohibitions, those who sought expanded rights for disabled Americans, and those who wished to protect the environment. It also legitimated the efforts by economic conservatives to curtail the role of government and expand free choice, the realm of the marketplace, especially in the Reagan and Thatcher era. The 1960s is, of course, also the era in which the constitutional right to privacy was fashioned out of the penumbra of the Constitution, drawing on the reproductive rights cases, *Griswold* v. *Connecticut*, *Eisenstadt* v. *Baird*, and, ultimately, *Roe* v. *Wade*.[13] (Previously, privacy in the American jurisprudence was largely limited to torts, drawing on what is considered the most influential law review article on the subject, "The Right to Privacy," published in 1890 by Warren and Brandeis,[14] and on some state laws.)

By 1990, American society had been transformed from a nation with a very strong core of values (albeit many that today are considered unacceptable) to one in which rights dominated and individualism overwhelmed community bonds. This development is such standard communitarian fare that it needs to be only briefly sketched here. Mary Ann Glendon showed in her book *Rights Talk* that the growing tendency to turn differences of interests, needs, or wants into offenses of rights made it difficult to resolve conflicts and turned America into a litigious society.[15] Robert Bellah and his associates showed that civic culture waned as Americans became preoccupied with the self.[16] Legal transgressions and moral offenses were increasingly disregarded because the laws or mores involved were said to violate a right of the parties charged with these violations. It became more important to nurture self-esteem than good behavior. In my own work, I showed that as the old values, many of which deserved to be abandoned, were washed out, no new ones were formulated, leading to widespread anomie, as well as higher rates of crime, drug abuse, divorce, and teen pregnancy, all of which were very low in the 1950s. I argued that moral dialogues were needed to lead to new shared understandings of virtue.[17]

In the same period, between 1960 and 1990, not only was a whole new constitutional right to privacy fashioned, but the privacy obligation was also weakened. As mores and laws that reflected social values – that which society views as virtuous – waned, privacy as an obligation practically disappeared from many legal and moral texts, and even from social parlance. The concept was peeled away from the society at large as more and more conduct that was previously required or expected to be carried out in private was legitimately exposed to the public eye.

"Let it all hang out" was a slogan of the 1960s, well heeded in the decades that have followed. Dress codes have greatly relaxed, to the point of practically vanishing. Exhibitionism in the media and in the public square has become rampant. Intimate behavior in public is tolerated, if not welcomed. The media has been pushing the envelope, showing more and more conduct that previously had been considered improper to display on the tube, especially at times when children are up and about. (Showing people using urinals and frontal nudity have become increasingly commonplace in recent years.) The internet has pushed the boundaries still further. True, there are still a few items of behavior that, even in those states with the most liberal laws and mores, are required or expected to be carried out in private. Thus, having sexual intercourse in public, in broad daylight, especially next to a playground, is not considered acceptable, even in Scandinavia or California. Nor is defecating in public. Indeed, every state still has some kind of law on the books concerning indecent exposure,[18] although these laws are rarely enforced. Instead, by and large, the trend in the United States (and increasingly in other free societies), at least until very recently, has been to thin out both mandated and expected privacy, although some attempts have been made to reverse this trend since the beginning of communitarian efforts in the 1990s.[19]

The question remains as to whether such a development is detrimental to individual and social well-being. If the answer to this question is in the affirmative, what kinds of behavior should we expect or mandate be carried out in private, and how is this to be determined? Surely, few would seek to simply restore old forms of privacy, such as those that outlawed breast-feeding in public spaces.

The issue is not an historical one; there is little question as to whether the privacy obligation has declined sharply in the same period during which other social values greatly weakened. The question is whether the trend is liberating, harmless, or harmful, and, if the latter, needs to be reversed to some extent. We have gotten used to public kissing, necking, and partial nudity; the sphere of what is considered acceptable public exposure has been expanding. Is it merely a matter of cultural lag that we have not removed the last vestiges of mandated and expected privacy? Or, are there profound reasons to move in the opposite direction, forming new shared understandings, first morally and then ensconced in law, about what one ought to keep out of sight and earshot? More importantly, does increased exposure of private parts and matters undermine the moral foundations of society and harm civility?

A Rights-Centered Society

The preoccupation with privacy as a right is so strong in contemporary America that privacy as an obligation is, as a rule, not mentioned, even when it is a key element of the issue at hand. In common American parlance, privacy is considered first and foremost a right. The *Miriam Webster's Dictionary* defines privacy as "the quality or state of being apart from company and observation" and adds "freedom from unauthorized intrusion."[20] A search in the Lexis-Nexus news research area for articles with "privacy" in the headlines that appeared during a one-month period turned up 140 articles, all of which concerned privacy as a right, including the privacy rights of patients, convicts, or consumers.[21] Scores of public opinion polls take it for granted that when they ask about privacy, their audience will understand that the reference is to a right.[22]

Books on privacy, often written by law professors, but also accessible to the public at large, typically (with some noted exceptions)
deal with privacy as a right. These include *The Transparent Society*,
by David Brin; *The Unwanted Gaze*, by Jeffrey Rosen; *Right to Privacy*, by Ellen Alderman and Caroline Kennedy; and *The End of
Privacy*, by Charles J. Sykes, just to name a few.[23] My own book,
The Limits of Privacy, deals with privacy as a right that needs to be
balanced with concerns for the common good; mandated privacy is
only very briefly mentioned.[24] The same is true for legal literature.
A search in the Lexis-Nexus legal research area for articles with
"privacy" in the title that appeared during one month in 2000 turned
up 114 articles, all dealing with the right to privacy and none with
privacy as an obligation to the common good or to protect social
mores and values.[25]

Legal essays dealing with mandated privacy – for instance those
dealing with indecent exposure, nudity on beaches, nude dancing,
and so on – are, reflecting the general culture, very rare. Those few
that deal with matters concerning mandated privacy tend to treat the
issue with reference to one right or another. One example is the
discussion of two Supreme Court cases, *Barnes* v. *Glen Theater, Inc.*
and *City of Erie* v. *PAP's A.M.*, both of which dealt with public
ordinances prohibiting nude dancing.[26] Though in both cases the
Court did recognize the need to balance the protection of free speech
and the protection of public morals, the discussion in legal literature
has tended to focus overwhelmingly on the former to the neglect of
the latter.[27] David Cole, for example, discusses nude dancing from
the viewpoint that it is a form of sexual expression, and thus, like all
other forms of speech, it cannot be regulated in keeping with the
First Amendment:

> The regulation of sexual expression cannot be justified under trad-
> itional speech doctrines and indeed inverts two of the First Amend-
> ment's most fundamental principles. . . . [T]hat the Supreme Court has
> endorsed such an inversion of First Amendment values suggests that
> the Court considers the benefits served by policing the public/private
> line to outweigh First Amendment principle.[28]

Timothy Tesluk begins his article on the Barnes decision with the
statement that it "is not a case about nudity; it is about the freedom of
expression," and ends with the conclusion that the Court's ruling in
Barnes "gives legislatures a blank check to control content in communication for all. What a blatant violation of the Constitution!"[29]

To reiterate, the matter is framed as a question of whether or not the right to free speech is intruded upon, with little regard for the question of whether there is any antisocial impact from whatever conduct is newly allowed to take place in public, and the scope of this impact, if there is any. One may argue that what one sees here is merely evidence of the very high regard in which freedom of speech is held, and the implicit assumption that almost anything else should give way to avoid violating it. However, in an era less focused on rights and more concerned with crumbling commitments to the common good, an author should be more inclined to explore the extent of the sacrifice society is expected to make to accommodate the expanded interpretation of the right at hand, and possibly to seek ways to protect what remains standing of privacy as an obligation – ideally in ways that would not undermine First Amendment protections.

In some other cases, the "right" to nullify laws or expectations concerning privacy obligations has been questioned, not because of the possible ill-effects on the moral culture of the society, but out of concern for some other individual right. David Kushner begins his examination of court cases and comments by Supreme Court Justices on nude sunbathing with a telling question: "Does one have a right to enjoy the beach in the nude? Or, conversely, does one have a right to enjoy the beach without being subjected to the nudity of other bathers?"[30] In the 1975 case *Williams* v. *Hathaway*, in which the National Park Service sought to ban nudity on Cape Cod National Seashore, the federal district court found that nude conduct is "fundamentally individualistic and personal" and thus falls within the realm of personal liberty and is entitled to at least some constitutional protection.[31] In the cases at hand, against this right of individual expression the courts weigh only the right of other individuals not to be perturbed by the said behavior. (Tangible damage to public property may be considered, but not such intangible matters as harm to the social fabric.) Thus, in several cases, courts upheld bans on nudity on beaches that are easily seen from the street or that closely adjoin non-nude beaches – on the grounds that it is likely to cause offense to individuals.[32]

In still other cases, the clash between the "right" to undermine whatever existing standards of virtuous privacy still exist and the "rights" of those who might be offended is "solved" by calling on those offended to retreat in one way or another, again without awareness of any possible effects on the moral culture. Harm can be avoided by people "averting their eyes" to avoid offensive speech, views, or behavior.[33] For example, in 1968 a man was arrested on the grounds of "offensive conduct" for wearing a jacket in the Los Angeles courthouse with the words "Fuck the Draft" written on it. Much of the argument for convicting him was based on the stated desire to protect bystanders, especially women and children, from viewing language that they would find offensive and unwelcome in a public place.[34] In *Cohen* v. *California*, the Supreme Court eventually overturned this conviction, stating that "the mere presumed presence of unwitting listeners or viewers does not serve automatically to justify curtailing all speech capable of giving offense.... Those in the Los Angeles courthouse could effectively avoid further bombardment of their sensibilities simply by averting their eyes." The opinion of the court, written by Justice Harlan, displays a high degree of moral relativism. He writes: "Surely the State has no right to cleanse public debate to the point where it is grammatically palatable to the most squeamish among us.... For while the particular four-letter word being litigated here is perhaps more distasteful than most others of its genre, it is nevertheless often true that one man's vulgarity is another's lyric."[35]

Social philosopher Hadley Arkes writes that this decision "resolved for the first time that the preservation of civility was simply not substantial enough as an interest of the state to warrant any restrictions on speech that has even the slenderest pretense of being 'political.'"[36] Arkes does not suggest that no one in the US since the 1960s has taken the other side. But it seems clear that books and articles that examine damage to public morals rather than rights are at best rare. There are, however, some important partial exceptions.

Priscilla Regan, in her book *Legislating Privacy*, at first seems to be a sterling exception. She criticizes the tendency, in both American philosophical and legal discourse, to view privacy as a wholly individual right, and thus to frame it in terms that emphasize "separateness and self-interest" without developing a concept of the broader social importance of privacy. She argues that the public policy debate has been influenced by this individualistic view, and thus the goal in law and policy has only been to protect an individual's interest in privacy.[37] Where recognition of the social value of privacy does exist, it exists because of, as Edward Bloustein put it, "community concern for the preservation of an individual's dignity."[38]

Regan identifies three bases for the *social* importance of privacy. First, she argues that privacy is a common value, a value shared by all individuals to some extent. Second, privacy is a public value – it is of value not just to the individual, but to the democratic political system. Lastly, Regan holds that privacy is a collective value because new technologies or government polices affect everyone, making it difficult for any individual to safeguard his or her own privacy without securing a similar level of privacy for all others.[39] However, although she discusses privacy as a social value rather than as a right, she uses this argument to show why an individual's right to privacy must be safeguarded against outside threats – not to discuss whether there are some realms where privacy is (or ought to be) an obligation rather than a right.

Anita Allen is a rare contemporary American scholar who recognizes the category of mandated privacy and dedicates two essays to exploring it. In "Coercing Privacy," Allen describes the erosion of the desire for and expectation of privacy in American society, caused, she argues, by opportunities both to give up one's own privacy for a profit – for example, women who set up web cameras in their bedrooms and allow paying customers to watch them – and to consume other people's privacy through tabloids and TV talk shows.[40] Allen continues this discussion in a later article, "The Wanted Gaze." Here, she traces the lack of attention to the problems of exhibitionism to the tendency in American society to treat privacy as completely voluntary, believing that "we have a right to give up privacy if we want to and a duty to respect the privacy other people want, but we have no duty to be private or to respect the privacy people do not want."[41] Allen identifies places in US law where privacy is enforced (such as public indecency statutes and requirements to provide single-sex public bathrooms), but notes that such non-voluntaristic privacy is "nonetheless overshadowed by the pronounced voluntarism of the modern-American liberal mainstream."[42]

Allen rejects this notion that privacy is an "optional good," and instead sees it as "a foundation, a precondition of a liberal egalitarian society."[43] She points out that the government forces us to be free by not allowing such things as slavery and forced marriages, and she asks about the issues for which it can similarly force us to be private. While her thinking meets mine by suggesting that certain forms of privacy should be considered expected and even mandated – she suggests "regulatory measures that aim at curbing the culture of exposure for the sake of 'forcing' people to love privacy and to live privately"[44] – she arrives at this conclusion via a quite different path. Whereas I hold that some measures of privacy are required to shore up the moral culture of society, Allen believes that privacy serves another, albeit very important, social good – the rights-centered liberal society. That is, when all is said and done, like other rights-centered arguments, Allen's ultimate focus and source of legitimation is the rights-bearing individual. She goes further, though, than the other American legal scholars I uncovered in recognizing the very existence of privacy as a social and legal obligation.

Roots in Political Theory and Social Philosophy

The recent tendency in the West (especially the United States) to focus on privacy as a right and not as an obligation reflects more than historical trends. It also reflects dominant philosophies, which have a deep influence on law, public policy, and public thinking. Indeed, the focus on this particular right is but one incidence of a general approach that is rights-centered and has no place for a moral culture or shared conceptions of the common good.[45] I refer especially to utilitarians, libertarians, and, to a significant extent, several contemporary liberal political theorists. (To save breath, I shall refer to them as individualistic approaches). These approaches are next examined from a critical, communitarian viewpoint that seeks to combine concerns with rights with concerns for nurturing the moral culture, and searches for the appropriate balance between the two.[46]

Act vs. exposure

Before the discussion can proceed, a crucial distinction must be introduced between acts themselves and their exposure to others, either directly or via a cultural representation. Take violence. We disapprove of most forms and outlaw many. We are particularly offended when it occurs in such a way that people other than the victims are exposed to it, rather than when it takes place out of sight and audibility (the sociological definition of privacy here followed).[47] When a teacher is killed in front of her class, a parent in front of his children, or children in front of their parents, we are especially troubled. The reason is that, aside from the harm done to the victim, additional harm is caused, under these circumstances, to those exposed to the crime. I refer to these effects as secondary harm. (One may say that no privacy issue is involved if the act occurs, say, within a home. However, just as we consider it a violation of privacy when someone peeps into a bedroom from another room in the house, or a parent reads the mail of a teenager of the same household, so violations of privacy as an obligation can occur within what has traditionally been considered a private space.[48])

The distinction between acts and their exposure to others comes into focus in situations where we have no way of preventing the act, but we can avoid or curb secondary harm by keeping the cultural representations of the act (including pictures, movies, electronic images, and drawings) under wraps. A case in point is the tape made of the brutal beheading of *Wall Street Journal* reporter Daniel Pearl in Pakistan by assassins who afterwards shook his head before the eyes of a video camera. No media source has shown the entire video, and CBS was heavily criticized, by both the State Department and other networks, for airing a 15-second segment that did not involve the actual murder.[49] When Iraqi television showed the pictures of American prisoners of war in 2003, it was considered both a violation of international law (the Geneva Convention) and of social mores, and American networks did not air the tape. If one grants that the decisions on the part of the media not to broadcast these pictures were good decisions, one in effect holds that keeping some cultural representations of select acts private and not exposing them to the public is a social good.

In these instances, because the media's restraint was fully voluntary and self-imposed, free-speech concerns did not arise. These were merely cases of expected privacy. In many other situations involving the mandated privacy of cultural products, First Amendment issues do arise. For instance, issues are raised when the government outlaws not only the production of child pornography using real children (on the grounds that it violates the children involved and the act itself is a crime), but also the distribution and even the mere possession of the resulting cultural representation of the acts involved.

When we consider secondary harm, it makes little difference whether the events are true or fictionalized. It should be noted in passing that the line between these two forms of representation is increasingly blurred as pictures of real events are very readily and often greatly manipulated, and fictionalized events can be made to seem very real. Thus, from my viewpoint, allowing virtual child pornography (as the Supreme Court did when striking down the Child Pornography Protection Act[50]) while banning circulation of real child pornography makes little sense unless one assumes that the harm and offense to our values caused by child pornography is limited to that caused by the act of production (where "real" children are involved) and there are no secondary ill effects that stem from merely being exposed to this form of pornography.

Granted, social science data are not yet available, as virtual child pornography is a rather new phenomenon. However, I draw on 50 years of sociological experience to predict that such pornography, by making depictions of sex among adults and minors much more commonly available, will gradually make such relationships seem less abnormal, and will thus make acts of pedophilia more common and the public's view of it more permissive.

In short, aside from keeping acts private (e.g., we teach children to close the bathroom door) and keeping private the cultural representation of certain acts (e.g., by banning the distribution of child pornography), we also seek to keep under wraps some cultural products that do not necessarily represent any "real" acts (e.g., curbing children's access to R- and, especially, X-rated movies).

What is meant by a privacy obligation when one deals with fictionalized cultural representations, where there is no act, but only images? What is required is to keep those cultural representations of items that generate significant secondary harms out of the sight and hearing of children and, in some instances, of most adults. This is achieved when the media, out of self-restraint or under government pressure or mandate, broadcasts whole categories of movies and TV shows only during hours when children are typically asleep; when X-rated videos are kept in special divisions in video shops; when filters on computers in public schools and libraries prevent children from accessing certain material; and when labels are placed on music disks and ratings on TV programs and V-chips into TV sets, all to allow parents to keep certain materials out of the sight and hearing of their children.

We assume that adults are more resilient, but we still favor protecting them from some material that individuals or the community finds offensive. This is the reason many jurisdictions require that nude dancing be kept in certain specified quarters,[51] and behind opaque glass, with heavy curtains at the entrance – i.e., in private places – and some publications be kept behind the counter at newsstands, or in wrappers.[52] In these ways, these items can be kept out of sight for most of society, and only those who wish or need to can access them – in private.

Discouraging the media from producing certain content even for adults (rather than merely limiting the access of children), following what I call "expected privacy," is quite common when one or more of our values is engaged. You will not find racial or ethnic slurs on contemporary TV shows or in movies of any significant circulation, unless they are very carefully framed to make clear that they are introduced in order to show how offensive they are, or how they were historically abused. No air time is given to the "N word" or to Holocaust deniers. The use of other words has led to the firing or resignation of more than one radio announcer.[53] People surely continue to use such expressions in private conversations in homes, and cars, and even in some small groups. While society would prefer that such conversations did not occur in the first place, it still considers it virtuous to keep the public from being exposed. More generally, we understand civility to mean that people should not shout out whatever comes to mind.

Nor is mandated privacy unknown. For a while, hate speech has been banned from public expression by force of law on many American campuses.[54] Canada has laws banning hate speech, and numerous European nations attempt to regulate hate speech.[55] These bans show that even freedom of speech, considered the most revered of rights, can be made to yield to some normative considerations about the good in society.

One may argue that all these incidents set back-to-back do not amount to much, that they are all exceptions to the rule of unlimited exposure. It should be noted, however, that even these rather few and limited incidences of mandated (and even merely expected) privacy have encountered considerable opposition from individualists. Therefore, the principles that justify privacy obligations deserve to be articulated as a step toward explaining whether such privacy has become too thin.

Is there harm? If so, to whom and what?

In determining whether privacy obligations need to be made more robust, two questions must be addressed. First, what is the validity of the argument that cultural representations of vile and violent material cause no harm, and that they in fact help vent unavoidable antisocial urges and prevent them from turning into antisocial acts? Second, if there is harm, can it be properly addressed in terms of rights – or need one add considerations of the common good? These two questions are addressed here in reference to children, adults, and the society at large.

This is the subject of a huge literature, and one that is greatly contested.[56] Researchers commonly, and wisely, reject simplistic notions that the media is "the" cause of violence and sexually inappropriate conduct, but they tend to agree that the said exposure does have significant ill effects.

1 Harm to children

A large number of studies show harm to children from media violence, though some are based on one-time observations or are merely
illustrative. There are few studies on the effects of pornography on
children because researchers are reluctant to expose children to
pornographic materials in even controlled settings. These social science data are surveyed in some depth in the next chapter; for the
time being, it suffices to say that while the data is controversial,
several major professional organizations in the field of health have
concluded that there is a causal connection between media violence
and aggressive behavior in some children. The preponderance of
scientific opinion points to the conclusion that exposure to media
violence is detrimental to childhood development.

2 Harm to adults

While the question of whether and to what extent there is harm from
unbounded exposure to violent and pornographic material is the
subject of considerable study and controversy, a question that is just
as hotly contested is whether or not this harm should lead to us to
establish mandated privacy for adults. Some feminists argue that
pornography portrays women as objects to be used, that sex and
violence cannot be separated in pornography, and that pornography
is a form of rape – and hence should be banned.[57]

While many in the TV industry try to discredit claims that the
media has negative effects on adults, new research contradicts the
industry's position. A study published in *Science* on the effects of
violent TV programming on adolescents and young adults reaches
conclusions similar to those regarding the effects of television on
children.

A meta-analysis of 46 studies conducted between 1962 and 1995
on the effects of pornography on adults sought to determine whether
exposure to pornography had an effect on sexual deviance, sexual
offending, intimate relationships, and attitudes regarding rape
myths. The results of the analysis indicated pornography is "one
important factor which contributes directly to the development of
sexually dysfunctional attitudes and behaviors" and that "exposure
to pornographic material puts one at risk for developing sexually
deviant tendencies, committing sexual offenses, experiencing difficulties in one's intimate relationships, and accepting the rape myth."[58]

Other meta-analyses found similar effects from pornographic exposure. For example, a 1995 study shows that pornographic stimuli increase aggressive behavior and that media depictions of violent sexual activity induce more aggression than do depictions of non-violent sexual activity.[59]

3   Social fabric and moral culture

Beyond values that lead society to call for the government to demand that certain matters be kept private for the protection of specific "real" children and adults, there is also a concern to protect the stock of values – the moral culture – that society at large seeks to uphold.

A case in point is the way executions are carried out. Aside from the question of whether the death penalty should ever be handed out, there is the question as to whether the public should be allowed to witness executions, either in person or on TV. Public executions were common in early American history, but during the nineteenth century they increasingly fell into disfavor. Historian Louis Masur writes that the public began to regard public executions as inhumane, and public officials became "disgusted by a 'loathsome exhibition.'"[60] Public executions are believed to dehumanize the public, coarsen society, and make it more prone to violence.[61] Anthony Lewis writes that televising executions would "trivialize" them and "reduce them to the level of entertainment, to be clicked on and off." He further suggests that "the First Amendment in my judgment does not require access to scenes whose broadcast would further coarsen our society and increase its already dangerous level of insensitivity."[62]

Rights and values?

Individualists in effect argue that when a community seeks to keep some matters private, values are not involved, but rather the rights of some are weighed against the rights of others. The whole matter can be addressed in terms of the calculus of harm. One either yields to those who suffer the greatest harm, or tries to compensate those who are harmed when the others have their way.

Typical of such individualistic approaches, philosopher R. M. Hare deals with the issue not by recognizing a common good that might call for mandated or expected privacy, but by reducing the

issue to a conflict between individual rights. In examining the case of
nude beaches, he sums the problem up as the rights of the "nudes"
versus the "prudes." He uses a utilitarian analysis, weighing the
pleasure derived from nude bathing against the distress caused to
offended onlookers. Though he admits that he leaves out the important consideration of "the general effect on public morals of a relax-
ation of standards," he dismisses this concern, by stating that
he does not believe that "if people make the habit of looking at
other naked people of the opposite sex on beaches, then they
will tend to become more lascivious or in general immoral," but he
does not support this claim with empirical evidence or in any other
way.[63]

There is little doubt that, *to some extent*, the issue does involve the
balance of relative rights and interests, a balance that can be dealt
with in terms of the calculus of harm. But I will attempt next to
show that this calculus itself reflects society's values and that some
privacy considerations cannot be accounted for in any other way
than through the moral culture. For instance, the United States pays
much more mind to curbing vile material than to curbing representations of violence. There are several Supreme Court cases upholding
laws that limit the production or distribution of vile materials such
as obscenity and child pornography,[64] but in response to the few
state statutes attempting to limit the access of minors to depictions
of violence, the courts have explicitly ruled that cultural images of
violence are protected by the First Amendment.[65] In the case of
Video Software Dealers Association v. *Webster*, which challenged a
Missouri statute prohibiting the sale or rental to minors of videos
containing violent material,[66] the district court stated that "unlike
obscenity, violent expression is protected by the First Amendment."[67] The US differs here from many other free societies, reflecting remnants of the Victorian values American society held in earlier
eras, as well as stronger contemporary social conservative and religious commitments.

Also at issue is how highly one regards the First Amendment. Free
speech is itself a value that different societies hold to varying degrees
of intensity (and even in the United States it was less highly regarded
before the 1920s than it is currently). The fact that the United States
is less inclined to mandate limits to protect children from exposure
to violent and vile material in the media than are other free societies
suggests a difference in values – not that American children are more
resilient or less endangered. In short, a legal calculus based on the
weighing of rights claims is insufficient. Other values are clearly rele-

vant, including what society as a whole determines should be private behavior.[68]

Conceiving of and protecting moral culture

Concern for the common good (or the public interest) is, of course, widely recognized throughout the law, but the moral culture is not typically considered a public interest in the same way public safety and health are.

This tendency is illustrated by the body of nuisance law, which traditionally protects individuals from interference with the use or value of their property, such as noise from nearby industry, aggravation by a neighbor's pet, or damage caused by pollutants.[69] These torts focus on harms done to specific individuals, not on the effect on the common good. Some attempts are made to use nuisance law to protect the common good, but they tend to concern damage to the natural environment, economic loss to a community, or threats to community safety – but not harm to the moral culture.[70]

Moral-nuisance claims, which have been used to prosecute in cases such as nude beaches and crack houses, constitute an exception.[71] Moral-nuisance torts allow individuals or communities to take action against behavior that is offensive to them. If the basis of a moral-nuisance claim lay solely in an individual's right not to be offended, then disapproval of an activity by the community at large would not be necessary. Some do recognize that for a certain activity to constitute a moral nuisance, it must violate the mores of the community at large, not just the individuals attempting to prosecute it. John Copeland Nagle writes:

> Those who possess unusual moral sensibilities cannot rely upon a nuisance action to protect them. The sights, embarrassment, and fear that arise from the moral objections to an activity should be actionable only where there is a consensus in the community that the offending activity is immoral and objectionable.[72]

Indecency statutes provide another illustrative example. Indecency statutes have historically banned, and in some cases still do so, public sexual activity and nudity.[73] Justice Rehnquist wrote, "Public indecency statutes reflect moral disapproval of people appearing in the nude among strangers in public places," and pointed to the deep roots of indecency statutes in English common law, under which public nudity was considered an act *malum en se*, or bad in and of itself.[74] However, some of those who examine the issue skirt the effects of public nudity on the moral culture, attempting instead to prove harmful effects on an individual or to link nudity to public disturbances.[75] Jeffrey Narvil argues that while old indecency statutes were based on notions of privacy and modesty, today they should be based on concepts of intent and harm to an individual. The issue, he writes, is not whether nudity in public is immoral, or if nudity is something that belongs in the private realm, but rather whether the intent of the person who exposes him or herself is to cause harm to another person.[76] Such thinking is reflected in the indecency laws of many states, including Washington and Hawaii, where exposure is illegal only if the perpetrator knowingly causes affront or alarm.[77] Similar tendencies also appear in cases dealing with pornography, as well. In the case of *Redrup* v. *New York*, the Supreme Court overturned the conviction of a man who sold pornographic books on a New York City newsstand because the action did not constitute "an assault upon individual privacy by publication in a manner so obtrusive as to make it impossible for an unwilling individual to avoid exposure to it."[78] To a communitarian, the concern, on the face of it, is the moral culture and the virtue of keeping some things private, above and beyond whatever effects they have on the individuals involved.

The communitarian position is reflected in the *Barnes* ruling, in which the Supreme Court upheld the notion of a moral culture that should be protected through laws. Writing in concurrence with the decision, Justice Scalia rejected the idea that nudity should be banned only if it is offensive to others: "There is no basis for thinking that our society has ever shared that Thoreauvian 'you-may-do-what-you-like-so-long-as-it-does-not-injure-someone-else' beau ideal – much less for thinking that it was written in the Constitution." He goes on to argue that an event at a public place involving public nudity could be prohibited "even if there were not an offended innocent in the crowd."[79]

Moral culture as a core good

From a communitarian viewpoint, there is a whole array of major common goods, not just exceptional goods few and far between. These are goods that are not the property of any individual, and that are of value to the future, including generations not yet born, whose interests can hardly be aggregated and measured without engaging in some very scholastic and far-fetched calculations. The environment is a prime example. To argue, as some do, that trees or beaches have rights is a contrived attempt to preserve the validity of an individualist rights calculus.[80] Such an effort serves as an example of the pains to which people will go, and the conceptual contortions to which they will subject themselves, in order to avoid recognizing that some good things do not belong to a particular person or group, but to the community at large, including future generations.

Moral culture is the core of values shared by a given community or society.[81] Moral culture provides the criteria by which members of a society differentiate between right and wrong. It is reflected in various mores and norms. Laws that reflect these values are honored much more willingly. Certain material, whether or not it harms children and adults, may be banned or discouraged if it degrades that culture.

Particularly relevant to this matter is the "broken windows" approach to crime reduction.[82] This approach is based on the notion that when the moral culture of a community can be restored – by, among other things, mandating some privacy obligations – crime subsides significantly. For instance, police may work to restore local conceptions of civility by suppressing not only drug dealing, but also minor infractions that previously have been ignored, such as playing boom boxes loudly and urinating in public. These restorations of civility, in turn, would lead to public spaces being reoccupied by what has been called the "prom brigade" – parents, children, and other law-abiding citizens – further enhancing the restoration of mores. The resulting change in culture was widely reported to have been a major factor in the reduction of serious crime in some cities.[83] Still other studies by leading social scientists, including Robert Sampson of the University of Chicago, show that if a neighborhood's culture is strong and intact, the community will mobilize to curb drug abuse and other crimes.[84] In short, there is considerable evidence to support the idea that nurturing moral culture is significant to the common good. Such nurture entails establishing what is of value and undergirding it with mores and laws.

Maintaining some kind of privacy obligation is part of such a moral culture. When obligatory privacy wanes, the moral culture is harmed – whether or not there are immediately discernible effects. It is like chipping away at the foundations of a building: for quite a while, one is able to do with thinner pillars, but that does not mean that the building is unaffected. A non-privacy-related issue might serve to illustrate the point. Sissela Bok argues that one ought not to lie; aside from whatever damage it does to ego and to alter, it diminishes the stock of trust that exists as a good in society. As this stock is depleted, society becomes not only less civil and good, but less stable.[85]

Barrington Moore, in *Privacy*, surveyed the concept of privacy as it existed in cultures all around the world. He found that nearly every culture had the customs that required certain bodily functions, namely excretion and sexual intercourse, to take place in private, to the extent that it was made possible by the environment. Moore found a "panhuman desire to cast a veil of privacy over the sexual act." He rejected the idea that in every culture defecation takes place in private for purely sanitary reasons. He pointed out that all societies have an interest in making sexuality a private thing, not because sex is considered immoral in itself, but because sexual passions can be disruptive to relationships and to productivity, and are therefore best left out of the public arena.[86]

Warren and Brandeis, in their famous law review article of 1890 "The Right to Privacy," wrote that the right to privacy exists not only "to prevent inaccurate portrayal of private life, but to prevent its being depicted at all." They establish privacy as a right unto itself, not linked to other interests, and they considered it a "spiritual" value, one that is essential to human dignity. They wrote: "Each crop of unseemly gossip, thus harvested, becomes the seed of more, and, in direct proportion to its circulation, results in a lowering of social standards and of morality.... Violation of privacy, unlike libel, slander, and property law, *is not just about the injury done to one party, but about the damage to all of society*."[87] (Note, though, that in limiting gossip, reportedly the motivation for Warren and Brandeis' article,[88] the issue again concerns violating the privacy of others, rather than demanding people to keep some things private.)

Among legal scholarship, Harry Clor's essay on the subject is a rare find, not only because he fully recognizes the importance of moral culture, but also because he is one of very few legal scholars who examines the relationship of moral culture to mandated privacy. Clor defines "public morality" as "an ethic of decency or civility (not simply rights and liberties) which is public in the sense that it is generally acknowledged as requisite to the well-being of the community as such – and is therefore recognized in public policy, and (periodically at least) supported by law." He illustrates the point by discussing the regulation of such activities as dueling, gambling, drug use, prostitution, public indecency, vulgarity, and drunkenness –

activities regulated even when "consenting adults" are involved and no physical harm comes to non-consenting persons. Though Clor does not call for the mandating of virtue or moral excellence, he envisions "an intermediate ethic demanding of us something less than nobility but aiming higher than a mere set of minimal rules (abstention from violence, theft, and fraud) instrumental to life, liberty, and prosperity." For Clor, this ethic is embodied in the concept of decency, a "set of rather modest ethical demands." This ethic of decency, Clor says, "serves to stigmatize the grosser violations of certain proprieties which have a significant social function." In this vein our society has traditionally "tried to protect sexual intimacies with a veil of privacy," outlawed no-holds-barred prizefighting, and kept anti-obscenity laws on the books.[89]

John Copeland Nagle argues that "some conduct which many regard as immoral is beyond the scope of the Constitution's protections. Outside the Constitution's boundaries – wherever they are – the state possesses police power to regulate for the protection of the public morals, just as it protects the public health."[90]

The courts have not ignored the relationship of moral culture to mandated privacy. In *United States* v. *O'Brien*, in which it determined that certain conduct contains both speech and non-speech elements, the Court ruled that "a sufficiently important governmental interest in regulating the nonspeech element can justify incidental limitations on First Amendment Freedoms."[91] In *Barnes*, the Court applied the principle set out in *O'Brien* to the protection of public morals. Chief Justice Rehnquist concluded, "The State's traditional police power is defined as the authority to provide for the public health, safety and morals, and such a basis for legislation has been upheld. This governmental interest is unrelated to the suppression of free expression, since public nudity is the evil the state seeks to prevent, whether or not it is combined with expressive activity."[92]

In the Supreme Court case of *City of Erie* v. *PAP's A.M.*, the city of Erie, Pennsylvania adopted an ordinance making it illegal to appear nude in public.[93] An establishment that featured totally nude erotic dancing challenged this ordinance, which was eventually overturned by the Pennsylvania Supreme Court, which found that the ordinance violated the constitutionally protected freedom of expression.[94] The Supreme Court of the United States reversed this decision, finding: "First, the ordinance is within Erie's constitutional power to enact because the city's efforts to protect public health and safety are clearly within its police powers," and, second, that "the ordinance furthers the important government interests of regulating conduct through a public nudity ban and of combating the harmful secondary effects associated with nude dancing." The purpose of the ordinance banning nudity in Erie, Pennsylvania, as stated by the city council, was to limit "a recent increase in nude live entertainment within the City, which activity adversely impacts and threatens to impact on the public health, safety, and welfare by providing an atmosphere conducive to violence, sexual harassment, public intoxication, prostitution, the spread of sexually transmitted diseases and other deleterious effects."[95]

In the *Barnes* case, the Court found that the crux of the case was the "substantial governmental interest in protecting societal order and morality," rather than the issue of freedom of expression. Chief Justice Rehnquist, in announcing the Court's decision stated, "This and other public indecency statutes were designed to protect morals and public order. The traditional police power of the States is defined as the authority to provide for the public health, safety, and morals, and we have upheld such a basis for legislation."[96]

In *Barnes*, unlike in *Erie*, the Supreme Court specifically asserted a "substantial government interest in protecting public order and morality," as established by their ruling in the 1957 case *Roth* v. *United States*. The language in this case was more clearly moral. Chief Justice Rehnquist called public nudity "the evil the state seeks to prevent," and Justice Scalia, writing in concurrence, asserted, "Our society prohibits, and all human societies have prohibited, certain activities not because they harm others but because they are considered, in the traditional phrase, 'contra bonos mores,' i.e. immoral."[97] Surely what applies to nude dancing applies to greater insults to the moral culture such as violence and sexual intercourse.

Changing Moral Culture and the Scope of Privacy Obligations

Restore, liberate, or habituate?

The observations that some measure of privacy is needed in order to undergird the moral culture, that certain forms of exposure are one force among several that cause numerous antisocial consequences, and that the moral culture may have to be shored up, raise a slew of new questions. Foremost among them is to what standards ought the moral culture be restored? Religious conservatives seek a return to traditional standards of mandated and expected privacy, sometimes giving stricter and more rigid interpretations of such standards than they have had in the past – for instance, the restrictions imposed by some Islamic regimes. Although the Koran gives no explicit command for women to cover their hair, and in fact seems only to ask them to conform to contemporary standards of modesty, it is interpreted in many Islamic countries to mean women must cover every part of the body except the face and hands These standards often are enforced harshly.[98]

In contrast, some liberals have suggested that whatever still offends our sensibilities today will cease to offend us with more exposure, just as conduct that was previously taboo to the moral culture is now acceptable. A strong example is public breast-feeding, once considered unacceptable, but now considered in the public interest because of the health benefits for the child. David Kushner suggests that "if it were generally acceptable to be nude on the beach, then the prudes would quickly get over the initial shock and the nudes could enjoy their right without causing distress."[99] Similarly, societies such as Communist China that once frowned on any public expression of affection rapidly got used to it. More and more exposure to violence and pornography in the media seems to trouble us less and less. Accordingly, one may argue that it is merely a question of time before we cease to mind whatever we now find offensive: say, intercourse during daytime, in a public park, next to a playground.

Moreover, some argue that, previously, we had an homogenous moral culture built on tradition, but now we live in highly diverse, multicultural societies. Jeffrey Narvil writes that "American notions of nudity as inherently indecent are strikingly ethnocentric," and that "traditional, historical notions of propriety may not exist in an increasingly diverse and multi-ethnic society."[100] There is no longer one set of community standards to uphold. If we seek to restore some kind of virtuous privacy, which community's values should mores or the law foster?

Others have suggested that it matters little which specific kinds of moral or legal restraints there are on displaying oneself – but that *some* are needed to instill the habits of self-denial or self-discipline, as in Alexis de Tocqueville's notion of the "habits of restraint."[101] Harry Clor, for example, argues that "public morality serves to endorse and enforce certain qualities of human character.... It is because these qualities require deliberate cultivation that we must concern ourselves with a public morality."[102] Ergo, it matters little which restraints, as long as there are some that can serve to build and reinforce character (as when a physician prescribes physical exercises to advance health, not caring which ones, as long as they are regularly carried out and are of sufficient vigor). As evidence that they are needed, one can point to the fact that practically all cultures through history have had some such self-restraints.

Assumptions about human nature

One's assumptions about human nature determine whether one sides with those who see the gradual destruction of mandated and expected privacy merely as a matter of transition, or with those who argue that privacy obligations ought to be restored. The sanguine school of human nature sees people as naturally positive, pro-social creatures who are perverted by the social inhibitions imposed on them by law or moral dictates. Psychological liberation is achieved when these oppressing mores are demolished. The SIECUS (Sexuality Information and Education Council of the US) position on sexual expression is a prime example. It holds that "sexuality is a natural and healthy part of living" and that "all persons are sexual," even, presumably, children. Furthermore, aggression and various obsessions are generated when sexual (or other) urges are repressed, as they have been by many religions and socially conservative Victorian codes.[103] Thus, we have the image, which Rousseau, among others, helped to propagate, of a happy – and healthy – savage, with the uninhibited but good nature of a child. According to the sanguine school of human nature, allowing the last mores of mandated privacy to fall would be a further step in human progression.

Although Freud is given to different interpretations, his position in *Civilization and its Discontents* is similar. He argues that while natural urges can be sublimated in favor of more pro-social (or civilized) expressions – and while such sublimation may well be unavoidable for civilization to persist – it exacts a psychic cost. This cost in turn leads to various unwholesome, infantile, and regressive behaviors, as well as antisocial outbursts.[104] Following this line, some privacy obligations might be necessary, but society benefits from keeping them fairly limited.

In contrast, in the dour view of human nature people are naturally aggressive and loaded with inappropriate sexual drives. A social order and a decent society are possible only if we "keep the lid on," not merely by teaching people about the merits of various forms of self-denial, but by habituating them such that self-government becomes part of their character. Moreover, the social veneer will have to be continuously reinforced, as people tend to regress toward their asocial natures. As Moore puts it, the root of privacy might be that "sexual passion is inherently threatening to cooperative human relationships and must therefore be kept out of sight."[105] If this is the case, privacy obligations had better be thick and firmly enforced.

I see room for an intermediate position – one that recognizes that we cannot live in a world in which people give their natural urges unfettered expression, but also that one can suppress excessively, to the point that efforts to maintain excessive social order cause disturbances of their own. The fact that many traditional mores have been allowed to die is not necessarily evidence that we can do without any. As we have approached a state of anomie – "letting it all hang out" – we have witnessed a very large increase in the type of antisocial behavior no civil society can condone, such as a 400 percent increase in violent crime, drug abuse, and teen pregnancy.[106]

A general communitarian thesis applies here – a good society provides a careful balance between social order and liberty.[107] A particular society in a given historical period can be too restrictive *or* too loose. To achieve the desired balance between autonomy and social order, different societies may well need to move in different directions. In societies where many of the old mores are long washed out, and which have been pushing the envelope ever closer to naked human nature, some restoration of the moral cultural, such as privacy and the habits of self-discipline in particular, may be called for. At the same time, some other cultures may require the lifting of many veils to move toward a good society.

What ought to be the specific core values of the moral culture, and what are their implications for new or renewed mores and laws concerning virtuous privacy? I am the first to acknowledge that I do not have a specific list of what kinds of privacy obligations need support or renewal. It is a matter not addressed here, not only because I believe that it matters less which values are upheld as long as there are some significant, well-supported, habits of self-restraint, but also because those values can arise only out of moral dialogues within the society that has to undergird such new or renewed values.[108]

3

Children and Free Speech

Introduction

When freedom of speech comes into conflict with the protection of children, how should this conflict be resolved? What principles should guide such deliberations? Can one rely on parents and educators (and more generally on voluntary means) to protect children from harmful cultural materials (such as internet pornography and violent movies), or is government intervention necessary? What difference does historical context make for the issue at hand? Are all minors to be treated the same? What is the scope of the First Amendment rights of children in the first place? These are the questions here explored.

The approach here differs from two polar approaches that can be used to position it. According to a key civil libertarian position, materials that are said to harm children actually do not have such an effect, and even if such harm did exist, adults should not be reduced to reading only what is suitable for children. Hence, as long as speech qualifies as protected for adults, it should be allowed. In short, the First Amendment should trump other considerations.[1]

Many social conservatives argue that pornography undermines the moral culture and corrupts character. Hence, such material should be barred, the way child pornography is, in order to protect children and adults alike – although additional protection of children is surely welcome. In short, according to this approach, protecting people and the community from harmful cultural products takes precedence over free speech when there is a conflict.

Neither of these positions focuses on the difference between children and adults. To put it strongly, quite a few civil libertarians lean toward treating children like adults, and many social conservatives focus on the child in all of us, on our vulnerabilities. Both focus on pornography and each, for its own reasons, is less mindful of the effects of exposure to violence.[2]

The position developed here[3] builds on extensive social science findings that there are cultural materials harmful to children – although we shall see that the greatest harm is not caused by the materials on which recent attempts to protect children have focused. I suggest the starting point of such deliberations should be an agreement that there be no a priori assumptions that either free speech or protection of children trumps the other, and that there are systematic ways to work out the relationship between these two core values.[4] I realize that to discuss the First Amendment in balance with something else is not a concept readily acceptable to those who treat free speech as the most primary right and who, while recognizing that it must be squared occasionally with other values, put the onus of proof completely on those making claims against it. My approach treats free speech as one of several values that must be balanced. Moreover, I hold that the balance between these two core values, like all others, is affected by historical context, in which excessive leanings in favor of one value (and neglecting the other) need to be corrected in the following time period if a reasonable balance is to be preserved. This principle guides us in exploring whether one can rely on voluntary means to treat the issue at hand or whether government intervention is needed. And I not only treat minors as having fundamentally different rights from adults, but also take into account differences among minors of various ages.

It should be noted that the discussion here focuses on the right to "consume" speech rather than to produce it. The main question is not whether children should be entitled to make movies, produce CDs, and so on, but whether their access to the harmful content found in some cultural materials should be limited.

The discussion proceeds by providing some background, and then extensively examining five case studies to provide key examples for explorations of the issues at hand. Readers familiar with the cases or less interested in the fine print may wish to turn to the discussion of the lessons drawn from these cases regarding the proper relationship between speech and the protection of children (see pp. 73ff.). I pay special attention to the merit of separating the access children have to cultural materials from the access adults have – or if this cannot be fully accomplished, the possibility of minimizing the extent to which limitations on children "spillover" onto adult access – rather than dealing with "all patrons" as if they were of one kind. Also, I take it for granted that commercial speech can more readily be limited than other speech, and that while voluntary means of curbing access are superior to semi-voluntary ones, there might be room for some regulation.

There then follows an examination of the evidence of the scope and nature of the harm some cultural materials inflict on children, with special attention given to the important differences in the effects of pornographic and violent content on children. The need to correct the delicate balance between speech and the protection of children is viewed in the historical context in which it occurs, followed by an examination of differences among children according to their ages. The chapter closes with a brief review of the implications of the conclusions drawn up to this point for political theory and with a discussion of whether the standards for limiting speech could be communal or must be national, and the implications of this factor for the protection of children.

Background: Content Controls Fail the Test

Congress has made several attempts to limit the access children have to materials that it considers harmful to them.[5] The constitutional challenges to these laws reveal a major flaw in these approaches and explain the current focus of other attempts to deal with the same problem. The issue has not been the need or legitimacy of taking special measures to protect children. In several cases, the Supreme Court has affirmed that the government has a compelling public interest in protecting children.[6] *Ginsberg* v. *New York* explicitly confirms that "the State has an independent interest in protecting the welfare of children and safeguarding them from abuses."[7] Moreover, it specifically recognized that some cultural products can cause harm to children, and that children are entitled to protection from such materials. The decision in *Ginsberg*, which upheld a New York State statute prohibiting the sale of pornographic magazines to minors under the age of 17, relied on two basic principles regarding children: that children should not be allowed the same access as adults to certain types of materials, and that the state is entitled to pass laws aiding parents in carrying out their duties. The Court ruled that though the materials in question were legal for adults, the Constitution permits the state to "accord minors under 17 years of age a more restricted right than that assured to adults to judge and determine for themselves what sex material they may read and see." Furthermore, it stated, "Constitutional interpretation has consistently recognized that the parents' claim to authority in the rearing of their children is basic in our society. . . . Those primarily responsible for children's well-being are entitled to the support of laws designed to aid discharge of that responsibility."[8]

The Court later reaffirmed this position in *FCC* v. *Pacifica Foundation*, which upheld an FCC (Federal Communications Commission) ruling restricting the broadcast of indecent speech to times of day when children were unlikely to be listening or watching unsupervised. The Court reasoned that "children may not be able to protect themselves from speech which, although shocking to most adults, generally may be avoided by the unwilling through the exercise of choice. At the same time, such speech may have a deeper and more lasting negative effect on a child than on an adult." The Court thus affirmed that "society may prevent the general dissemination of such speech to children, leaving to parents the decision as to what speech of this kind their children shall hear and repeat."[9]

The matter then became how to separate speech from which children should be protected from other speech. As in other attempts to separate two kinds of speech (such as "fighting words"[10]), this has so far proven next to impossible.

When Congress took up the challenge of protecting children on the internet, it first passed legislation attempting to shield children by controlling the content of the materials they could access. The most notable attempts, the Communications Decency Act of 1996 (CDA) and the Children Online Protection Act of 1998 (COPA), focused on restricting the type of content that could be posted on the internet. These attempts largely failed when they were challenged in the courts. The Supreme Court ruled that the CDA's prohibitions on "indecent transmission" and "patently offensive display" violated freedom of speech as protected by the First Amendment. Though it affirmed the compelling interest of the government in "protecting children from potentially harmful materials" on the internet, the Court found that "the CDA places an unacceptably heavy burden on protected speech, and that the defenses do not constitute the sort of 'narrow tailoring' that will save an otherwise patently invalid unconstitutional provision." The Court ruled that the scope of the legislation was too broad, attempting to shield those under the age of 18 from certain content at too great an expense to adults' access to protected speech.[11]

COPA was deemed unconstitutional by the District Court for the Eastern District of Pennsylvania and Court of Appeals for the 3rd Circuit, which issued an order blocking enforcement of the statute.[12] The Court of Appeals struck down COPA on the grounds that its use of the community standards test – established by Supreme Court precedent in earlier obscenity cases[13] – violated the First Amendment when applied to the internet. The case went before the Supreme Court, which overturned the previous decision, ruling that using "community standards" to determine what materials on the internet are "harmful to minors" was not a violation of the First Amendment.[14] However, the Supreme Court also recognized that COPA might be unconstitutional for other reasons, and thus allowed the order blocking its enforcement to stand and ordered the US Court of Appeals for the 3rd Circuit to review the other free-speech issues surrounding the statute.[15] Commentators speculate that the case will most likely return to the Supreme Court, and that it may well be ruled unconstitutional eventually.[16] Justice Anthony Kennedy stated that "there is a very real likelihood that the Child Online Protection Act is over broad and cannot survive."[17] In resolving the tension between free speech and the protection of children, we run into difficulties separating protected and unprotected speech and ensuring that the protection of children will not limit adults' access to speech. Given these rulings, our approach prefers measures that attempt to restrict the *manner* in which children can access harmful material rather than measures directly restricting the content itself.

I proceed by examining five cases in which the issue at hand comes to a head in order to provide grist for the mill of the examination that follows.

Five Cases

The five cases studied here – those of Loudoun County Library, Virginia; Kern County Public Libraries, California; the Children's Internet Protection Act (CIPA); restrictions on tobacco advertising; and television ratings and the V-chip – are not exhaustive. I have chosen them because they allow me to examine what I consider the two crucial dimensions of the issue at hand: (a) to what extent do the limitations succeed in curbing only the access of children, or are there also "spillover" effects that limit the access of adults? and (b) to what extent are the measures involved mandated by the government and designed to directly control (e.g. ban) certain forms of access rather than enhance the ability of parents and educators to guide their charges? The reason for choosing these two dimensions will become evident as the argument unfolds.

The issues in all of these cases are multilayered because, typically, when the access of minors is limited, the access of adults is also limited to some extent.[18] The Courts therefore tend to examine the issue in light of two different questions. In some cases, it is quite constitutional for the access of adults to be curbed for certain materials, such as child pornography.[19] The question then becomes whether or not those who put the limitations in place followed the proper procedures to determine that the material in question should be blocked. However, if the material in question cannot be constitutionally blocked from adults, the question still remains as to whether the same holds true for minors. In looking at the five cases at hand, I focus on the second question.

Loudoun County Library, Virginia

In July 1997, the Board of Trustees of the Loudoun County Library, in Virginia's conservative Loudoun County, adopted a policy requiring all library computers to have blocking software, but allowing the filters to be disabled when adults used the computers, or when minors were accompanied by a parent or guardian.[20] The policy was revised later that fall, however, after several members voiced their concern that it was not strict enough. The updated policy blocked access to all sexually explicit material, regardless of the patron's age, and required written permission from a parent or guardian for anyone under 18 who wanted to use the internet on a computer in a Loudoun County library.[21] Adult patrons who wished to have a specific site unblocked (not the filter itself disabled) needed to submit a written request providing their name, the site to be unblocked, and the reasons they wanted access. The librarian would then review the requested site and manually unblock it if she deemed it appropriate under the terms of the policy.[22] The stated purpose of the policy was to prevent a "sexually hostile environment" from forming as a result of the display of pornographic internet sites and to exclude pornographic materials from the electronic resources available at the library, as they had always been excluded from the print resources.[23] Whether deliberately or unwittingly, the policy clearly inhibited the access of adults by requiring that they disclose their name and preferences – in writing – before being able to access sexually explicit material.

Soon after, a grassroots group called Mainstream Loudoun County joined with several civil liberties groups to challenge the library policy in court, alleging that Loudoun County's policy, "as written and as implemented," violated the First Amendment rights of both the internet site providers blocked by the software and Loudoun County Library patrons wishing to access the internet by discriminating against protected speech on the basis of content. Furthermore, the plaintiffs argued, even if the library was justified in blocking the content in question, they did not follow the correct procedures in doing so; therefore the policy constituted unconstitutional prior restraint.[24]

In November 1998, the US District Court in the Eastern District of Virginia declared Loudoun County's policy overly broad and unconstitutional. The District Court found that the Loudoun County policy did involve First Amendment issues because use of blocking software was more akin to an active decision to remove materials from the library than to the passive decision simply not to acquire them. It also held that strict scrutiny was the appropriate standard by which any restriction of this kind of speech should be judged. The Court then proceeded to evaluate the specific speech prohibited by the policy: obscenity, child pornography, and material deemed "harmful to juveniles" by Virginia statutes. It found that while neither obscenity nor child pornography is protected by the First Amendment, the definition of "harmful to juveniles" in the Virginia Code includes speech that the courts have held to be constitutionally protected for adults. Having established that at least some of the content blocked by the Library was constitutionally protected, the Court then applied a three-prong test to determine whether the limitations imposed were constitutional. The Court asked: (1) whether the interests asserted by the state, in this case "minimizing access to illegal pornography and avoidance of creation of a sexually hostile environment," are compelling; (2) whether the limitations imposed by the policy are necessary to further those interests; and (3) whether the policy is "narrowly drawn to achieve those interests."[25]

The Court found that though the policy did claim to further a compelling interest, it failed to meet the second and third parts of the test. Loudoun County did not demonstrate to the Court's satisfaction that without the policy a sexually hostile environment might exist in the libraries, individuals would access obscene material or child pornography, or minors under the age of 18 would view materials that are harmful to them.[26] Nor was the Court persuaded that the means the County decided upon were narrowly tailored to meet the compelling government interests. The judges found that there were less restrictive means available to shield children from harmful material, such as privacy screens, casual monitoring of internet activity by librarians, or the installation of filtering software on only some of the computers.

They also ruled that the policy was "over inclusive because, on its face, it limits the access of all patrons, adult and juvenile, to material deemed fit for juveniles." Citing *Reno* v. *ACLU*, the Court noted that, in this instance, the spillover onto the ability of adults to receive protected speech and material was too great, for "[t]he interest in encouraging freedom of expression in a democratic society outweighs any theoretical but unproven benefit of censorship."[27]

In the case of Loudoun County, the policy promulgated by the Library Board empowered librarians to decide what speech to censor without providing "sufficient standards and adequate procedural safeguards."[28] In other words, librarians were given full discretion to determine which sites to unblock, with no established guidelines of any sort to help define what constitutes material that is harmful to minors, and no provisions for further review (i.e., by the Library Board or, perhaps more appropriately, by attorneys familiar with these legal standards).

The Court was particularly concerned with the lack of transparency in the blocking criteria used by Log-On Data Corporation, the makers of the X-Stop filtering software. Manufacturers like Log-On usually consider their blocking criteria to be proprietary information, and therefore protected trade secrets, in spite of the fact that this "entrust[s] all preliminary blocking decisions – and, by default, the overwhelming majority of final decisions – to a private vendor...that...does not base its blocking decisions on any legal definition of obscenity or even on the parameters of the defendant's Policy."[29]

Kern County Public Libraries, California

In 1996, the Kern County Board of Supervisors, in California, passed a resolution to "prevent disruption of the educational purpose and atmosphere of the public libraries of Kern County through the display of sexually explicit material and to restrict access by minors over the Internet at County public libraries to harmful material as defined in the California Penal Code."[30] Following the resolution, Kern County signed a contract with the N2H2 software company to supply BESS internet filtering software for more than 50 computers in the County's libraries. The Director of Libraries requested that N2H2 customize the blocking software so that it block only material defined as harmful to minors by the California Penal Code, in accordance with the clause in the resolution stating the intention to filter this type of content "to the maximum extent possible, consistent with constitutional principles and available technology."[31]

In the fall of 1996, N2H2 president Peter H. Nickerson informed Kern County that his company would be unable to customize the BESS filtering software to block out material based on the definitions of the California Penal Code, partly because "it seems that this is . . . a legal matter and I do not have the legal expertise in house to make that judgment" as to which websites did or did not meet the legal criteria for "harmful matter."[32] Despite this clearly stated inability to tailor the software to block only illegal material, Kern County installed BESS filtering software on all computers in all libraries with access to the internet.

Concerned with the inability of "BESS or any other software program to make distinctions between protected and unprotected speech" and the use of filtering software to prevent some library patrons from being offended by material accessed by other patrons, the ACLU claimed that the County knowingly denied access to "many sites on the Internet that are valuable and constitutionally protected both for adults and for minors."[33] Kern County repeatedly made assurances that the internet policy did not violate the First Amendment, while the ACLU argued that the technical limitations of the filtering software created the danger of censorship. Noting the American Library Association's opposition to blocking software in libraries[34] and recent policy decisions in San Jose and Santa Clara refusing to install filters on library computers, ACLU National Staff Attorney Ann Beeson wrote a letter demanding that Kern County remove the internet filters on library computers within ten days or face a legal challenge in federal court. Ms Beeson added a threat: the County would be liable for the ACLU's substantial attorney's fees if the ACLU prevailed in its claims, and removing the filters was the only way the Country could avoid costly litigation. The ACLU's demands were not qualified in any way. Rather than calling for the removal of filters from certain computers that would be accessible only to adults or for differing levels of filtering depending upon the age of the patron, the ACLU demanded that filtering software be removed from all computers.[35]

Although the County could have refused to comply with the ACLU's demands, it would then have faced a lengthy and expensive legal battle. Under these pressures, the Kern County Board of Supervisors decided to "resolv[e] any constitutional concerns or any intention of initiating litigation,"[36] and in January of 1998 it directed all Kern County libraries with one terminal with internet access to disable the filters and only enable them if requested to do so by a patron, noting that the County intended to install a second computer in these branches within two weeks. Branches with two or more online computers were ordered to disable filters on half of their terminals. But all patrons, both children and adults, had the choice whether or not to use the filtered or unfiltered computer.[37] The ACLU hailed this as a victory that would "allow all adult and minor patrons to decide for themselves whether to access the Internet with or without a filter."[38]

Children's Internet Protection Act

In 1996, several programs were established to make public funds available to schools and libraries to allow them to purchase computers and provide internet access. The e-rate program, which was established by the Telecommunications Act of 1996 and administered by the Federal Communications Commission, enables eligible schools and libraries to receive discounts on telecommunications and internet access services. The Library Services and Technology Act (LSTA) provides grants, administered at the state level, for the "purchase [of] computers used to access the Internet, or to pay for direct costs associated with accessing the Internet."[39] The purpose of these two programs is to provide internet access to people who cannot afford it themselves and to those living in remote or rural areas where high-speed internet access is unavailable.[40]

In 1999, Senators John McCain (R-AZ) and Fritz Hollings (D-SC) sponsored the Children's Internet Protection Act (CIPA), which was passed by Congress as part of an omnibus bill and signed by President Clinton in December 2000.[41] It requires schools and libraries that receive federal discounts on internet access or public funding for computers to install "technology protection measures" (i.e. filtering software) to block out material deemed "obscene, child pornography or harmful to minors."[42]

CIPA defines minors as individuals under the age of 17 and the phrase "harmful to minors" as "any picture, image, graphic image file, or other visual depiction that (a) taken as a whole and with respect to minors, appeals to a prurient interest in nudity, sex, or excretion; (b) depicts, describes, or represents, in a patently offensive way with respect to what is suitable for minors, an actual or simulated sexual act or sexual contact, actual or simulated normal or perverted sexual acts, or a lewd exhibition of the genitals; and (c) taken as a whole, lacks serious literary, artistic, political, or scientific value as to minors."[43]

CIPA's scope is rather modest. It does not impose a control on schools and libraries in general; it merely sets conditions for those schools and libraries that seek to use federal funds to connect to the internet, some 4,500 libraries and a large number of public schools across the United States.[44] To obtain these funds, a school or library must prepare a request that includes numerous details, and CIPA merely adds the one additional requirement that they commit to installing filters. Those schools and libraries choosing not to comply with CIPA, as well as those not demonstrating a good faith effort at compliance within a year and a half of the enactment of the law, will no longer receive the said discounts or subsidies.[45]

The ACLU and ALA joined to bring a legal challenge against CIPA, which was heard by a special three-judge panel in Philadelphia in March of 2002.[46] The ACLU and ALA contended that available filtering technology is not sophisticated enough to block only unprotected material and that even if it were, requiring it to be installed on all computers linked to the internet without first going through the proper procedures for determining what materials can be lawfully blocked constitutes "prior restraint."[47] According to the pretrial brief, CIPA was "lacking both narrow and reasonably defined standards, and without adequate (or, in fact, any) procedural safeguards."[48] They further alleged that the blocking programs are both over- and under-inclusive: they block constitutionally protected, but perhaps controversial, speech or websites containing arbitrary keywords[49] while allowing through vast quantities of the materials they claim to block.[50] They argued that CIPA also passed the buck on censorship to private companies that design and sell filtering programs. Decisions about which keywords to use and which sites to block were made by third-party, non-government entities, a fact which does not, they contended, exempt the restrictions of expression from constitutional scrutiny.[51]

Furthermore, the plaintiffs contended, CIPA's provisions for disabling the filtering software for adults allowed for, but did not require, librarians to approve exceptions for "bona fide" or other lawful research and contained no definition of these terms, leaving the decision to unblock software at the discretion of the librarian or administrator.[52] The ALA argued that, *de facto* if not *de jure*, this policy restricted the options of all patrons, leaving them with the choice of a computer with blocking software or no computer at all. In addition, the ALA argued, CIPA offered no such research exceptions to minors wishing to access constitutionally protected but technologically blocked material and speech in libraries that received e-rate funds.[53]

Finally, the plaintiffs pointed out that CIPA mandated that all patrons – both adults and minors – of the public libraries receiving discounts on internet access view only material suitable for children.[54]

The government's simple answer to the problems civil libertarians had with CIPA was: if you don't like it, don't apply. As stated in its pretrial brief: "Any library recipient that disagrees, as a matter of policy or principle, with the conditions imposed by CIPA simply may decline to accept the affected federal subsidies."[55] It is not discriminatory to ask that "federal money...[not] be used to give kids access to dirty peep shows," argued Janet LaRue, senior director of legal studies at the Family Research Council.[56] Donna Rice Hughes, a member of the Child Online Protection Commission and author of *Kids Online: Protecting Your Children In Cyberspace*,[57] agreed, stating, "If they don't want to use protection tools, fine. Then they don't get federal money for Internet access."[58] Installation of the filters was not wholly mandatory or compulsory; each library system could make its decision on an individual basis. The federal government's position was that, "under the Spending Clause, no putative federal subsidy recipient has the right to demand a subsidy, much less the right to demand that a subsidy be granted unconditionally."[59]

The ACLU and ALA contended that the government's arguments ran contrary to the e-rate program's mission to "bridge the 'digital divide' between those people with easy access to the Internet and those without."[60] Libraries in areas with wealthier and more liberal residents willing to forgo federal subsidies in favor of First Amendment principles could do so and still find the funds to remain open. Libraries in poorer areas, however, would be all but compelled to install filters or face losing what, for some, constitutes a majority of their budget. Judith Krug, director of intellectual freedom at the ALA, argued that this makes CIPA more than a poorly worded policy – it makes it discriminatory.[61]

Ultimately, many supporters of CIPA see the court case not as a dispute about legal precedent, but as a fundamental disagreement about society's role in protecting children. They hold that civil libertarians err too much on the side of protecting spillover into the First Amendment rights of adults at a heavy cost to children and allow for ideology to reach extreme levels. In an email debate with the ALA's Judith Krug, Mike Millen, an attorney affiliated with the Pacific Justice Institute, opined:

> for reasons that are mystifying to most Americans, these anti-filtering groups will not come out and say, "Yes, hard-core pornography in the hands of young children is harmful, wrong and ought to be stopped." ... While the American Library Association may not endorse children viewing obscene materials, it also refuses to condemn or do anything about it.[62]

Another CIPA co-sponsor, Rep. Ernest Istook (R-OK), concurs, writing in a letter to Congressional colleagues: "They [civil libertarians] treat it as 'someone else's problem' and falsely label it 'censorship' if they're not permitted to expose our children to the very worst things on the Internet, using federal tax dollars to do so."[63]

Lawmakers and advocates argue that it is irresponsible not to attempt to protect children from harmful materials that are available at the click of a mouse in a local library, and they see no realistic solutions being offered by an opposition that is focused only on First Amendment rights. Millen sums up their position as follows:

> I think our philosophical difference is again playing itself out here. If you believe that numerous children are being harmed daily by exposure to hard-core porn on the Internet, the trade-off of a child occasionally losing access to a blocked site (or having to ask for parental help to have it unblocked) is well worth having. However, if you believe that library-accessible porn doesn't hurt kids, then of course the balance would tip in favor of unfettered access. Most parents believe the former.[64]

In May 2002, the three-judge panel ruled against CIPA, and the Supreme Court heard arguments on the case in spring of 2003. The judges in Philadelphia justified their ruling in a 195-page statement that focused on content for all, but not on the question of the extent of minors' First Amendment rights – a bias which is a clear result of CIPA seeking filtering for all patrons rather than only for minors.[65] The ruling barely mentions minors, and the legal examination deals merely with First Amendment rights in general. Even when the Court discusses group-specific blocks, it briefly covers blocks on all kinds of content – racially offensive material, material that offends the employees of the library, or material that the librarians consider inappropriate (such as dating sites). The First Amendment rights of children were not the focus, although the protection of children is the purpose of the Children's Internet Protection Act.

The Court was impressed by the list of wrongly blocked sites provided by the plaintiffs, which included numerous websites for churches, health-related sites on topics ranging from allergies to cancer, and the websites of several political figures. Hence, the Court stated that filtering programs are "blunt instruments that not only 'underblock,' i.e., fail to block access to substantial amounts of content the library boards wish to exclude, but also, central to this litigation, 'overblock,' i.e., block access to large quantities of material that library boards do not wish to exclude and that is constitutionally protected."[66] Proponents of the filters argued that they are getting better all the time and that they are more than 99 percent accurate.[67]

The Court recognized but dismissed the argument that when one goes to a library one does not find all materials that are "protected" speech either – such as *Hustler* magazine or XXX-rated video tapes – on the grounds that providing internet access is more akin to opening up a public forum than to the process by which the library actively selects books to purchase. Once such a public forum is provided, the library cannot selectively exclude certain speech on the basis of its content without subjecting the exclusion to strict scrutiny.[68] I note that the Court also disregarded another issue: were a child to check out a pornographic library book, he would need to ask a librarian to retrieve it and would leave a record when he checks it out, thus creating a kind of barrier that does not exist when accessing information on computers.

Restrictions on tobacco advertising

It is not only violent and pornographic material from which parents, activists, and legislators have sought to shield children; the advertising of harmful products to minors has also been subject to regulation and subsequent debate and has raised First Amendment issues. (A wit once suggested that tobacco was pornographic because it has no redeeming social merit.) The marketing of tobacco products, in particular, has come under intense scrutiny, as new information about "Big Tobacco's" media campaigns aimed at children have come to light. RJ Reynolds Vice-President of Marketing, C. A. Tucker, made the tobacco industry's desire to reach this audience abundantly clear in a presentation to the RJR Board of Directors in 1974, stating: "This young adult market, the 14–24 group...represent[s] tomorrow's cigarette business. As this 14–24 age group matures, they will account for a key share of the total cigarette volume for at least the next 25 years."[69] A document from Philip Morris was uncovered providing information about how the company placed products in child-oriented entertainment like *Who Framed Roger Rabbit?* and *The Muppet Movie.*[70]

Given that 80 percent of adult smokers started smoking before they were 18,[71] getting youngsters addicted is of great interest to the industry in a period when adults have curtailed their smoking habits. Moreover, ads are a significant factor in promoting smoking among minors; it is not peer pressure alone that pushes minors to smoke, and the content of the peer pressure itself is influenced by ads.[72] Statistics indicate a strong correlation between certain tobacco advertisements and the numbers of young people who smoke. A study by the FDA found not only that "cigarette and smokeless tobacco use begins almost exclusively in childhood and adolescence," but also that there is "compelling evidence that promotional campaigns can be extremely effective in attracting young people to tobacco products."[73] Reports by the Surgeon General and the Institute of Medicine stated that "there is sufficient evidence to conclude that advertising and labeling play a significant and important contributory role in a young person's decision to use cigarettes or smokeless tobacco products," noting that kids smoke a smaller number of brands than adults and that "those choices directly track the most heavily advertised brands, unlike adult choices, which are more dispersed and related to pricing."[74] A 1991 study published in the *Journal of the American Medical Association* found that "30% of 3-year-olds and 91% of 6-year-olds could identify Joe Camel as a symbol for smoking."[75] Another study revealed that "the largest increase in adolescent smoking initiation was in 1988, the year that the Joe Camel cartoon character was introduced nationally."[76]

In 1997, the Federal Trade Commission (FTC) filed a complaint against RJ Reynolds Tobacco Company, charging that the company's deliberate attempts to target younger smokers in their advertising constituted a violation of the Federal Trade Commission Act and calling on the company to "cease and desist from advertising to children" through the Joe Camel character or others like it.[77] The FTC had considered banning Joe Camel as early at 1993, but free-speech concerns raised by civil libertarian groups led to the matter being dropped.[78] However, in 1994, four states sued the tobacco companies for reimbursement of healthcare expenses resulting from tobacco use. These states were gradually joined by others, until 41 states had filed lawsuits against the tobacco companies. In 1997, a group of state Attorneys-General drafted a settlement proposal that they hoped would settle all the suits. Soon after, Senator McCain drafted legislation attempting to make the proposed settle-ment law. In addition to requiring the companies to make payments to the states, this bill would have placed limitations on cigarette advertising.

As class-action lawsuits, litigation by states looking to recoup lost healthcare costs from smoking-related illnesses, and Congressional legislation to increase the price of tobacco products through taxes and restrict marketing practices all loomed in 1997, the tobacco in-dustry sought to broker a deal with state governments to stem the oncoming tide.[79] The terms of the 1998 settlement (after the initial 1997 proposal fell apart) specified that Big Tobacco pay states in excess of $240 billion over 25 years, embark on a $1.7 billion cam-paign to study youth smoking habits and fund anti-smoking adver-tising, and accept limitations on advertising practices that appeal to children. Among the tobacco industry's self-imposed restrictions, according to the 1998 settlement, are a complete ban on the use of cartoon characters in the advertising, promotion, packaging, or la-beling of tobacco products; a ban on tobacco industry brand-name sponsorship of events that have a substantial youth audience or of team sports (e.g. basketball, baseball, and football); and substantial restrictions on outdoor advertising, with the substitution of existing product advertisements with anti-smoking campaign material (on billboards and other displays).[80] Civil libertarians came out against the terms of the settlement, decrying the efforts to eliminate the marketing of tobacco products to youth as a violation of freedom of speech. The ACLU has stated that "we [should] allow consumers to make decisions for themselves and stop government from deciding for us what speech we should be free to hear about legal products." They also claimed that restrictions on advertising for minors would "effectively suppress a large amount of speech that adults have a constitutional right to receive."[81] Robert Levy of the Cato Institute went even farther, calling the restrictions on marketing contained in the settlement "ridiculous" and "draconian." Levy testified before

Congress that "there is no evidence" establishing a link between advertising and the decision of minors to begin smoking.[82]

Television ratings and the V-chip

Several measures have been introduced – either by law or by various industries under government or public pressure – to help parents and educators protect children from violent and pornographic materials. In the media, these include the ratings and labeling systems adopted by the movie, television, and music industries. The Motion Picture Association of America appoints a ratings board to set ratings (PG-13, R, etc.) for movies, and the National Association of Theater Owners supports these ratings by asking theaters to bar admittance of those under the recommended age limit.[83] In 1990, the Recording Industry Association of America introduced a uniform labeling system to inform parents if an album contains sexually explicit lyrics or foul language. Some stores voluntarily refrain from selling music with such labels to minors.[84]

Though the ratings system for movies has been in effect since the 1960s, television ratings did not exist until recently. The Telecommunications Act of 1996 set requirements that all new television monitors of a certain size be built with V-chip technology. V-chips allow a user to block all programming that carries a certain rating. The law also gave the FCC the power to set guidelines for rating television programs and to require broadcasters to transmit these ratings in such a way that individuals would be able to block programs with a certain rating using V-chip technology.[85] Since the law gave the television industry a year to enact a voluntary ratings system before the FCC would begin to set the ratings itself,[86] the National Association of Broadcasters, the National Cable Television Association, and the Motion Picture Association of America jointly created the *TV Parental Guidelines*, a voluntary rating system. Following criticism by advocacy groups, the associations revised the ratings system, which the FCC found to be acceptable.[87]

Though the rating system was voluntarily adopted by the industry, and blocking could only be activated by individuals who chose to use their V-chip and were free to determine on what setting to use it, civil libertarians were still not satisfied. The ACLU initially protested the Telecommunications Act's provision asking the FCC to set guidelines because government-set labels on TV programs would force "private individuals and companies to say things about their creative offerings that they have no wish to say, and even puts words into their mouths." They feared that FCC-prescribed ratings would "have the unconstitutional purpose and effect of restricting expression because it is unpopular or controversial."[88] When the industry released its voluntary ratings system, the ACLU called it "government-coerced censorship" and said it was "another example of the government's heavy-handed effort to dictate the use of our remote controls." They also objected to voluntary labeling of music albums on similar grounds, asserting that "even 'voluntary' labeling is not harmless" and arguing that labeling provides no help to parents.[89]

The ACLU also opposed the V-chip as "a heavy-handed attempt by federal bureaucrats to control what is aired on television" and worried that it would censor such important works as *Schindler's List*, *Roots*, and *Gone With the Wind* because they contain violence, and would "empower bureaucrats and television executives to make decisions for parents."[90] Marjorie Heins, formerly with the ACLU and now with the Free Expression Policy Project, claimed that there is no evidence "that explicit sex information and even pornography...by themselves cause psychological harm to *minors of any age*."[91] The ACLU also argued that the V-chip would be an "electronic babysitter" that robs parents of their ability to make choices for their children and to discuss programming with them.[92] Similarly, Rhoda Rabkin, arguing against government enforcement of age-graded ratings systems, contends that "parents know better than anyone else the level of maturity of their children and are therefore best equipped to judge the appropriateness of books, television shows, music, movies, and games."[93]

Civil libertarians have even criticized measures in which the government has no involvement whatsoever, such as the existence of commercial software programs like Cybersitter and Cyber Patrol that allow parents to block out harmful content on the internet. Though the ACLU admits that it prefers such programs to ratings systems or statutes restricting speech, it says they "present troubling free speech concerns."[94]

Lessons: First Approximation

In the first three cases discussed above, neither the courts nor civil libertarians have focused directly on a key question that policymakers (and the society at large) face, namely the subject of this examination: how to protect children from harmful cultural products.

In the Loudoun County, Kern County, and CIPA cases, this question was overshadowed by concerns over the extent to which the measures violated the First Amendment rights of *adults*. Hence, the relevant lessons must be drawn from secondary considerations. The Loudoun case, in which the Board of Trustees sought to ban access to pornography (and not just child pornography or obscenity, which are deemed unprotected by the Constitution) for everyone, not only for children, reflects – whether deliberately or inadvertently – a socially conservative position. In recent decades, the courts have tended to overthrow such restrictions.[95]

The Board of Trustees in Loudoun County retested, in effect, some of the issues raised by the CDA when it imposed filters on all computers and demanded gross violations of privacy for adult patrons who wished to access materials screened out by the filters (e.g. an adult wishing to read about anal intercourse and HIV would have to fill out a form giving his name, address, and the topic he wished to explore, then submit it to a librarian). If this policy would not have a chilling effect on adult access to speech, it is hard to imagine what would. Moreover, under the Loudoun County policy, the librarians – who are, given that we are dealing with public libraries, effectively government agents – would be free to determine whether or not such a request would be granted, without having to be accountable for the criteria used or subject to challenge. No wonder the question of children's rights was barely broached.

In Kern Country, the Library Board initially formulated a similar policy. Although it tried to limit the extent to which protected speech was blocked by seeking filters specially designed to screen out only unprotected speech and speech considered harmful to minors under California law, it did not provide separate computers for adults and children, but, as in Loudoun County, installed filtering software on all computers. The main issue was again whether the curbs are constitutional for anyone. When the County was challenged, it in effect swung to the opposite extreme, removing filters from half the computers and allowing all patrons – minors included – to choose whether to use a filtered computer or an unfiltered one, rather than attempting to distinguish between the First Amendment rights of adults and minors.

CIPA fails to draw a distinction between the access of adults and children, requiring that filters be placed on *all* computers in a school or library, regardless of the age of the patrons who would use them. Civil libertarians smartly challenged its use in public libraries, where adult patrons would have their access curbed, without mentioning schools, in which the issue of children's rights would have come into focus. The ruling against CIPA could have direct implications for the voluntary use of filters by public schools as well. Nancy Willard points out that the factual findings and analysis provided by the courts raise significant questions regarding the constitutionality of the use of these products in public schools.[96]

In dealing with these cases, the courts have focused first on whether the suggested curbs limit the access of adults to blocked materials that are constitutionally protected, and second on whether the proper (and rather strict) procedures to determine that the material was unprotected were followed. Given the inherent difficulties in sorting out which speech is or is not protected[97] and the high procedural hurdles, such curbs have been found lacking, not only by their critics, but also by the courts.

The courts have not pointed the legislature (or any other party) toward a third approach that would filter neither everything nor nothing, but would provide *separate computers for children and adults.* The courts either ruled in favor of the civil libertarians (as in the Loudoun County case) or were indirectly used to intimidate other libraries (as in the Kern County case), resulting in a situation where children were allowed the same rights as adults in choosing whether or not to use a filter. CIPA fell victim to the same weakness. The decision mentions briefly such a possibility, but places it among several other remedies, including the curious idea of librarians warning those looking at inappropriate material with a "tap on the shoulder."[98]

The first lesson that appears from the cases at hand, albeit indirectly, is that if the goal is to protect children and not to curb adult access to speech, the government should urge or require libraries to have *separate computers for children and adults* (the way many libraries have special sections for children's books or the way video rental stores have separate X-rated sections for adults only). Those computers set aside for children would be equipped with filters, while the others could provide unencumbered access to adults, or contain filters set to a different, much less stringent level (for example, to block only illegal materials, such as child pornography, to the extent technically possible). If a library has only one computer, there could be set-aside times for children and for adults. I shall refer to this as the *child–adult separation approach.* Such separation greatly reduces the conflict between protecting free speech and protecting children, although it leaves open the question of the scope of the harm done to children by the said material and what their own free-speech rights are, an issue I address below.

We must take into account two different situations. In one, whatever curbs are mandated are strictly for children, for example filters on computers in a primary school (to keep the case pure, let's say the computer in the teachers' lounge is left unfiltered). In the other situation, full separation of children and adults is not practical, hence any curbs advanced for children might limit the access of adults. (For example, if there are children's hours on the one computer at a library, the amount of time adults may have unencumbered access may be limited.) Eugene Volokh uses the term "spillover" to describe such a situation. He correctly points out that the proper way to frame the issue is not to ask whether there is any spillover, but to examine how significant the spillover is. Spillover rarely can be avoided completely.[99] The assumption is (as the courts have recognized) that there is a compelling public interest in protecting children from harmful material; thus, if a protective measure can be introduced that has minimal spillover, that small amount might be a price worth paying. This issue was not tested in the first three cases examined here because civil libertarians could argue that the spillover on adults was so considerable that even if there were benefits for children, the situation was not acceptable. (They did not have to unveil their argument that these materials do not harm children, a position that they correctly realize is much more difficult to sustain.) So far, I have suggested that the best public policies provide for full child–adult separation so that limitations on children's access will not spillover to adults; next best are those that *minimize* spillover to adults.[100] (In contrast, measures that involve significant spillover, especially if the gain to children is limited, are unacceptable.) Such balancing is commonly found constitutional in other areas in which two major values come into conflict, for instance privacy and the public interest.[101]

The restrictions imposed on tobacco advertising cast additional light on the criteria that might be applied in sorting out the First Amendment rights of children. The ACLU objected to these restrictions, arguing, "Adults cannot be reduced to reading only what is fit for children" and "attempts to reduce the exposure of minors to tobacco advertisements cannot avoid restricting the same information for the adult population."[102] In Justice Frankfurter's inimitable phrase, such limitations "burn the house to roast the pig."[103] But one may wonder if there would be a shortage of material enticing adults to smoke if cartoon characters especially seductive to children were no longer used and if tobacco ads were excluded from a few magazines popular with minors. The ability of adults to access information about tobacco products is thus not limited in any meaningful way.

From a constitutional viewpoint, it is important to take into account the *type* of speech being limited. Tobacco ads concern commercial speech, not speech that has political or social content, and therefore fall in the category of speech that the courts generally have recognized as having a lower level of First Amendment protection.[104]

Finally, there is the matter of who enforces the limitations. The restrictions on tobacco ads reflect an agreement reached between tobacco companies and state governments, not limitations legislated by the government. (One can fairly argue that the voluntary agreement was achieved under economic pressures exerted by the government. The same applies to poor neighborhoods that might find it more difficult than richer ones to pass up e-rate funds in order to avoid the restrictions included in CIPA. However, if one could deem any contract or voluntary agreement coercive whenever there is an economic incentive for one of the sides to enter, or the parties are not economically equal, there would very little left in American society that would be voluntary – and by ACLU and ALA lights, constitutional.) It follows that when speech is commercial and when the curbs are at least semi-voluntary, such measures should be more readily acceptable than curbs on other speech, for which children may not be ready (e.g. Mapplethorpe's photographs).

Labeling, the V-chip, and privately marketed internet filtering software allow further examination of the question of whether one can do without government intervention. These devices provide a continuum of the levels of voluntarism. Movie ratings and labeling on music are akin to tobacco ads in that they have been voluntarily introduced, but under considerable government pressure. Moreover, the criteria for what rating or label a film or album receives are set by the industry, and their use and standards are enforced by the industry, to the extent that they are enforced at all. Thus, unlike tobacco ads, which were part of a legal agreement and could therefore be enforced, the government does not determine what is labeled PG-13 versus R or force movie theaters to card teenagers or otherwise pay mind to the age of theatergoers. Still, the system is not fully voluntary.

The government did require that the V-chip be built into all TV sets. (Actually, a previous law required that decoder circuitry be built into all television sets to allow closed captioning, and nobody objected at the time. The Telecommunications Act of 1996 required that this circuitry also be fashioned so it could block programs based on content codes.[105]) But all that V-chips do is provide parents and educators with a tool for controlling what their charges may watch and the choice of whether or not to use it. The use of V-chips is not required or even actively fostered by the government through educational campaigns (despite the fact that most people seem unaware of the chip or how to use it) or by any other means.[106] Nor is the government monitoring who activates their chips and who neglects to do so. Furthermore, the government is not involved in either setting the ratings on specific programming or determining at what level an individual V-chip is activated, which in turn determines what is screened out.[107]

Finally, screening software that is sold on the free market, purchased at will by parents and activated in line with their educational preferences, is completely voluntary. Such software provides an ideal test of the issue at hand because no First Amendment rights are involved. Free-speech rights are claims people have against their government, not claims children have against their parents.[108] When a parent tells a child that he or she is not ready to read *Lady Chatterley's Lover* or *Mein Kampf*, the parent may be ill-advised, but he or she is not violating anyone's rights. On the contrary, parents and other educators are discharging a duty in this situation. Though public school teachers are government actors – which means that students could make First Amendment claims against them – there is Supreme Court precedent that allows teachers and administrators to use their judgment in limiting a student's speech rights under certain circumstances. In *Tinker* v. *Des Moines Independent Community School District*, the Supreme Court held that First Amendment protection does not extend to student speech which "materially disrupts class work or involves substantial disorder or invasion of the rights of others." Later, in *Bethel School District No. 403* v. *Fraser*, the Court held that a *student's* right to speech must be "balanced against the society's countervailing interest in teaching *students* the boundaries of socially appropriate behavior."[109]

Civil libertarian objections to many of these voluntary devices, including labeling and television ratings, are difficult to fathom and draw heavily on such rhetorical devices as claiming that they constitute "censorship"[110] – a claim that makes people see red, even when no censorship is actually involved. (To be accurate, there is one form of voluntary filtering that even the ACLU does not mind: in the Multnomah County library system, a person turning to use a public computer would first be asked if he wants to use a filter or not. ACLU attorney Chris Hansen, who is a member of the CIPA plaintiff's legal team, simply allowed, "We don't have a problem with that."[111])

Does it follow that the best way to proceed is to rely merely on systems that are voluntary and thus avoid the constitutional issues involved? Few would disagree that voluntary treatments are preferable to government interventions that contain coercive elements and public costs. Persuasion is clearly more effective than the imposition of mores – if it can be made to work. However, when it comes to the protection of children from harmful cultural materials, voluntary protections are highly ineffectual. Most parents and educators do not activate the V-chips in their televisions; movie theaters, and most assuredly CD shops and video rental stores, often do not enforce the rating and labeling systems in place; and only a minority of parents purchase protective filtering software.[112] One may argue that a major educational campaign could alter this behavior, but experience with other such campaigns suggests that one cannot avoid the question of whether or not additional measures are justified.

To review the discussion so far: the courts ruled that there is a compelling public interest to protect children from harmful cultural products which should remain freely accessible to adults.[113] (This, in turn, implies that children have lesser free-speech rights than adults.) However, they found that controlling content does not allow the desired separation between children and adults.[114] Separation of access should avoid this issue. If complete separation is not possible, systems that have little spillover on adult access seem justified, while those that have significant spillover may not. Voluntary measures are to be preferred per se, even if enhanced, but do not provide adequate protection of children. Therefore, government interventions are needed.

The Scope and Nature of the Harm

The examination so far has taken for granted that the courts correctly ruled that there are cultural products that harm children. The discussion now turns to the relevant evidence addressing not merely the scope, but also the nature, of that harm. A recurrent theme running through civil libertarian arguments is that exposure to cultural materials causes no discernible harm – while limiting access does. For instance, in response to efforts to label music with offensive lyrics, the ACLU asserted that "no direct link between anti-social behavior and exposure to the content of any form of artistic expression has ever been scientifically established."[115] Although the ACLU recognizes the existence of social science studies showing harm, it challenges or attempts to invalidate these studies and argues that they do not justify regulating television. For instance, arguing against the voluntary ratings system for television, the ACLU testified that "the social science evidence is in fact ambiguous and inconclusive" and that "the effects of art and entertainment on human beings are more various, complex, and idiosyncratic than some political leaders or social scientists would suggest."[116]

The question of whether there are elements in our culture that harm children is the subject of a huge literature.[117] As far one can determine, there is a considerable, although by no means universal, consensus among those who have studied the matter that significant harm is caused.[118] The next question is what specific items of culture cause significant harm. Here, social science evidence, the courts, and the legislators are at considerable odds. While the courts and legislators focus almost exclusively on pornography, by far the strongest data concerns the effects of depictions of violence.[119]

In response to the few state statutes attempting to limit the access of minors to depictions of violence, the courts have explicitly held that cultural images of violence are protected by the First Amendment.[120] To wit: In the case of *Video Software Dealers Association* v. *Webster*, which challenged a Missouri statute prohibiting the sale or rental to minors of videos containing violent material, the district court stated that "violent expression is protected by the First Amendment."[121]

In contrast, researchers have much stronger evidence about the harms caused by violence depicted in the media and on the internet than they do on the harms of pornography. While they commonly and wisely reject simplistic notions that the media is "the" cause of violence and sexually inappropriate conduct, they repeatedly and systematically find that unfettered exposure is "merely" one major cause for several forms of anti-social behavior.[122]

While a large number of studies are simple one-time observations, several rigorous longitudinal studies have been conducted. For instance, the study conducted by Lefkowitz et al. determined that "the relation between boys' preferences for violent television at age eight and their aggressiveness revealed itself *unequivocally in our study*." They also found that *"the greater was a boy's preference for violent television* at age eight, *the greater was his aggressiveness* both at that time and *ten years later*," and later found greater incidents of serious crime at age 30.[123] The results here are consistent with other studies that have shown aggressive tendencies in children who view violent material.[124]

In another study, researchers compared the aggression levels of children in three Canadian towns. The first town (Notel) had no television service due to its geographical location in a valley, the second town (Unitel) had received only one station for the last seven years, and the third town (Multitel) had received Canadian and American broadcast television for 15 years.[125] The researchers found that following the introduction of television in Notel, both boys and girls at various age levels were more physically and verbally aggressive than they had been before the introduction of television. Researchers also found that children in Multitel exhibited higher levels of both verbal and physical aggression than those in Unitel.[126]

A report by the Senate Committee on Commerce, Science, and Transportation summarizes research in this area and concludes that watching significant amounts of televised violence negatively effects human character and attitudes, promotes violent behaviors, influences moral and social values about violence in daily life, and often results in a perception of a nastier world and an exaggerated probability of being a victim of violence.[127] On a similar note, University of Michigan psychologist Leonard Eron has testified that meta-analyses of current research estimate that "10 percent of all youth violence can be attributed to violent television."[128]

Several studies followed children into adulthood and concluded that viewing violent material increases the likelihood of aggressive behavior and, in some instances, criminal behavior. For example, one study found greater incidence of serious crime at age 30 in young people who watch violent television at age 8.[129] A recent study in *Science* comes to similar conclusions. Johnson et al. found that those who reported watching higher amounts of television in adolescence later reported higher rates of aggressive behavior in late adolescence and early adulthood. The authors also found a higher rate of aggressive acts at a mean age of 30 in those who reported heavier television viewing at a mean age of 22.[130]

James P. Steyer, who examined well over a hundred studies conducted over 30 years, identified four particular ways that media violence has been shown to impact on children, which he sums up in simple language as follows:

> It can make them fearful and lead them to believe that the world is a mean and violent place. It can cause some kids to act violently and aggressively toward others. It can teach them that violence is an acceptable way to deal with conflict. And it can desensitize them toward the use of violence in the real world.[131]

The effects of exposure to pornography on minors are much less established: ethical considerations prevent researchers from conducting experiments that directly test the effects of pornography on children. Even if correlative studies existed, they would not allow for causal inferences.[132] Because of the paucity of such studies, those who make strong arguments about why it is undesirable to expose children to such materials must do so without evidence supporting their claims.[133] However, studies do exist on the effects of pornography on young, college-aged adults, and these show that young adults exposed to pornography that is combined with violence hold more callous views toward rape and sexual coercion than those not exposed.[134] The *Report of the Surgeon General's Workshop on Pornography and Public Health* hypothesized that "it is certainly reasonable to speculate, however, that the results of such exposure on less socially mature individuals with less real world experience to counteract any influences of this [pornographic] material would be equally (or more) powerful than those seen in college students."[135] A meta-analysis of 46 studies conducted between 1962 and 1995 on the effects of pornography on adults found that pornography is "one important factor which contributes directly to the development of sexually dysfunctional attitudes and behaviors" and that "exposure to pornographic material puts one at increased risk for developing sexually deviant tendencies, committing sexual offenses, experiencing difficulties in one's intimate relationships, and accepting the rape myth."[136]

Overall, the social science data strongly support the need to protect children from harmful material, especially from exposure to violence in the media and on the internet. (The argument that exposure to violence itself, in the home and in the streets, has a worse effect is a valid one, but it does not invalidate the additional harm done by the violence portrayed in cultural materials. Moreover, portrayals of violence in the media constitute one factor that breeds and nurtures actual violent behavior. All this is not to suggest that pornography is not harmful; only that it seems – in the absence of evidence – less so than images of violence.) There is no reasonable doubt that exposure to a torrent of images of violence in the media harms children significantly. The evidence on pornography (which itself may contain violence) is less strong. When considering how to protect children, the current preoccupation with curbing pornographic material and not violent material should be reversed.

The reasons both civil libertarians and social conservatives tend to focus on pornography rather than on violence require a separate examination. Civil libertarians may realize that their case is much weaker when it comes to the effects of depictions of violence; social conservatives may associate violence with manhood. But these are merely speculations. Whatever the reasons, both sides push the public dialogue, legislators, and the courts to focus on the lesser harm, drawing attention away from the greater harm.

A colleague, reviewing a previous version of this chapter, raised several cogent questions. How is violence defined? Should children be protected from all forms of violence? And would not such a ban prevent their being exposed to a large variety of novels, books of history, and even news? Defining violence is surely not more difficult than pornography, and is probably easier. Violence, for the purposes at hand, is best defined as the use of physical force with the intent to harm, maim, or kill. Which kinds and forms children should be protected from (and what difference age makes) is an issue we face only once we move away from the current position that all of it constitutes free speech, including, say, showing a sadistic movie to children aged 6 years or younger. Once we are ready to curb access to violent content, several rules, often suggested before, come to mind. We can limit the showing of such material on television to late hours; we can discourage the use of gratuitous violence in the media as well as in video games; we can urge that its depictions be negatively framed; and so on. More details require, and deserve, a separate study.[137]

Historical Context

Societies tend to lose their balance between conflicting core values in one direction or another.[138] They then move to correct, often tilting too far in the opposite direction because they lack a precise guidance mechanism. Through much of American history, until the 1960s, rights were neglected, including those of women, minorities, and the disabled. However, communitarians have shown that during the next generation, rights were pushed to the point where the public interest and the moral culture were undermined.[139] As of the early 1990s, a counter-correction set in, which arguably went overboard in the opposite direction, especially in the wake of September 11, 2001.[140]

Viewed in this context, since the 1920s civil libertarians have worked to promote rights in general, and the right to free speech in particular, as profound self-evident truths. Typically, the First Amendment is presented as if it were semi-sacred, and any attempts to curb it as sacrilegious and outright offensive. Civil libertarians believe it self-evident that the right to free speech ought to trump all other considerations – or at least that the onus of proof is on those who seek to advance other values, and that the test for such proof should be set very high indeed. Moreover, the very suggestion that free speech (and rights in general) reflects but one set of societal values, albeit a very important one, and that there is such a thing as the common good (above and beyond that invested in rights), such as the well-being of children, may well seem strange, if not false, to civil libertarians and others imbued with the values of a rights-centered society.[141]

Communitarians have repeatedly pointed out and documented that individualism has been excessive since the 1970s and the common good in general has been neglected.[142] In the same period, children's rights have been pushed too far. One sees that the time has come to restore a better balance between rights and the common good in general, and in matters concerning the balance between free speech and the protection of children in particular. To put it differently, various measures to protect children become much more acceptable once one realizes that free speech can be highly valued even if one ranks it somewhat lower than it has been recently held and that children are now to be more highly regarded. Free speech can be ranked a notch or two lower – as is the case in all democratic societies other than the USA – without that freedom being compromised or society becoming illiberal. Indeed, as Richard Abel shows in his outstanding book *Respecting Speech*, we often limit speech for other purposes, including commercial ones. One may ask, perhaps a bit too rhetorically: are children less worthy than intellectual property?

In the same vein, the more value a society puts on the well-being of children, the more it would be willing to curb free speech under certain circumstances. The argument advanced here is not that American society does not value children highly, but that it arguably does not value them as highly as other liberal democratic societies do relative to other concerns. Not surprisingly, these societies have fewer difficulties introducing measures to protect children from violent and pornographic materials. Surely child care policies in the United States offer further support for this thesis.[143] As Eugene Volokh has noted, civil libertarians believe that "perhaps children's increased vulnerability is a price worth paying for extra freedom for adults."[144]

America's rights-tilt, developed between 1960 and 1990, is gradually being corrected in response to communitarian urging. Society has been willing to pay more mind to social responsibilities, the common good, and the moral culture than in the preceding decades.[145] The attempt to better protect children from harmful material – as reflected in poorly drafted laws such as COPA and CIPA – fits into this societal agenda. To put it differently, the Constitution is a living document, the understanding of which responds to the changing needs of the times and has never been fully specified,[146] and for which the implications are constantly being reinterpreted. The understanding of the First Amendment currently prevalent was fashioned largely after 1920, in response to Americans who were arrested for criticizing US involvement in WWI – a drive led mainly by the ACLU, to its credit. Now that society has moved from being too restrictive to being too permissive, the time has come to realize that the First Amendment was not, in either text or spirit, intended to apply to both children and adults.

The Constitutional Implications of Age-Graded Protections

Are children entitled to the same First Amendment rights as adults, or are they entitled only to lesser free-speech rights? This question is crucial, because if they have the same rights, none of the ideas of separation and spillover would apply. Practically no one would argue that minors have no free-speech rights. Few, if any, would favor banning a 17-year-old from making a political speech at a Young Republican club meeting.[147] At the other extreme, however, some do hold that children of any age should have First Amendment rights identical to those of adults, including the right to be exposed to harmful cultural materials. The question hence stands as to the scope of protected speech when we deal with children. Or, conversely, from what speech are they to be protected – and in what manner?[148]

One's response is greatly affected by how one perceives children in general. There are greatly different views, historically and culturally, as to whether childhood should be considered a unique category, or whether children are "mini-adults" able to make their own decisions. There is also disagreement as to what age childhood concludes and children are able to act as autonomous adults.[149]

In further discussion of this matter it is crucial to distinguish between several terms often used interchangeably – minors, children, and teenagers – each of which has rhetorical consequences. Those who favor full First Amendment rights for children of all ages tend to use the term "young people," "youngsters," or "students" and point to examples of the harm done when teenagers' access is limited to information about, say, HIV or abortion.[150] Those who favor controls tend to call all minors "children" and point to the harm done to toddlers when they are exposed to pornographic or violent material on television.

To allow for a clearer discussion, from here on the following terms will be used: "children" refers to those aged 12 and under and "teenagers" refers to those between the ages of 13 and 18. "Minors" is used to refer to both groups together. The age at which a person reaches majority differs for different matters, such as being eligible to drive or to vote, although in the US 18 is often considered the age at which one becomes an adult. However, there would be nothing sociologically shocking to set a different age, say 17, as an age for less-protected cultural access. The age-differentiated approach is at the heart of this matter.

The discussion so far has followed the way the issue is typically argued by both sides, with relatively little attention given to age differences among minors. Although rating systems are age-graded and parents are free to set their V-chips to age specifications, government-set protections are not usually age-specific. CIPA requires filters on all computers, whether used by adults or children, as do the policies that were implemented in Loudoun and Kern counties. Nor are the curbs on tobacco ads age-graded.

Civil libertarians demand not only the removal of various protective devices for teenagers, but also unencumbered access for children of all ages – as if they were adults. (Social conservatives, in turn, want to treat all minors – and sometimes adults – as children.) Writing on the outcome of the battle over filters in Kern County, Ann Beeson, an ACLU National Staff Attorney, praised the County's decision to "allow all adult *and minor* patrons to decide for themselves whether to access the Internet with or without a filter."[151] In its basic charter, the American Library Association (ALA) demands that "the rights to minors shall in no way be abridged," in regard to internet access.[152] This position is based on the Library Bill of Rights, which states, "A person's right to use a library should not be denied or abridged because of origin, age, background, or views."[153] Any age. It leads to a position most people would consider not only unreasonable, but also unbelievable for any serious professional association. According to the ALA, if a child of age 7 loses a library book, the parents are responsible for replacing it.

However, if the parents wonder which book their child has lost, the library should not (according to ALA recommendations) disclose this information.[154]

One may argue that such a policy is concerned with the child's privacy rather than with First Amendment rights. Disregarding the question of whether children have privacy rights against their parents, there is a connection. The ALA fears that if parents can find out what their children read, this may "chill" the children's choices and thus undermine freedom of speech. Children may fear to access material their parents find objectionable. Indeed, this is a matter of concern for teenagers, especially older ones, but not for those 12 or younger. Laura Murphy, the director of the Washington DC office of the ACLU, evoked the case of a 12-year-old who wants to read about homosexuality or HIV but fears to do so at home. Let us grant that there are some such cases. But it does not follow that millions of children ought to be harmed by unlimited exposure to all manner of sexually explicit material in order to accommodate these few cases. Such children should be encouraged to discuss the matter with a school nurse, a public clinic, or some other source which will help them get the information they need without exposing all others to objectionable material.

Nor did the ACLU ever suggest or hint, as it was fighting CIPA and two previous attempts to protect children from internet pornography using internet filters, that it would accept them if they were limited to schools or even to only primary schools. On the contrary, in other situations, civil libertarians state the opposite position quite explicitly. The ACLU has written that "if adults are allowed access, but minors are forced to use blocking programs, constitutional problems remain. Minors, especially older minors, have a constitutional right to access many of the resources that have been shown to be blocked by user-based blocking programs."[155] The same position was struck by the ACLU when it charged the Loudoun County Library Board of Trustees in Virginia with "'removing books from the shelves of the Internet with value to both adults *and minors* in violation of the Constitution."[156]

These positions are difficult to entertain, as minors clearly are developmental creatures whose capabilities change a great deal as they mature. Children – according to practically all of a huge social science literature and elementary common sense – are different from adults in that they have few of the attributes of mature persons that justify respecting their choices. Children have not yet formed their own preferences, have not acquired basic moral values, do not have the information needed for sound judgments, and are subject to ready manipulation by others. In the same vein, parents and educators are discharging their social duties when they shape the cultural environments in which children develop, which includes choosing the material to which children are exposed. The underlying assumption is developmental. Children begin life as highly vulnerable and dependent persons, unable to make reasonable choices on their own. Stanford Law Professor Michael Wald writes, in reference to the social science findings on the subject:

> Younger children, generally those under 10-12 years old, do lack the cognitive abilities and judgmental skills necessary to make decisions about major events which could severely affect their lives. . . . Younger children are not able to think abstractly, have a limited future time sense, and are limited in their ability to generalize and predict from experience.[157]

As children develop they gradually become capable of making moral judgments and acting on their own, and only then are they ready to be autonomous. As Colin McLeod and David Archard put it: "children are seen as 'becoming' rather than 'being'" and "the basic idea that children must be viewed as developing beings whose moral status gradually changes now enjoys near universal acceptance."[158]

The Constitution basically deals with adults. Its application to children needs to be specifically worked out, rather than assumed to apply to them in the same way. Otherwise, a police officer who asks a child wandering in the streets where he is going could be charged with a violation of privacy (or maybe with age-profiling). Thus, to stop an adult a cop would need "reasonable suspicion." A young child roaming the streets alone, however, is unusual enough to provide reasonable suspicion in and of itself. This issue has been visited explicitly in *Horton* v. *Goose Creek Elementary School District*. Although the court ruled that students should not be considered to have lower expectations of privacy, and that "society recognizes the interest in the integrity of one's person, and the Fourth Amendment applies with its fullest vigor against any intrusion on the human body," it also recognized that standards of reasonableness differ for children and adults.[159] There seems no reason to treat the First Amendment otherwise. The same point is also evident when it comes to "unlawful detention;" it hardly applies to parents keeping their kids at home or sending them to their rooms.

To put it differently, whatever one considers the purpose and merit of the First Amendment – whether to ensure a free exchange of ideas, to maintain liberty, to enrich one's life, and so on – none of this applies to toddlers. To speak of the right to free speech of a 2-year-old is ludicrous, but that is precisely what happens when one speaks of all minors as if they are of one kind. One may say that it is obvious that when one talks about "minors" one does not mean to encompass toddlers. Still, the term avoids engaging the question of the age at which children command First Amendment rights, and what the scope of those rights is. One should assume that those who are somewhere between infancy and age 13 have much lower capacities to contribute to and benefit from speech and are more vulnerable to harm from certain materials.

Since one's ability to deal with certain types of material increases as one grows older and develops, protections of minors should be age-graded. Ideally, there would be many different types of labels and screening software that could take into account age differences (as well as other factors, such as the values of those who issue them.) Some might be issued by teachers' colleges, some by religious groups, and some by the media, leaving parents and educators free to choose among them. (Given that age is merely a reasonable approximation for maturity, some parents may choose protections that have been prepared for somewhat older or younger children.)

When it comes to government-introduced measures, which we argued are needed at least for now, such complexity may not be possible. Hence, a minimum of two gradations should be provided to take into account gradual maturing: one for children and one for teenagers. It is difficult to justify treating high school students the same way as children in primary schools and kindergartens, and vice versa. But in no case should children or teenagers be treated simply as adults.

Roots in Liberalism

To understand the underlying assumptions of civil libertarians' case against protective measures, one needs to examine the roots of these assumptions in political theory and social philosophy. The tendency of civil libertarians to treat children as adults when it comes to First Amendment issues is not accidental. It is rooted in contemporary liberal political theory, especially in its more extreme libertarian version, and it clearly differs from the classical liberal theorists. John

Locke, writing in his Second Treatise of Government, noted, albeit somewhat reluctantly: "Children, I confess are not born in this full state of Equality, though they are born to it. Their parents have a sort of Rule and Jurisdiction over them when they come into the World, and for some time after." He goes on to comment later, "Children being not presently as soon as born under this Law of Reason, were not presently free."[160]

Nathan Tarcov notes that Locke's concept of "parental power" derives from parental duty to take care of children, which extends until children become capable of taking care of themselves.[161] Until a child reaches an "Age of Discretion," when he has acquired reason, "some Body else must guide him, who is presumed to know how far the Law allows a Liberty."[162]

Similarly, John Stuart Mill immediately follows his assertion that "over himself, over his own body and mind, the individual is sovereign," with the qualification that "this doctrine is meant to apply only to human beings in the maturity of their faculties. We are not speaking of children, or of young persons below the age which the law may fix as that of manhood or womanhood. Those who are still in a state to require them to be taken care of by others, must be protected against their own actions as well as against external injury."[163] This is not a text embraced by contemporary liberals or libertarians. Most avoid the issue by simply not discussing children from this viewpoint, as the indexes to scores of their books show.[164]

Contemporary liberals, especially libertarians, hold that we are to honor people's choices and avoid paternalism because it is the individual who must live with the consequences of his or her own actions. But children are not prepared to assess the consequences of their choices, and families are deeply affected when kids abuse drugs, shoplift, or are dehumanized by harmful material. Paternalism means treating adults like children, not treating children as children. Paternalism is exactly what the law and society expect from parents, and we hold them accountable when they fail. Of course, as children grow older, they can and ought to be given more leeway to learn and to exercise their own judgment – with parents and other educators looking over their shoulders until they learn to fly solo.

Ultimately, the reason liberals shy away from dealing with children in political theory and social philosophy is that children threaten the very foundations on which their theory rests. Once one grants that they are human beings whose preferences are deeply affected by outside agents, including culture and values, in ways that they are unaware – that there are individuals who can be influenced, persuaded, or swayed by peers and leaders – it is hard to respect their choices as truly their own. Such cultural and social influences do not suddenly vanish when a minor achieves a given age and is called an adult. Thus, children point to the need for a social theory that can accommodate the role of profound external influences on individuals much better than liberalism does.

It also follows that dropping all protections from harmful cultural material is not justified even for adults, as is certainly the case with child pornography. So far, the legal justification for banning child pornography has been that "the distribution network for pornography must be closed if the production of material which requires the sexual exploitation of children is to be effectively controlled."[165] The 2002 decision in *Ashcroft* v. *Free Speech Coalition*, in which the Supreme Court overturned the Child Pornography Protection Act, weakened this precedent by allowing the distribution of "virtual" child pornography because no "real" children were harmed during its production.[166] However, virtual child pornography causes real harm by normalizing the kinds of behavior it portrays, which would be illegal if carried out by real people, and thus we argue that there are grounds for banning child pornography, both real and virtual, based on its effects. Determining how and in what way to limit the access of adults – and determining what material should be limited – is a subject for another discussion altogether.[167]

Whose Standards?

Finally, we must address the difficult question of how to go about determining what specific cultural materials are so harmful that we must block them for children. One argument against protecting children from harmful material is the lack of consensus regarding what is offensive. Although there were shared, historically fashioned community standards in the past, our current pluralistic society is said to preclude widespread agreement about what is objectionable. Jeffrey Narvil writes: "American notions of nudity as inherently indecent are strikingly ethnocentric," and "traditional, historical notions of propriety may not exist in an increasingly diverse and multi-ethnic society."[168]

The concept of "contemporary community standards" was introduced in the 1957 case *Roth* v. *United States*, in which the Supreme Court established a test for determining what is obscene and therefore outside the protection of the First Amendment.[169] This test was modified in *Memoirs* v. *Massachusetts* and then in *Miller* v. *California*.[170] The test established by *Miller*, and then tweaked in numerous succeeding cases, included the yardstick of whether "the average person, applying contemporary community standards would find that the work, taken as a whole, appeals to the prurient interest."[171]

The crux of civil libertarian objections to "contemporary community standards" lies in the argument that, although a community might be able to limit its own members based on what is agreed to be unacceptable in that community, in the cases at hand the limitations are set nationally. As the Supreme Court pointed out in its ruling striking down the CDA, when "community standards" are applied to something like the internet, which is viewed by members of many communities, they will reflect the views of those with the lowest threshold of offense, thereby limiting the access of those in other communities who would not be offended by the same materials.[172] Thus the ACLU defended the song "Cop Killer" (in which rap artist Ice-T fantasizes about killing a police officer) as reflecting "a radical attitude held by some inner city residents" and said that it is "impossible to know exactly what message a particular listener takes" from it. They further charged that voluntary plans to label music were an attempt to "impose on all Americans the tastes and standards of political power brokers who don't connect with the experiences and concerns of the young, the alienated, and minorities."[173]

A similar argument involves the global nature of the internet. Kelly Doherty writes:

> the community standard is extremely difficult to apply to the Internet because the Internet's reach is worldwide. When someone in a country with a conservative community standard receives sexually explicit material via the Internet from a country that permits and encourages bigamy or nudity, for example, it becomes difficult to determine which community standard should govern.[174]

Philip Lewis goes farther, arguing that for the internet "such communication would be impossible, or at the very least, greatly restricted, by the application of the arbitrary and antiquated 'community standard' that Congress has advocated in its two attempts at Internet regulation (the CDA and the COPA) thus far."[175]

These arguments, when critically examined, seem unsustainable. First, in reference to the notion that "as goes the internet so goes the world," one notes that the Loudoun and Kern County public libraries, and most others, are still very much local institutions. So are schools and many other institutions. Community standards are by no means merely historical relics, non-applicable to the internet, as the Supreme Court reminded us in its partial ruling on COPA.[176]

Nor are we without national standards. Justice O'Connor, writing in concurrence with the COPA ruling, countered skeptics who believe that a national standard is "unascertainable," noting: "It is true that our Nation is diverse, but many local communities encompass similar diversity.... Moreover, the existence of the Internet, and its facilitation of national dialogue, has made jurors more aware of the views of adults in other parts of the United States."[177] Most relevant, the very Constitution and its First Amendment that liberals rise to defend reflect national values that some communities may well not endorse if left to their own devices, but we hardly exempt those communities from abiding by it. Of course, Congress is an institution authorized to speak for nationwide preferences and values. So is the Supreme Court.

Aside from upholding national standards in the protection of minors, communities should be given some leeway, in gray areas, to add some standards of their own. The term "gray areas," to be defined by Congress and the courts, is used to indicate that communities would not be free to ignore the First Amendment, but only to add some measures or provide further definitions, for instance what they consider harmful, which movies should receive R rating, and whether moviegoers should be carded before entrance. And, just as local governments can ban people from drinking alcohol in public or running around nude, they should also be allowed to ban rental of XXX-videos to children in their libraries. Those who argue that the internet makes it impossible to impose local standards should take heart from the fact that it is technically possible. At least they should agree that, if possible, the internet should not be given license to expose children in ways no other institution is allowed. In short, if there are any reasons to refuse better protection of children in the media and on the internet from harmful material, the lack of standards cannot be counted among them.

In Conclusion

The position that children have full speech rights is untenable in the face of the intentions and interpretations of the First Amendment. Our laws in general do not mechanically extend to children, but take into account that their capacities are still developing. There is no reason for the right to free speech to be treated any differently. Children are clearly developmental creatures. Initially, they have few if any of the attributes of mature persons. For children to develop properly, parents and educators, and society at large, have not merely a right but a duty to shape the cultural environment in which they grow. Unbounded exposure to harmful cultural material undermines their proper development, especially, as data show, representations of violence (aside from violence itself). As children grow older and their capacities increase, they are entitled to broader speech rights, but they still require some protections. Thus, protections of children (and, to a lesser extent, of teenagers) are best set in ways that separate the various limitations by age, and that "spillover" as little as possible onto the access of adults. However, if protecting children requires some limitation on adults, especially their commercial speech, then these measures are justified when the harm is substantial and well documented. We see this more clearly once we recognize that the First Amendment does not trump all other considerations, and begin to value children more than we may have in the recent past.

4

Privacy and Safety in Electronic Communications

Introduction

Are the new measures that have been introduced to protect America from terrorism too extensive, undermining our rights, or are they not extensive enough, leaving the nation vulnerable to future attacks? This chapter addresses these questions only with regard to those public safety measures, of the more than 150 introduced after 9/11/01,[1] that concern communications surveillance, and among these only the measures relevant to the use of six technologies: cellular phones, the internet (as a means of communication), high-power encryption, Carnivore, the Key Logger System, and Magic Lantern. The chapter examines the effects of the measures on the use of these technologies and on individual rights and the public interest. The main rights at issue are privacy, anonymity, and due process. The main areas of public interest at issue are public safety and public health, especially prevention of terrorism and response to terrorist attacks once they occur, including bio-terrorism.

I take for granted that both individual rights and public safety must be protected, and, given that on many occasions advancing one requires some curtailment of the other, the key question is what is the proper balance between these two cardinal values. The concept of balance is found in the Constitution in the Fourth Amendment, which refers to people's right not to be subjected to unreasonable search and seizure, hence recognizing a category of searches that are fully compatible with the Constitution: those that are reasonable. Historically, to be considered reasonable, searches have had to serve a compelling public interest, especially public safety or public health.

Much of the debate about the issues at hand in the public arena (by legislatures, opinion makers, and some legal scholars) is conducted in a format familiar in American court rooms: strong advocacy by opposing sides. Thus, one side argues that public safety requires new laws, regulations, and court rulings that would give the government greater surveillance powers, and warns that major calamities will strike if the government is not accorded these powers.[2] Moreover, the advocates of public safety and health claim that the best way to defend liberty is to provide the government with more authority. Dead people are not free. The other side does not oppose making concessions to public safety, but puts the onus on the government to prove that such concessions are needed and sets the bar very high for such proof, calling for an approach resembling "strict scrutiny."[3] Although, in the debate since 9/11, the civil libertarians' opening position has been to demand a tighter definition of the conditions under which the new technologies can be applied and closer supervision of the expanded governmental powers, ultimately the classical civil libertarian position is that the government needs no additional powers, and moreover cannot be trusted to use any of them legitimately.

From the viewpoint of the paradigm used here, each side is speaking for just one side of the needed balance rather than seeking to find the point (or better, zone) at which a carefully crafted balance can be found between protecting the public interest and individual rights.[4]

The quest for balance reflects a new (or responsive) communitarian position developed in the 1990s.[5] Its starting point is that there are two valid claims each society faces: the requirements of the public interest (which most obviously encompasses public safety and health, but also encompasses other elements of the common good, such as the protection of the environment) and the requirements of liberty (individual rights included).[6] The "turf" does not belong a priori to either claim. It is a gross misconception to argue that public safety measures entail a sacrifice of rights – or vice versa, that respecting individual rights entails sacrifices of the common good. First, in some situations, both can be advanced, such as when restoring law and order to a crime-ridden neighborhood or an anarchic country. Second, when the public interest and rights pose conflicting demands, criteria must be developed as to which should take priority, without assuming a priori that one automatically trumps the other.[7] Judge Richard Posner put the same basic idea in the following way: "I'll call them the public-safety interest and the liberty interest. Neither, in my view, has priority. They are both important."[8]

Such general positions are best examined within an historical context. There is a tendency by societies and polities to tilt in one direction or the other, to lean excessively toward the public interest or liberty. Moreover, curbing such imbalances tends to lead to overcorrection. For example, the limitations the Church Commission imposed on the FBI in the 1970s, following the abuses of civil rights that occurred during the years J. Edgar Hoover was the director, seem to have excessively curbed the work of the agency in the following decades.[9] The public safety measures enacted since 9/11 have removed many of these restrictions and granted the FBI and other public authorities – such as the Central Intelligence Agency, the National Security Agency, and the military – new powers, arguably tilting excessively in the opposite direction. There have almost always been attempts immediately afterwards to rebalance such powers. e.g., limiting the conditions under which military tribunals can be used and spelling out procedures not included in their preliminary authorization).[10] At the same time, historical conditions change the point at which we find a proper balance; the 2001 assault on America and the threat of additional attacks constitute such a change.

I will begin by introducing the relevant aspects of three of the six technologies – cellular telephones, the internet, and encryption – which have expanded people's free choices, and in this sense their liberties, but have limited the ability of public authorities to engage in the kind of activities they are legally entitled to engage in, especially intercepting communications following court approval. I shall refer to these technologies as *liberalizing technologies*. I will then examine the arguments in favor of and against changing laws and regulations to enable public authorities to cope with, if not overcome, the hurdles posed by the liberalizing technologies in the post-9/11 context.

Next, I will turn to the three new technologies that help public authorities – Carnivore, the Key Logger System, and Magic Lantern – which have the opposite profile of the first three: they enhance public safety but it is feared that they curb people's rights. I refer to these as *public protective technologies*. These technologies are then also examined with regard to new laws and regulations and to their effect on the balance between the public interest and individual rights in the post-9/11 context.

Finally, I will call attention to measures that might help increase public safety while minimizing the threat to individual rights, focusing on the concept of accountability. It should be noted from the outset that the position outlined entails a measure of trust in the government, or at least in some elements of it.

New Liberalizing Technologies

New and multiple means of communication

Before the discussion can proceed, it is essential to note that no attempt is being made here to describe fully or to analyze the technologies at issue, but merely to point to features of them relevant to the issues at hand. The year 1980 is used as a baseline. At the time, the most convenient, and by far the most commonly used, way to communicate instantaneously with a person at a different location was through a wired telephone. Cellular phones existed, but they were not yet commercially viable nor were they available in models lightweight enough to put in a pocket; fax machines had not yet come into wide use.[11] Telegraphs required, as a rule, going to a post office or Western Union location. Most people had one phone line, even if they had more than one extension. The internet was still the ARPANET, a government-sponsored network that mainly linked universities and research centers.[12] In 1980, all necessary communications surveillance could be carried out easily by attaching simple devices to a suspect's one landline telephone.[13]

In the following two decades, many millions of people acquired several alternative modes of convenient, instantaneous communication, most significantly cellular telephones and email. By July 2000, there were more than 100 million cell phone subscribers in the United States.[14] Email and internet usage became similarly pervasive. Nielsen/Net Rating estimated that by July 2001, 165.2 million people in the United States had home internet access.[15]

These technological developments greatly limited the ability of public authorities to conduct communications surveillance using traditional methods under old laws (those in effect before the passage of the USA Patriot Act, the provisions of which will be discussed later on in this chapter). Attempts were made to apply old laws to new technologies, but they did not fit well. To proceed, it must be noted that there are two types of communications surveillance: public authorities get "pen register" and "trap and trace" orders to obtain only the numbers dialed to or from a specific telephone, or they get full intercept orders to listen to the content of a telephone call.[16] Because the information involved in the first type is less sensitive, these orders are much easier to get than the latter.[17] The terms "pen register" and "trap and trace" refer to the devices originally used to carry out the trace orders.[18] Though the technologies they refer to have been replaced, these terms are still commonly used. From now on, I will use the term "pen/trap" to designate the type of communications surveillance that involves gathering only the numbers dialed to and from a telephone, or their email equivalent. The term "full intercept" will refer to wiretaps and other means of intercepting the full content of a communication. The term "communications surveillance" will include both pen/trap and full intercept orders.

The law governing full intercepts, contained in Title III of the Omnibus Crime Control and Safe Streets Act of 1969, required that court orders for intercepts specify the location of the communications device to be tapped and establish probable cause that evidence of criminal conduct could be collected by tapping that particular device. Hence, under this law, if a suspect shifted from one phone to another or used multiple phones, the government could not legally tap phones other than the one originally specified without obtaining a separate court order for each.[19] Once criminals were able to obtain multiple cell phones and to "dispose of them as used tissues," investigations were greatly hindered by the lengthy process of obtaining numerous full intercept authorizations from the courts.[20]

The rise of internet-based communications further limited the ability of public authorities to conduct communications surveillance under the old laws. Because Title III did not originally apply to electronic communications, email was often treated as analogous to an older form of communication in the courts.[21] Because emails used to travel largely over phone lines, laws governing interception or traces for telephones were extended to govern interception and traces of emails as well. However, the language of the old legislation governing pen/trap orders was not clearly applicable to email communications.[22] Though police used pen/trap orders to trace email messages, there was a possibility that, if it were ever challenged legally, a court would rule that email did not fall under pen/trap orders.[23]

Furthermore, deregulation of the telecommunications industry created additional complications in carrying out pen/trap orders. When the old legislation was enacted, a unified phone network made it easy to identify the source of a call.[24] But email may pass through multiple service providers in different locations throughout the nation on its way from sender to recipient. This means that a service provider might only be able to inform public authorities that a message came from another service provider. In this case, public authorities would have to obtain a new court order from the jurisdiction of that provider to find out where the message came from.[25] Thus, until recently, if a message went through four providers, four court orders in four different jurisdictions would be needed to find out the origin of that message.

As with pen/trap orders, the original laws governing full intercept orders did not initially apply to email. However, the Electronic Communications Privacy Act of 1986 extended the full intercept laws to apply to electronic communications.[26] Email messages differ from phone conversations in important ways that have made the old laws, at best, an imperfect fit.[27] Emails do not travel over phone lines in discrete units that can just be plucked out. They are broken up into digital packets and travel over the internet through different routes and mixed together with the packets of the messages of other users. This creates a challenge for law enforcement agents attempting to intercept or trace the email of just one user without violating the privacy of other users.[28]

Problems also occurred when agents received the same search warrants to obtain saved email that they would use in any other physical search. Under old laws, a warrant must be obtained from a judge in the jurisdiction where the search will take place.[29] Email, however, is not always stored on a personal computer, but often is stored remotely on the servers of internet service providers (ISPs). This means that if a suspect, say, in New Jersey had email stored on a server located in, say, Silicon Valley, an agent would have to travel across the country to get a warrant to seize the email.[30]

In short, the introduction of both cellular phones and email created new challenges to the ability of public authorities to conduct communications intercepts, even if they were fully authorized by a court – intercepts that had been an important tool of law enforcement. Another technological development has made communications intercepts much more difficult still. Before it is introduced, a brief digression. There is a tendency in parts of the literature on privacy to argue that new technological developments have gravely undermined privacy, if not killed it altogether.[31] In effect, though, the situation in this area is akin to an arms race: as new means of attack are developed, so are new means of defense, although in any given period one side or the other may be the leading beneficiary of new technological developments.

To return to our subject, a major technological development that greatly enhances privacy – and potentially sets back the ability of public authorities to intercept communications – is high-power encryption.[32] Although codes have existed for thousands of years, only over the last few have programmers developed encryption systems that use codes 128 bits or longer, which are said to be impossible to crack, even by the National Security Agency (NSA).[33] Moreover, these programs are readily available to private parties at low costs. Stewart Baker, former general counsel for the NSA, said that "encryption is virtually unbreakable by police today, with programs that can be bought for $15."[34] Indeed, these programs are increasingly being routinely built into computers.[35] This means that the privacy of encrypted messages is much higher than that of any messages historically sent by mail, phone, messenger, carrier pigeon, or other means. (The same encryption also allows the storing of information in one's computer – personal or corporate – that is much better protected than it ever was under lock and key, or even in safes.[36])

High-power encryption has caused a very major setback for law enforcement.[37] Even when granted a court order, public authorities simply seem unable to implement it.[38] The consequence of this development has been different from others created by new technologies. In contrast with the situation concerning the multiplication of means of expeditious communication, in which the main factor that constrained public authorities was the obsolescence of laws, in the case of high-power encryption, the new technology imposes a barrier all its own. In the other instance, a change of law was sufficient to enable law enforcement to deal with the new challenges posed by the new technologies. Here, the horse was out of the barn by 9/11. It seems impossible to break high-power encryption, whatever the courts may authorize.

Legal responses

All in all, these technological developments have provided law-abiding citizens and criminals, Americans and people of other nations, including terrorists, greater freedom to do as they choose, and in this sense they are "liberalizing." At the same time, they have significantly hampered the ability of public authorities to conduct investigations. Some cyberspace enthusiasts welcomed these developments, hoping that cyberspace would be a self-regulating, government-free space.[39] In contrast, public authorities clamored for changing the laws to enable them to act in the new "territory" as they do in the world of old-fashioned, landline telephones.[40] Their pressures led to some modifications in the law before the 2001 attack on America, although the most relevant changes have occurred since. We will now examine jointly both the pre- and the post-9/11 changes to expand the relevant intercept powers of the authorities.

1   Roving intercepts

The Electronic Communications Privacy Act of 1986 (ECPA) attempted to update the laws governing communications intercepts to be able to deal with the limitations put on them by the technological developments already discussed by allowing for what are known as "roving wiretaps" in criminal investigations.[41] Roving wiretaps are full intercept orders that apply to a *particular person*, rather than to a *specific communications device*. They allow law enforcement to obtain a court order to intercept that person's communications, without specifying in advance which facilities will be tapped, allowing officers to intercept communications from any phone or computer that the person uses.[42]

The process for obtaining a roving intercept order is more rigorous than that for obtaining the old kind of phone-specific order. The Attorney-General's office must approve the application before it is even brought before a judge.[43] Originally, the applicant had to show that the suspect named in the application was changing phones or modems frequently with the *purpose* of thwarting interception,[44] but the Intelligence Authorization Act for Fiscal Year 1999 made it easier to obtain a roving intercept order by replacing the requirement to show "purpose to thwart" with the requirement to show that the suspect is changing phones or modems frequently, and that this practice "could have the effect of thwarting" the investigation.[45] Although roving intercepts have not yet been tested in the Supreme Court, several federal courts have found them constitutional.[46]

Prior to 9/11, the FBI could not gain authorization for using roving intercepts in gathering foreign intelligence or in investigations of terrorism. The USA Patriot Act allows for such roving intercept orders to be granted under the Federal Intelligence Surveillance Act (FISA).[47] FISA was passed in 1978 and provides the guidelines under which the executive branch – not only the President but also the Department of Justice – can obtain authorization to conduct surveillance for foreign intelligence purposes.[48] Agents who wish to conduct surveillance under FISA submit an application first to the

Attorney-General's office, which must approve all requests (as with roving intercepts under ECPA). If the Attorney-General finds the application valid, it will be taken to one of seven federally appointed judges, who together make up the Federal Intelligence and Security Court (FISC), for approval. The FISC allows no spectators, keeps most proceedings secret, and hears only the government side of a case.[49]

Initially, FISA was limited to investigations for which foreign intelligence was the sole purpose. USA Patriot modifies FISA so that foreign intelligence need be only a "significant purpose" of an investigation.[50] This change effectively allows FISA to be used as part of "multi-faceted responses to terrorism, which involves foreign intelligence and criminal investigations."[51] Because FISA was originally designed for use in gathering foreign intelligence, communications surveillance conducted under FISA differs from that conducted under Title III criminal investigations in several other ways. Under normal Title III intercepts, anyone whose communications have been intercepted has to be notified after the fact that this happened. Under FISA, people do not have to be notified unless evidence obtained through the interception is to be used against them in court.[52] When FISA evidence is used in court, it is difficult for the defendant to challenge it because he or she cannot see the information that agents relied on in making the application for surveillance – this is secret for national security reasons.[53]

2   Email surveillance

USA Patriot includes provisions to make it easier for public authorities to trace or seize email messages. It explicitly allows pen/trap orders for computer communications (as already discussed, previous orders had to rely on stretched interpretations of the statutes governing pen/trap for telephones).[54] Traces on telephone lines can usually be fulfilled by the local phone company that issued the line. Tracing email messages, which travel through a variety of routes and may go through multiple carriers, often requires access at different points across the country.[55] As previously explained, following the phone model requires gaining warrants in several locations in order to trace one email message. USA Patriot establishes what are de facto nationwide pen/trap orders,[56] allowing one court order to be used on all the carriers through which messages from an individual pass. When a law-enforcement agent discovers that an email message was forwarded to (or from) any carrier, he can serve the original court order to this carrier without getting an additional order from the court in whose jurisdiction the carrier is located. Moreover, because agents cannot know in advance which carriers will be involved, the court order needs to specify only the initial facility at which the pen/trap order will be carried out.

USA Patriot also allows a judge in the district with jurisdiction over the crime under investigation to grant search warrants to seize electronic communications stored outside that judge's jurisdiction. This means that an agent can obtain a warrant from a judge in the jurisdiction where the investigation is taking place to seize email stored by an ISP physically located in another jurisdiction.[57]

3 Dealing with encryption

Previous administrations tried to have "back doors" built into encryption software that would enable public authorities, when needed, to decrypt reportedly unbreakable codes.[58] They also attempted to get legislation passed that would require users to deposit a copy of their key with third parties (referred to as "escrow") or public authorities, who would not be able to look at or use the key unless authorized to do so as part of an investigation.[59] A combination of civil liberties groups and high-tech corporations successfully fought off both of these attempts.[60] No attempts to deal with this matter were included in the USA Patriot Act. Further discussion of law-enforcement tools to cope with encryption must be deferred until the public protective technologies are discussed.

4 Evaluating the changes in the law

(a) General The adaptations of the laws governing communications surveillance (which include both pen/trap and full intercept orders) and seizures of stored communications have been subject to both general and detailed debates by the adversarial advocates already mentioned. On the general level, these adaptations were lumped together with numerous other matters, including indefinite detention of aliens, allowing the government to listen in on attorney–client conversations, and military tribunals.[61] The nature of the debate on this level is illustrated by statements such as Senator Patrick Leahy's that some of the measures are "shredding the Constitution" and Morton Halperin's reference to the legislation as "Striking Terror at Civil Liberty."[62] On the other side, Senator Hatch dismissed such misgivings as "hysterical concerns" and said the American people do not want to see

Congress "quibble about whether we should provide more rights than the Constitution requires to the criminals and terrorists who are devoted to killing our people."[63] Attorney-General John Ashcroft suggested that criticisms of the new powers being requested by the executive branch serve only to "aid terrorists" and "erode our national unity and diminish our resolve."[64]

(b) Fourth Amendment issues   There has been some debate in the courts and among legal scholars as to how to apply the Fourth Amendment to the new technologies, as well as to the constitutionality of the new legislation governing these technologies. Before 1967, the Supreme Court interpreted the Fourth Amendment in a literal way, as applying only to *physical* searches. In the 1928 case of *Olmstead* v. *United States*, the Court took a strict interpretation of the Fourth Amendment and ruled that telephone wiretaps did not constitute a search unless public authorities entered a home to install the device and that therefore the Fourth Amendment did not apply to them. The justices wrote in their decision that a person is not protected under the Fourth Amendment unless "there has been an official search and seizure of his person, or such a seizure of his papers or his tangible effects, or an actual physical invasion of his house."[65]

In 1967, in *Katz* v. *United States*, the Court replaced this interpretation of the Fourth Amendment with the view that it "protects people, not places." The Court established a new guideline for determining what falls under the protection of the Fourth Amendment and one that is still in use today – that of a reasonable expectation of privacy. Justice Harlan, in his concurring opinion, set out a two-part test for determining if Fourth Amendment protection applies: the individual must have shown an expectation of privacy, and society must recognize that expectation as reasonable.[66]

Legal scholars have criticized reasonable expectation as the cornerstone of the legal privacy doctrine on a number of grounds that need no reviewing here,[67] but the doctrine is generally still used as a guiding principle. As new technologies emerge, however, the question of what constitutes a reasonable expectation of privacy has to be re-examined in this new context. In the 1996 case of *United States* v. *Maxwell*, the courts determined that there was a reasonable expectation of privacy for email stored on a server, giving this email, in essence, the same protections given to paper documents stored in an office. In the case of *United States* v. *Charbonneau*, however, the courts determined that the extent to which one can expect privacy in email communications depends on the context of the situation.[68]

Lieutenant-Colonel Joginder Dhillon and Lieutenant-Colonel Robert Smith argue that because email messages reside on numerous servers between the sending and receiving server, and because on many networks duplicate copies of all emails are sent to the system administrator, there may not be a reasonable expectation of privacy for email.[69] This interpretation is backed up by the Supreme Court case *Smith* v. *Maryland*, in which the Court found that there is no reasonable expectation of privacy for the telephone numbers one dials because those numbers must be conveyed to the phone company.[70] Dhillon and Smith conclude that, at the very least, *Smith* v. *Maryland* should mean that recording the addressing information of email does not require a full intercept order.[71]

There is some question as to whether or not roving intercepts are in compliance with the Fourth Amendment's *particularity* requirement. The requirement that intercept orders specify the place of the intercept comes from the Fourth Amendment, which states that "no warrants shall issue, but upon probable cause, supported by oath or affirmation, and particularly describing the place to be searched, and the persons or things to be seized." Because roving intercepts do not name the location to be tapped, there is some question as to whether or not they are constitutional under the Fourth Amendment.

The argument in favor of their constitutionality is that the particularity of the *person* to be tapped is substituted for the particularity of the *place* to be tapped. In the case of *United States* v. *Petti*, the Ninth Circuit Court of Appeals upheld the use of roving intercepts, arguing that the purpose of the particularity requirement was to prevent general searches.[72] So long as a warrant or court order provides "sufficient particularity to enable the executing officer to locate and identify the premises with reasonable effort" and there is no "reasonable probability that another premise might be mistakenly searched," it is in compliance with the Fourth Amendment.[73] A court order to tap all phones used by a specific person *does* describe particular places, but in an unconventional way. Public authorities cannot use the order to tap any location they wish, but only a set of specific locations, which they can show are used by a specific person.[74]

Not everyone agrees that this substitution of particularity of person for particularity of place is sufficient to satisfy the Fourth Amendment. Tracey Maclin cites the Supreme Court case of *Steagald* v. *United States* in which the Court concluded that an arrest warrant that specifies a person cannot be used to search private places not named in the warrant in pursuit of that person. She interprets this decision to mean that the Court found warrants to be flawed that specify only the target of the search, but leave police to determine which particular locations to search. Maclin argues that although roving intercepts are issued for one person, once public authorities decide to "tap" a telephone or computer, everyone using that telephone or computer will be subject to surveillance, so there is no true particularity of person maintained.[75]

In his analysis of the issue, Clifford Fishman finds that although relevant Fourth Amendment case law does not give conclusive support either for or against roving intercepts, there are strong arguments in favor of their constitutionality. He holds that roving intercept orders "describe the 'place' to be searched in a somewhat untraditional, but still sufficiently particular way" and argues that "if the Fourth Amendment is flexible enough to protect privacy against technological developments far beyond the contemplation of the founding fathers, then it must also be flexible enough to permit investigators to preserve the basic mandate of the amendment's particularity requirement in a novel way."[76]

Numerous additional questions arise regarding the difference in applying the new laws, as well as the old ones, to non-citizens as opposed to citizens, to terrorists as opposed to criminals, and to international as opposed to domestic terrorists. These are huge issues that concern the extent to which the Constitution applies to non-citizens, in the United States and elsewhere, and what rights non-citizens have. These issues raise potential problems, such as how to define terrorism and whether that definition should extend to citizens, as well as the danger that a loose definition might allow ordinary criminals to be encompassed by terrorism laws. These issues go well beyond communications technology and the laws related to it – the focus of this chapter – and are not covered here, although they have implications for the issues at hand.

(c) Other critiques Proponents of roving intercepts argue that without them authorities will see a "whole operation frustrated because a terrorist throws away a telephone and picks up another phone and then moves on."[77] Critics argue that the new law will ensnarl many innocent people unrelated to investigations. Civil libertarians like Nadine Strossen argue that the new law, as it relates to roving intercepts, "goes far beyond" facilitating investigations based on individual suspicion. She uses the example of a suspected terrorist who sends email from a public library computer terminal. If the computer is tapped, any of the other users, who have no connection to the

suspect, will also have their communications intercepted.[78] The same critics contend that issuing nationwide warrants just allows law-enforcement agents to "shop for friendly judges."[79] Senator Hatch counters that these provisions and others merely fix parts of the criminal code that formerly treated terrorists "with kid gloves."[80]

It is worth noting that although the ACLU does not exempt the laws at issue from its blanket criticism of all the new measures, when explicitly asked whether it would at least recognize that allowing public authorities to tap all phones used by the same person was eminently reasonable, it hinted that it is somewhat less troubled by the changes in the laws under discussion here than by many of the other measures.[81] Alan Dershowitz, a longtime defender of civil liberties, even went so far as to concede that roving intercepts are "a very good idea."[82]

The ACLU criticizes changes in FISA, which it charges allow authorities to "by-pass normal criminal procedures that protect privacy and take checks and balances out of the law."[83] Civil libertarians worry about USA Patriot's extension of the reach of FISA, which provides fewer protections than are provided for criminal cases, as the discussion above regarding full intercepts under FISA illustrates. (Civil libertarians' concerns about pen/trap orders for email are discussed in the next section.)

I shall defer my own assessment of the legitimacy of the new legal adaptations to the liberalizing technologies and of their effects on the balance between individual rights and public safety and health until the next three technologies and the laws concerning them are reviewed. For now it might serve to remind that this chapter does not deal with the general legitimacy of FISA or the USA Patriot Act, but with some elements of these laws, specifically those that concern communications surveillance. This is significant to keep in mind, because conclusions about other elements – military tribunals and indefinite detention of suspects, for instance – may be different from those about the surveillance laws at issue.

Public Protective Technologies

The discussion now turns to three technologies that have the opposite profile of those explored so far: they enhance the capabilities of public authorities and raise fears that they will curtail individual rights.

Carnivore

Carnivore is a computer program that was unveiled by the FBI in July 2000 and is used to trace and seize internet communications. To capture a suspect's messages or trace messages sent to and from his account, public authorities must sort through a stream of many millions of messages, including those of many other users as well as those of the suspect. Some ISPs have the capability of doing this sorting themselves and will simply pass the appropriate information on to agents after a warrant or court order is presented. If an ISP is not capable of doing this kind of sorting, the FBI uses Carnivore to do it.[84]

Carnivore runs as an application program on an operating system and works by screening emails and sorting them based on a "filter," which tells the program which information to capture and which to merely let pass by. The filter can be set to sort out messages from a specific computer or email address, or it can scan various packets to find a specific text string. Carnivore can be set to operate in two different modes: "pen" and "full." In pen mode it will capture only the addressing information (which includes the email addresses of the sender and recipient, as well as the subject line) while in full mode it will capture the entire content of a message.[85] Carnivore is designed to copy and store only information caught by the filter, thus keeping agents from looking at any addressing information or email content not covered in the court order.[86]

Carnivore's pen mode is of value to public authorities even if the messages themselves cannot be read, such as in the growing number of cases in which high power encryption is used, because the government benefits from an analysis of the addresses. For instance, it can use pen/trap orders to trace to whom a group of suspects address their email. When used in this capacity, it would make more sense to call Carnivore (which hardly devours the messages, despite its name) a communications traffic analyzer.

As of the fall of 2000, the FBI said that it had used Carnivore "approximately 25 times in the last two years."[87] The Carnivore program is stored in an FBI laboratory and only brought out when needed to fulfill a specific court order. After the court order has expired, the program is returned to the laboratory.[88]

The Key Logger System and Magic Lantern

Despite the introduction of Carnivore, the government seems to be greatly hobbled by its inability to decrypt a rapidly growing proportion of all messages. To overcome this limitation, the FBI is introducing two new technologies to obtain a suspect's password. A password can enter or exit the encryption/decryption process in four ways: going over a modem, retrieval from storage, entry into a keyboard, or a process working within the computer itself.[89] The Key Logger System (KLS), developed by the FBI, has several components that work together to obtain someone's password.[90]

Once agents discover that information they have seized through a warranted search or intercepted with a proper court order is encrypted, they can obtain another warrant to install and retrieve the KLS.[91] In the case of Nicodemo Scarfo, who was suspected of racketeering, agents had to show both probable cause that Scarfo was involved in crime and probable cause that important information was installed on his computer in encrypted form. As in any warrant, the FBI had to specify the exact location of the computer on which the KLS would be installed.[92]

Once installed, the KLS uses a "keystroke capture" device to record keystrokes as they are entered into a computer. It is not capable of searching or recording fixed data stored on the computer, or of intercepting electronic communications sent to and from the computer (which would require an intercept order, which is more difficult to get than a warrant). In order not to intercept inadvertently the content of communications, the KLS is designed so that it is unable to record keystrokes while a computer's modem is in operation.[93]

Because the KLS must be installed manually and covertly on a suspect's computer, which involves breaking and entering, it is arguably more invasive than "back doors" and key escrow (which, as previously discussed, are not available, due mainly to opposition by civil libertarians and high-tech business interests).[94] Those who are shocked by this technology should consider the effects of high-power encryption. As the *Boston Globe*'s technology reporter commented: "techno-libertarians rightly howled when the feds tried to bar access to encryption software; now we must live with the consequences. The bad guys have encryption. The good guys must have counter-encryption tools."[95]

Recently, the FBI has revealed that it has been developing a less invasive technology. In November 2001, the Bureau admitted that it had developed, but not yet implemented, a remote-control approach called Magic Lantern that allows it to put software on a computer that will record keystrokes typed without installing any physical device.[96] Like the KLS, Magic Lantern does not by itself decrypt email, but it can obtain the suspect's password. The details of how it does this have not been released.[97] It is said to install itself on the suspect's computer in a way similar to a Trojan horse computer virus. It disguises itself as ordinary, harmless code, then inserts itself onto a computer. For example, the FBI will have a box pop up when someone connects to the internet reading something like "Click here to win." When the user clicks on the box, the virus will enter the computer.[98]

Evaluating the new technologies

Just as laws were put in place both before and after 9/11 to limit the concerns that new liberalizing technologies posed for public safety, measures have also been introduced that limit the use of new protective technologies and address the concerns they pose for individual rights. Most of the limitations on the use of Carnivore and the KLS were put in place as these technologies developed and before they were used, though there have also been "additions" to the checks placed on them. The shift from the KLS to Magic Lantern can be considered an improvement from a rights viewpoint because it will not require covert breaking and entering by a law-enforcement agent to install it on a suspect's office or home computer.

Nevertheless, both Carnivore and the KLS have raised concerns on the part of privacy advocates and civil liberties groups. Critics are skeptical that the programs operate the way the FBI claims they do and are troubled by the degree of secrecy the FBI maintains regarding how the programs work.

Groups like the Electronic Privacy Information Center (EPIC) and the Center for Democracy and Technology (CDT) have multiple arguments for why Carnivore should not be used at all. They argue that because, for email, it is much harder to separate addressing information from content than for a phone call, Carnivore will not allow the FBI to do a pen/trap without seizing more information than authorized.[99] Privacy advocates also worry that Carnivore will scan through "tens of millions of e-mails and other communications from innocent Internet users as well as the targeted suspect," thus violating the Fourth Amendment.[100] The ACLU compares a

Carnivore search to the FBI sending agents into a post office to "rip open each and every mail bag and search for one person's letters" and to "tapping the entire phone exchange system, listening to all the conversations, and then keeping only the ones that are incriminating, instead of tapping a single phone line."[101] A *USA Today* editorial stated that "once it's in place, Carnivore acts as an unrestrained Internet wiretap, snooping through every Internet communication that comes within its reach."[102]

Officials at the FBI respond that Carnivore, when it is used properly, will pull out only the appropriate emails, and that its use is subject to strict internal review and requires the cooperation of technical specialists and ISP personnel, thus limiting the opportunities an unscrupulous agent might have to abuse it. In Donald Kerr's words, the FBI does not have "the right or the ability to just go fishing."[103]

A review of Carnivore conducted by the Illinois Institute of Technology concluded that although it does not completely eliminate the risk of capturing unauthorized information, Carnivore is better than any existing alternatives and should continue to be used. However, the panel also determined that the FBI's internal audit process is insufficient to protect against improper use. Specifically, the operator implementing a Carnivore search selects either pen or full mode by clicking one box on a computer screen, and because the program does not keep track of what kind of search has been run, it is difficult to determine if an operator has used the program only as specified in the court order.[104] The head of the panel commented: "Even if you conclude that the software is flawless and it will do exactly what you set it to do and nothing more, you still have to make sure that the legal, human and organizational controls are adequate."[105] I turn to this matter below, when accountability is discussed.

There is a tendency to attribute to computers human characteristics and to talk or write about them as if they "sniff" and "snoop," violate privacy, and so on. One day computers may achieve such human capabilities, but for now a computer does not ogle, snicker at, or get aroused by a picture of a nude person because it does not "see"; its "mind" processes merely ones and zeros. Thus, if millions of messages flow through a computer running Carnivore, none of them is "read" *unless* it is caught by the filter and passed on to a human observer.[106] Computers do not "read" or "scan" messages any more than phones "listen" to messages left in their voicemail box. The issue is what humans do – not what machines do. True, if new technological capabilities did not exist or if their use were fully banned – an old Luddite argument[107] – the problem would not arise in the first place. However, as long as new technologies are available to criminal elements, it is hard to argue in favor of privileging them and blocking the government from using counter-measures under the proper conditions.

The legality of the KLS was tested in the case of Nicodemo Scarfo, in which the FBI used the KLS to decrypt records implicating Scarfo in racketeering. Scarfo's defense argued that the KLS records keystrokes typed in electronic communications and sent over a modem, and should therefore have required a full intercept order, rather than an easier-to-obtain search warrant. Though the FBI says that the KLS cannot record while a modem is in operation, thus protecting against the capture of electronic communications, Scarfo and the privacy advocates interested in the case were skeptical. During the trial, Scarfo was shown a hard copy of all of the keystrokes intercepted, but was unable to pick out anything that he recognized as being part of an electronic communication.[108]

Scarfo also argued that the warrant used to install the KLS violated the particularity requirement of the Fourth Amendment and therefore constituted a general search because it did not describe specifically what could be searched and seized.[109] The warrant in the case authorized FBI agents to "install and leave behind software, firmware, and/or hardware equipment which will monitor the inputted data entered on Nicodemo S. Scarfo's computer in the TARGET LOCATION," which was specified in great detail. The same warrant authorized the surreptitious breaking and entry into the target location to install and retrieve the KLS, and also authorized the FBI to seize business records "in whatever form they are kept."[110] David Sobel of EPIC said that since the warrant was issued to get one password, but the KLS recorded every keystroke typed, it was comparable to if a police officer got "a warrant to seize one book in your house, but was also allowed to haul out everything that's in there."[111] Although it is true that in the Scarfo case agents had to look through all keystrokes entered after the installation of the KLS in order to pick out the string that was his password, the FBI argues that this is similar to any search. If public authorities have a warrant to get someone's account book from their office, they may have to look through many drawers and shelves before finding it.[112] In December of 2001, the judge in the Scarfo case ruled that the use of the KLS to obtain his password was legal and constituted neither a general search nor a form of surveillance.[113]

Accountability

Accountability, the second balance

The article opened by calling attention to the need for balance between individual rights and public safety and health, rather than allowing one or the other to predominate. When the polity tilts too far toward safety or rights, it is best to correct the imbalance. The question hence arises what effects the new technologies have on the balance. There can be little doubt that the liberalizing technologies have greatly hindered the work of public authorities in the area of communications surveillance and that new protective technologies to some extent overcome these difficulties. The same might be said about new legislation that did adapt the old applicable laws to the new technologies. Finally, 9/11 changed the point (or zone) of balance by posing a new, credible threat to public safety and health. This still leaves open the question of whether the new measures, whether technological or legal, provide for much-needed enhanced public safety or excessively intrude into individual rights.

This, in turn, raises the question of how generally to determine whether or not the polity is in the zone of balance. This is an issue with which the courts have struggled for generations; it would take volumes to begin to do it justice. I have dedicated some text to this issue elsewhere.[114] Briefly, I concluded that the course of a nation's laws should not be corrected unless there is a compelling reason (a concept akin to "clear and present danger," although not necessarily one that meets this criterion technically); unless the matter cannot be addressed by non-legal, voluntary means; and unless one can make the intrusion small and the gain (either in safety or in rights) considerable. Further specification draws on what a reasonable person would find sensible, taking into account that the Constitution is a living document whose interpretation has been adjusted through the ages.

These criteria can be applied to the issues discussed here. For example, in the post-9/11 context, it is clear that the government should have greater powers to decrypt email because: terrorism does pose a major threat; voluntary means to fight encrypted terrorist messages have not sufficed on the face of it; and enabling and allowing the government to decrypt email messages is not more intrusive than tapping a phone and can be allowed under similar conditions. The authority to use roving wiretaps may pass the same test.

(To reiterate, other public safety measures recently introduced that do not concern communications surveillance, such as requiring protestors to remove their disguises, are not discussed here and may very well not meet the criteria listed.[115])

To complete the judgment whether or not a given new measure that enhances the powers of public authorities is called for, I suggest that a second form of balancing needs to be considered that, arguably, in the matters at hand, may turn out to be decisive compared to the first form already discussed. It concerns not whether the government should be accorded new powers, but how closely it is held accountable regarding the ways it uses these powers. From this viewpoint, the key issue is not whether certain powers – for example, the ability to decrypt email – should or should not be available to public authorities, but whether or not these powers are used legitimately and whether mechanisms are in place to ensure such usage. This is similar to passing over the question of whether there is too much money in a vault in favor of asking how strong the locks are. (One may argue that, in effect, this is really one question, because whether the sum is "too much" depends on the locks. Some would argue that whatever the quality of the locks, too much of one's money should not be located in one bank, mutual fund, etc. This is surely the argument about government data banks. However safeguarded, libertarians oppose concentrated national databases.)

Although these two forms of balance have some similarities and points of overlap, they are quite distinct. Thus, to argue, as cyberlibertarians did, that the government should not be able to decrypt encoded messages, should not be allowed to demand from an ISP the addressing information for email sent to and from a suspect's account, and so on, is different from agreeing that such powers are justified so long as they are properly circumscribed and their use is duly supervised.

The balance sought here is not between the public interest and rights, but between the supervised and the supervisors. Deficient accountability opens the door to government abuses of power; excessively tight controls make for agents reluctant to act.

Thus, a case can be made that in the decades preceding the Church Commission, under most of Hoover's reign, the FBI was insufficiently accountable, and that after the Commission's rules were institutionalized, until 9/11, the FBI was excessively limited in what it was allowed to do, in the area of communications surveillance. Agents, fearing reprimands and damage to their careers, were often too reluctant to act.

To elaborate a bit: it seems difficult to sustain the argument that the government should be unable to decrypt any messages or be unable to gain the authority to do so. After the first bombing of the World Trade Center in 1993, one of its principal masterminds used encryption to protect files on his laptop computer, even as he plotted to blow up commercial airlines.[116] (Encrypted files were found on a computer used by Osama bin Laden's lieutenants in the Afghan capital.[117]) Few would argue that public authorities should be unable to decrypt such files, even, say, after obtaining a warrant based on probable cause that the files included important information.

The issue hence becomes which limits will be set on what messages can be decrypted, who will verify that these limits are observed, and by what means. Similarly, regarding roving intercepts, the issue is not whether the government should have to get a warrant for each instrument of communication that the same suspect uses, but by what means it will be ensured that the government does not collect information about other people who use the same instruments of communication or the same computer terminal. The key issue is not whether communications in cyberspace should be exempted from the same type of public scrutiny to which mail and phone calls have historically been subject, as cyber-idealists had hoped,[118] but whether there are proper controls in place to protect against abuse.

The next step in assessing whether or not the American polity, in matters concerning communications surveillance, is currently excessively attentive to public safety or not willing to take needed measures out of excessive concern for rights, is hence to determine to what extent accountability has been built into the new powers granted to the government in response to the new technologies at hand and in reaction to 9/11.

Layers of accountability

1   Limitations built into the law

Limitations on the use of new powers are written into the laws governing them and limitations on protective technologies are often built into the technologies themselves. Roving intercepts, and indeed any intercepts, are not granted without limits. Title III lays out a requirement for "minimization," stated as follows: "Every order and extension thereof shall contain a provision that the authorization to intercept shall be executed as soon as practicable, shall be conducted in such a way as to minimize the interception under this chapter, and must terminate upon attainment of the authorized objective, or in any event in thirty days."[119]

Such built-in guidelines are intended to limit the ability of public authorities to gather and use information not directly related to their investigations.[120] Practically, this means that agents are not allowed to record conversations that are unrelated to the subject of the investigation and should stop listening when irrelevant matters are being discussed. If agents are unsure if a seemingly innocent conversation might touch on a relevant subject at some point, agents are to conduct "spot-monitoring," in which they tune in every few minutes to check, but only begin to record when appropriate.[121]

In *Scott* v. *United States*, the Supreme Court found that an agent's implementation of such guidelines must be evaluated under a "standard of objective reasonableness," so that if circumstances make minimization difficult, failure by an agent to attempt it does not constitute a violation of the law. In addition, if investigators have reason to suspect a conspiracy involving a large number of people, they are justified in recording and listening to all conversations until they are certain who is innocent and who not.[122] Many critics point out that under any circumstances, minimization is voluntary and we must rely on our trust in law-enforcement officers to do it properly, highlighting the importance of further layers of accountability, such as the exclusionary rule.[123]

Although telephone wiretaps rely on human judgment in implementing minimization, new public protective technologies, if properly used, carry out much of the minimization function automatically. Carnivore's filters, if set properly, act as a built-in minimization process, intercepting only what is appropriate. Although it might be capable of collecting all content that passes through it, in compliance with court orders it should be set to capture only data sent to and from a specific user. As mentioned before, data that does not fit the filter settings just passes through without being saved by Carnivore, and is therefore not seen by public authorities.[124]

2 Supervision within executive agencies

Numerous accountability mechanisms are built into the executive agencies of the government. Of course, FBI field agents are subject to numerous guidelines and supervisors whose job includes ensuring that these guidelines are abided by. They, in turn, report to still higher-ranking supervisors. Moreover, when agents cross the line, internal reviews take place. In addition, the Attorney-General's office to some extent supervises what the FBI does.

For instance, as already mentioned, requests by the FBI to conduct communications surveillance under FISA must be approved by the Attorney-General's office before they are submitted to the FISC. In some cases, court order or warrant requests never get past internal FBI approval procedures. For example, in the investigation prior to 9/11 of Zacarias Moussaoui, the possible "20th hijacker" who did not make it onto an airplane because he was arrested before 9/11 on immigration charges, the request by field agents to search his computer never made it past FBI attorneys, who found insufficient evidence to justify it.[125]

3 The courts

Once surveillance technology is available that makes possible such actions as scanning email or gaining keys to decrypt messages, and once it is established in principle that the government will have access to such technology, the question for both sides becomes: under what conditions should the government be allowed to use it? Often the contest on this second-level issue centers on the issuance of warrants and court orders.

Civil libertarians hold that court orders are issued too liberally, without due scrutiny. They argue that agents cannot be trusted to abide by minimization guidelines, so it is best not to grant them court orders in the first place. Jerry Berman stated that some 1,000 intercept orders a year are approved under FISA, suggesting that this is a very large number.[126] In fact, only around 10,000 intercept orders have been granted under FISA since its creation in 1979,[127] amounting to fewer than 1,000 a year.

Civil libertarians point to the fact that the FISC has only denied one request for surveillance in its entire history as evidence that the standards for receiving a FISA intercept order are lower than for receiving a Title III order.[128] Though applications for intercept orders are rarely turned down by the FISC, public safety advocates point out that it is embarrassing and damaging to one's record and career to be turned down by the FISC, and as a result agents are reluctant to request warrants even when they seem justified.[129] Moreover, if the FISC finds that there is not sufficient justification, it tends to return the request for further documentation rather than denying the request outright, which accounts for there being next to no outright refusals.[130] As mentioned above, some requests never get past the Attorney-General's office. Also, FISA applications need to meet preset guidelines and must include a statement of the means by which the surveillance will be conducted, as well as a statement of proposed minimization procedures.[131]

Although civil libertarians typically are much more favorably disposed toward courts than toward the administrative parts of the government, they fear that judges might be unable or disinclined to curb law-enforcement agents.[132] First, judges are either elected or politically appointed, making them subject to the influence of public opinion, especially since 9/11. In addition, it has been suggested that judges are less accountable outside their home jurisdictions and might thus be less cautious in granting, and less diligent in enforcing proper implementation of, warrants and court orders they issue that apply to other jurisdictions, as allowed by the USA Patriot Act. Judge Meskill, in his concurrence with the ruling in *United States* v. *Rodriguez*, warned:

> Judges may be more hesitant to authorize excessive interceptions within their territorial jurisdiction, in their own back yard so to speak, than in some distant, perhaps unfamiliar, part of the country. Congress determined that the best method of administering intercept authorizations included territorial limitation on the power of judges to make such authorizations.[133]

If this is true, it would weaken the courts as an accountability mechanism for nationwide warrants.

In addition to the requirements that need to be met to get a warrant or court order in the first place, courts ensure that law-enforcement agents act within the limits of the power granted to them by suppressing evidence that is collected illegally. The exclusionary rule – that evidence collected in violation of the Fourth Amendment must be excluded from a trial against the suspect – was not originally written into the Constitution, but was established in the Supreme Court case *Boyd v. United States* and later re-affirmed in *Weeks v. United States*.[134] It has since been diluted in more ways than one.[135] Still, evidence collected illegally will be suppressed. This serves not only to protect the suspect after a violation occurs, but also to deter inappropriate searches, because agents know that if they do not follow the correct procedures, the culprits might go free.

4 Congress

Under the US system of checks and balances, Congress, of course, is supposed to oversee the work of the executive branch and its agencies. It has many instruments for doing so, including requiring heads of agencies and other high-ranking officials to respond to written questions, testify before congressional committees, and turn over documents; conducting hearings in which civil libertarians and others can make their case; ordering the General Accounting Office to conduct a study; and more.

A survey of the extent to which Congress provides another layer of accountability regarding issues such as those covered here, above and beyond what is provided by the agencies themselves and by the courts, is well beyond the scope of this chapter. It should be noted, though, that civil libertarians argue that many of the measures included in USA Patriot (including those explored here) were enacted in a great rush, without the usual hearings and deliberations.[136] Supporters of the public authorities point out that after 9/11 it was assumed that there were other "sleeper" terrorist agents in the United States and that other attacks were imminent, and argue that therefore the rush was justified. Indeed, they held that expanded powers should have been given well before 9/11.[137] Moreover, hearings and other reviews of the issues at hand, such as Carnivore, were conducted before 9/11.[138]

5 The public

The ultimate source of oversight is the citizenry, informed and alerted by a free press and civil liberties advocates and briefed by public authorities about their needs. To be fully effective in overseeing the issues at hand, civil libertarians argue that the public must be informed about the inner workings of the protective technologies, while public authorities claim that such disclosures would inform terrorists and other criminals about how to circumvent the technologies, thus rendering them useless. Specifically, since the existence of Carnivore was made public, numerous parties have demanded access to information about how it works. The ACLU filed a Freedom of Information Act (FOIA) request to get its source code, which reveals what a program is intended to do and how it operates.[139] The Electronic Privacy Information Center, a privacy advocacy group, filed an FOIA request to gain a copy of *all* documents relating to Carnivore.[140] In addition, numerous ISPs that might be asked to cooperate in installing Carnivore wanted guarantees that the program worked as claimed and that there would be sufficient controls to keep law-enforcement agents from capturing more than what was covered in the court order.[141]

In the Scarfo case, the judge joined civil liberties groups in demanding that the FBI release information on how the KLS works, arguing that he could not rule on whether or not its use was legal without knowing how the technology worked. The judge said he would review the technology secretly.[142] This solution satisfied neither the civil libertarians nor the FBI. David Sobel of EPIC said the matter raised "very basic questions of accountability. The suggestion that the use of high-tech law enforcement investigative techniques should result in a departure from our tradition of open judicial proceedings is very troubling."[143] Donald Kerr, assistant director of the FBI's laboratory division, stated that the disclosure of certain information about the KLS would "compromise the use of this technology . . . and jeopardize the safety of law enforcement personnel."[144]

Secrecy also remains one of the key objections to the use of roving intercepts under FISA. FISA was established in the mid-1970s, after the public was alarmed to learn of the activities of President Nixon and to discover that the NSA had been illegally intercepting telegraph and telephone calls.[145] A congressional committee was created to investigate, and found that nearly every president had authorized warrantless communications surveillance, often for political purposes.[146] Essentially, agencies such as the FBI, CIA, and NSA were able to conduct surveillance without going through normal criminal procedures. The Department of Justice launched its own in-house investigation, resulting in new guidelines for both domestic and foreign intelligence investigations. To prevent future abuses, Congress passed FISA in 1978 to spell out what the NSA (and other intelligence agencies) could and could not do.[147] The NSA had insisted that its activities – especially regarding its methods and technologies – would be severely compromised if discussed in open court. In response, FISA authorized the formation of a special federal court whose proceedings could be completely secret.[148]

In short, while the public cannot be informed about all the workings of all the protective technologies, such as Carnivore, because this would impair the usefulness of the technologies, the public can act as the ultimate enforcer of accountability.

In conclusion

To determine whether or not a specific public policy measure is legitimate entails more than establishing whether or not it significantly enhances public safety and is minimally intrusive, whether it further undermines already endangered civil rights, or makes it more difficult to deal with public needs. It entails rendering a judgment as to whether or not those who employ any new powers are sufficiently accountable to the various overseers – ultimately the citizenry. Some powers are inappropriate no matter what oversight is provided. However, for those at issue here, the main question is whether there is sufficient accountability. The remedy, if accountability is found deficient (or excessive), is to adjust accountability and not to deny the measure altogether.

Whether the specific powers given to the government in regard to the matters at hand are sustaining or undermining the balance between rights and safety depends on how strong each layer of accountability is, whether higher layers enforce lower ones, and whether there are full complements of layers or not. It is true that there can be too much accountability, such that law-enforcement agents would be reluctant to act out of a fear that they might be penalized by superiors, by the courts, or by Congress, or be skewered by the press. However, there have been no signs of this since 9/11.

The Ultimate Question

Accountability is ultimately a matter of trust. Plato is said to have raised the issue when he asked: "who will guard the guardians," or, as it is put in Latin, "*Quis custodiet ipsos custodes?*"[149] Others attribute the question to the Roman satirist Juvenal, who wrote around 2000 years ago.[150] The issue, though, is very much with us. If we do not trust the cops on the beat, we may ask their captains to keep them under closer supervision. If we do not trust the police, we may call on the civil authorities, such as mayors, to scrutinize the police. We may call on the other branches of government – the courts, especially – to serve as checks and balances. However, if we believe that the mayors are corrupt and the judges cannot be trusted either, we have little to fall back on other than the fourth estate. Yet the media, too, is often distrusted.[151]

The question, then, is whom we should distrust and how much. If basically no authority or media figure is trustworthy and "The System" is corrupt, we face a much larger challenge than if, in a few instances, public authorities intercept more email than they are supposed to, or tap some phones they ought not. Anyone who believes the former should either move to another country or fight for an entirely new political system. In contrast, if only some cops, captains, mayors, and other public authorities are corrupt, we have good reason to watch out for such individuals, but not to doubt the political system. We ought, then, to work to improve the various layers of accountability, but also realize that the fact that critics can always come up with some horror stories does not necessarily mean that they are typical of the system.

Although I cannot justify it within the confines of this volume, I hold the latter position. Hence, I suggest that it is best to ignore both claims by public authorities that no strengthening of accountability is needed and the shrillest civil libertarian outcries that sound as if no one is to be trusted. Instead, we should favor reforms that will enhance accountability, rather than denying public authorities the tools they need to do their work (although not necessarily granting them all those they request) in a world in which new technologies have made their service more difficult and in which the threat to public safety has vastly increased.

5

DNA Testing and Individual Rights

Introduction

This chapter examines several issues raised by extensive use of DNA tests and databases in advancing public safety. The examination draws on a communitarian perspective that balances the common good with individual rights rather than presuming that rights routinely trump the common good.

Specifically, the chapter examines major arguments made by critics who oppose extensive usages of DNA tests and especially the keeping of results (or the samples from which the results were drawn) in databases for law-enforcement purposes. (To save breath I shall refer to "DNA usages" from here on.) Most of the criticisms are by civil libertarians. While none seems completely to oppose DNA usages, all demand that the state be greatly limited in conducting such tests, in storing the results, and in drawing on them. The critics' basic approach is to combine a general distrust of the government with a strong commitment to the value of being let alone.

I start with a response to the challenge that DNA usages will usher in eugenics, because this claim is so detrimental that until it is set aside, there is little point in dealing with other criticisms. I then turn to assess the extent to which DNA usages serve the common good, and to assess claims that numerous DNA usages violate the Fourth Amendment, violate privacy, and contribute to the development of a surveillance state. In the last section, I analyze the question of what kinds of material should be kept in DNA banks (if any), and whether inmates should be granted a new right – to be tested.

The Threat of Eugenics

The most severe criticism hurled at DNA usages is that they will lead to Nazi-like policies in which people will be killed or discriminated against according to their genes. For instance, Barry Steinhardt, Associate Director of the American Civil Liberties Union, stated before the House Judiciary Committee's Subcommittee on Crime: "It is worth recalling that there is a long unfortunate history of despicable behavior by governments toward people whose genetic composition has been considered 'abnormal' under the prevailing societal standards of the day."[1] And the National Research Council Report in DNA Technology in Forensic Sciences raised the same issue in reference to an earlier America: "The eugenics movement in this country...resulted in thousands of involuntary sterilizations ..."[2]

In response, one notes first that the availability of DNA tests and banks did not cause the rise of totalitarian regimes or their introduction of eugenics, as is evident from the fact that the Nazis implemented such policies on a very large scale before DNA tests existed. The same holds for whatever eugenics policies were introduced by other governments, including that of the United States. Nor are there any signs that totalitarian tendencies or interest in eugenics have increased in those democratic societies that have introduced DNA testing. To put it more sharply but not less accurately, eugenics has only so far been implemented before the existence of DNA tests and not since their development.

It is true that, as new biotech procedures and databases are further developed, they will make it easier for a future government to abuse these tools. But the same holds for many new scientific and technological developments, including most if not all modes of communication and transportation. It makes little sense to forgo or severely limit the use of a new device that yields major benefits out of a fear that some day some government may abuse it. To suppress DNA usages because they might be abused is akin to arguing that we should not allow the building of rapid trains because they may be used to transport victims to concentration camps, or should refrain from developing computers because Big Brother might benefit from them. This last analogy is particularly apt because such objections were raised in the early days of computers by some of the same groups that now object to DNA usages, using rather similar arguments. (One may say that critics do not oppose all DNA usages and thus the analogies do not apply. Fair enough. Let's just say that they advocate so many limits on their use that it is akin to limiting the trains' speed to 10 miles an hour.)

Second, a government that would introduce eugenics is likely to inflict numerous other abuses on its people. This is what has invariably happened in the past. In the USA, eugenics was practiced when the society used its laws to discriminate against women, minorities, and gay people, and was at least a bit authoritarian. The best protection against the abuse of DNA tests and other basically beneficial products and devices is to work to ensure that the institutions and values that undergird free societies are strong, and to defend them vigorously.

In addition, civil libertarians ignore the fact that DNA tests can help ward off totalitarianism. Totalitarian governments arise in response to breakdowns in the social order, when basic human needs, especially public safety, are grossly neglected. When a society does not take steps to prevent major social ills and to strengthen social order, an increasing number of citizens demands strong-armed authorities to restore law and order. By greatly helping to sustain law and order, DNA tests and banks play a significant role in curbing the type of breakdown in social order that can lead to totalitarianism.

Two Approaches: Libertarian and Communitarian

Civil libertarians often take the position in reference to DNA databases, as they do in reference to most other law-enforcement techniques, that individual rights must be vigorously protected. They state that they do not in principle oppose considerations of the common good, especially public safety, but, given their great distrust of the government, they demand that all such considerations be carefully scrutinized. Public safety procedures are presumed to be guilty (of abuse by government) until proven otherwise, and the standard of proof is set very high.[3]

The approach followed here, which relies on responsive communitarian thinking,[4] treats individual rights and the common good as two profound legitimate moral claims and seeks to work out a carefully crafted balance between these two. When possible, as is to some extent the case with DNA as we shall see shortly, both claims should be satisfied. And when they conflict, one should yield if a limited and carefully circumscribed reduction of it yields a substantial gain for the other. This should be allowed only if strong "notches" are developed to prevent sliding down a slippery slope.[5]

Accordingly, the examination turns next to assess the scope of benefits to the common good DNA usages provide, followed by a discussion of its contribution to the *protection* of individual rights, and then to an assessment of claims that such usages violate such rights.

Benefits for the Common Good

As one source put it: "For a decade, DNA tests have been the most powerful tool available to police and prosecutors investigating new crimes, helping to pinpoint suspects in rape and murder cases, while alerting authorities when they were on the wrong track."[6] Paul Ferrara, the director of Virginia's DNA database program, said: "It is revolutionizing the way police do their work."[7] Christopher Asplen, the federal prosecutor who is serving as the executive director of the National Institute of Justice's National Commission on the Future of DNA Evidence, calls DNA testing "the most significant advancement in investigative tools at least in this century.... It's one of the most accurate technologies we have. It has an incredible ability not just to convict the guilty but also to exonerate the innocent."[8] Walter Rowe, a leading academic forensic scientist, has gone even further, saying that DNA testing "may be the greatest advance in forensic science in history."[9]

In the short period in which DNA databases have been in use for forensic purposes, they have played a significant role in taking large numbers of criminals off the street. Numerous old "cold" crimes, which had long occupied the time and resources of law enforcement, have been solved. Serial killers and rapists have been much more readily identified. As tests and databanks – which currently encompass but a small number of criminals – are expanded, the benefits of DNA usages will be greatly increased.

There seems to be no data on the deterrence effect that DNA usages have. However, it would be very surprising if, as it becomes increasingly evident (once much more of the DNA material collected is introduced into the DNA banks and many more criminals are encompassed) that if a criminal leaves behind even one hair or drop of sweat, he or she may identified, this does not begin to have a deterrence effect. It is hence likely that DNA usages will lead not only to more convictions, but also to fewer crimes being committed in the first place, which is the best of all worlds.

In short, benefits to public safety are very substantial.

Advancing Individual Rights

DNA tests and databases do not merely serve to dramatically increase public safety, but also to protect individual rights. One of the strongest and indeed noblest claims of free societies is that it is better to let a thousand guilty people go free than to imprison one innocent person. This is a very powerful commitment that attests to how abhorrent a free society holds incarceration of the innocent. Extensive and accessible DNA testing and databases can be strongly justified on this ground alone: they already have freed from prison – even death row! – a substantial number of innocent people who had been falsely convicted and incarcerated.

Moreover, by making it possible to identify quickly the guilty person from among a group of suspects (a process to be much further accelerated as handheld, quick response DNA tests become available), DNA usages greatly reduce the humiliation and costs entailed in being a suspect in a police investigation.[10] (Dr. Paul Ferrara, Director of the Virginia Division of Forensic Science, reports, "We typically and routinely eliminate approximately 25 percent to 30 percent of the suspects who the police have centered on in their investigation using our DNA analysis."[11]) Picture the following situation, which is based on a real case. A rape occurred in a hospital. Eleven people had ready access to the room overnight. Before DNA tests were available, the police would have quite legitimately questioned all eleven people – asking them to provide alibis, checking their records for past offenses, interviewing their supervisors, friends, and family members. If the rapist were not identified, the case might linger for years; none of the suspects would be cleared and a cloud would hang over them at work and in the community despite the presumption of innocence, which is guaranteed in trial court but not in the court of public opinion. In the new world of rapid DNA testing, the police would ask each of the eleven to provide a sample of saliva, or a hair, and all suspects (or all but one) would be completely cleared almost on the spot, without any other measures having to be taken, and without the undesirable effects of people being long suspected.

Granted, this hypothetical case makes several assumptions. It assumes that some semen (or hair or saliva) was left behind; that it belonged to the rapist;[12] that the suspects voluntarily provide the samples or that the police would be granted the right to collect them; and that the police sweep would be limited to "true" suspects (more about all these points later). However, none of these assumptions is unrealistic.

There are other ways in which DNA tests and databases greatly help to better protect individual rights (as well as public safety). DNA tests are many times more reliable than the police procedures that heretofore were very often relied upon to make people into suspects (and convicts). If one compares using DNA tests to identify a perpetrator to using eyewitnesses and police line-ups, which are notoriously unreliable,[13] one immediately sees the double virtue of DNA testing: it vastly enhances the probability both that those who are guilty will be convicted and that those who are innocent will be rapidly cleared, despite the early indications that made them into suspects.

The reliability of DNA tests, which was contested when they were less developed, is now considered so high that, as a rule, it is not contested. (There have been, worldwide, fewer than a handful of cases, reported in the press, in which mismatches occurred, but most, if not all, were due to mishandling in labs and other such errors. These were readily corrected by re-testing and by examining other evidence.[14])

In its few years of operation, the British National DNA Database, which was the first national DNA database in the world, has provided more than 16,000 links between suspects and DNA left at crime scenes. At this point, the database matches around 600 crimes to suspects or to other crimes each week.[15]

In the United States, where DNA databases are newer and much less developed than in Britain, the FBI's multitiered DNA database system, CODIS, had "assisted in over 1,100 investigations in 24 states" by March 2000.[16] Many of the benefits of the databases have yet to be realized because large numbers of DNA samples that have been collected have not yet been analyzed and coded, and hence are not included in the databases.[17] And DNA has yet to be collected from many convicted criminals.

DNA evidence has already exonerated a considerable number of convicts. In a report sponsored by the US Department of Justice, in which 28 cases of wrongful conviction are documented, Edward J. Imwinkelried, Professor of Law at UC Davis, notes: "In all 28 cases, without the benefit of DNA evidence, triers of fact had to rely on eyewitness testimony, which turned out to be inaccurate." He also pointedly asks: "if we impose a unique restriction on scientific testimony, on balance are the courts more likely to reach just results – or are we condemning the courts to reliance on suspect types of testimony that call into question the caliber of justice dispensed in our courts?"[18]

Even though it took several years for DNA testing to become admissible in US courts, and even though DNA databanks are only now being set up on a large scale in the US, a significant number of wrongly convicted people have already been freed. Barry Scheck reported in a statement before the Senate Judiciary Committee on June 13, 2000: "There have been at least 73 post-conviction DNA exonerations in North America; 67 in the United States, and 6 in Canada.... In 16 of these 73 post-conviction exonerations, DNA testing has not only remedied a terrible miscarriage of justice, but led to the identification of the real perpetrator." He correctly added that, "With the expanded use of DNA databanks and the continued technological advances in DNA testing, not only will post-conviction DNA exonerations increase, but the rate at which the real perpetrators are apprehended will grow as well."[19]

In short, one should first note that DNA often can be used to enhance both individual rights and public safety. If one truly places a great deal of importance upon the release of innocent people from jail, what is considered righting the ultimate wrong, and on limiting the exposure of innocent suspects to police interrogation, one should welcome the extensive use of DNA testing on this ground alone.

Threats to Individual Rights

Having established the very considerable extent to which the common good is served by DNA tests and databases, and their contributions to the protection of individual rights, the discussion turns to claims that DNA usages impinge on these rights. The question of balance hinges upon whether rights are greatly harmed or, alternatively, barely affected.

Critics of DNA usages raise numerous objections that are intertwined and shade into each other. Although they differ regarding the specifics, critics employ the same arguments: that DNA usages violate basic rights such as the constitutional protection against unreasonable search and seizure, that they constitute a particularly gross violation of privacy, and that by adding to the rapid development of a surveillance society they undermine the right to be let alone. Given that no critic seems to favor banning *all* DNA usages (for criminal justice purposes), although they often sound as if they do,[20] the contested issues are what kind of evidence may be collected, from whom, what is to be done with the DNA material and analyses once available, and who may have access to these materials and analyses. In short, how can DNA testing and databases be effectively utilized without significantly offending individual rights?

Fourth Amendment concerns

The Fourth Amendment establishes the most communitarian of all the rights enumerated in the Constitution because, on the face of it, it recognizes the public interest. By banning unreasonable searches and seizures, it recognizes that there are reasonable ones – those in the public interest. (Compare its text to the First Amendment, which reads in part, "Congress shall make no law . . . " and hence is widely recognized as more absolute than the Fourth Amendment.) However, this still leaves much room for differences of opinions about where the point of balance lies, about what makes a search reasonable or unreasonable in general, and specifically in the area at hand. Civil libertarians almost invariably argue in regard to any new law-enforcement technique and procedure (and about many old ones) that it constitutes an unreasonable search.

Most DNA usages are not treated any differently. For instance, most DNA usages are opposed by the New York Civil Liberties Union on the ground that they violate the Fourth Amendment.[21] And Dorothy Nelkin and Lori Andrews recount claims by Virginia inmates whose DNA was collected for a database that "in the absence of individualized suspicion, mandatory extraction of DNA samples violated their Fourth Amendment right against search and seizure."[22]

Opponents of this and other DNA collections for databases point to the lack of "individualized suspicion" because this is the general standard for probable cause. (It is said to draw the line between reasonable and unreasonable searches.) However, searches lacking individualized suspicion have repeatedly been upheld by the courts if there are good reasons for them. Indeed, for decades millions of innocent Americans have been routinely "searched," and legal challenges to many public policies that entail so-called "suspicionless searches" have been rejected by the courts. Suspicionless searches that have been deemed constitutional include drug testing of whole categories of people (e.g., train engineers) without any suspicion of prior drug use. It might be said that such searches are "job-related requirements," and that those who accept these jobs agree to them. But we still might ask if these are fair requirements or abusive ones, the way we do, for instance, about email screening by employers. It seems to me that what justifies such tests for some professions and not for others is the scope of the public interest involved.

For the same reason, sobriety check points that stop all or randomly chosen drivers, rather than only those whose driving shows signs of being intoxicated, are justified, as is the use of metal detectors in airports, public buildings, and many other places that search the belongings and persons of millions of people each day. (One may say that people agree to be searched if they decide to travel by air or to enter a public building or travel on a public road, but often people have no choice at all, such as when they appear in court, or they have no real choice, e.g., when their job requires them to travel large distances.)

Moreover, the Constitution is a living document that has always been reinterpreted to take into account the changing social and historical situation. Without such recalibration, there would be no constitutional right to privacy (articulated only in the mid-1960s); the right to free speech would have a rather more limited meaning than attributed to it today; and African-Americans would not count as full persons. Similarly, searches of whole categories of people, when they are not based on ascribed status such as race and gender, are permitted by a modern adaptation of the Fourth Amendment, reflecting modern needs to deal with large numbers of people and new kinds of threats to their safety.

Additional reasons are given by the courts that DNA usages do not offend the Fourth Amendment. In *Jones* v. *Murray* (the case referred to by Nelkin and Andrews), six inmates challenged a Virginia DNA databank statute. The district court rejected the inmates' challenge, relying upon the "special needs" exception that is used to justify administrative searches. In these cases, heavily regulated industries are considered to have a low expectation of privacy, and the regulation of these industries is a special need that requires surprise, albeit suspicionless, searches. Moreover, while the appeals court in the same case argued that the special needs exception was not relevant, it also ruled that it was not needed. The appeals court upheld the statute, basing its judgment upon the fact that convicted criminals have reduced rights (and a reduced expectation of privacy), and on the weighty public interest in maintaining a DNA database of convicted felons.[23]

Whatever legal argument one relies upon, the fact is that the courts found such searches legitimate. This is in line with the communitarian conception articulated earlier. DNA tests are, in principle, justified on the same grounds as other suspicionless searches, but the question remains: who may legitimately be subject to them? Just as mandatory drug testing of one and all is not justified because there is no compelling public interest, DNA testing of all people is not justified. The question becomes: when *is* there a compelling public interest, and, in these cases, which if any rights are violated?

Criminals, suspects, and innocents

Rights issues differ in their relation to three categories of people: convicted criminals, suspects, and innocent people.

There is relatively little disagreement that, given the high propensity of criminals to commit additional crimes once released from prison, given that their DNA may help to solve crimes they committed before they were caught, and given that there is a well-established legal tradition of greatly scaling back the rights of felons even when there is much less public interest (for instance, they are not allowed to vote), collecting DNA material from them and keeping the evidence is very much in line with the American constitutional tradition. People who commit crimes surrender many of their rights, from their liberty to their privacy.

Which criminals should be included in DNA databanks? Only violent ones? Or also those who commit non-violent crimes such as burglary and car theft? According to one article, in state investigations, "more than half the DNA investigations of unsolved violent crimes led to burglars."[24] At that time Ferrara said, "People think of burglars as these...'gentlemen bandit' types, but that is often not the case."[25] Since the early 1990s, Virginia and Florida have compared the DNA of convicted offenders, including burglars, to the DNA found at the scenes of unsolved crimes. In Virginia, 60 percent of the crimes solved through DNA matching have been matched with convicted burglars, while about 50 percent of such crimes in Florida have been matched to burglars.[26]

"Research in England and the United States in recent years has shown that violent criminals such as rapists frequently commit felonies such as burglary before they turn to violence. Limiting the routine collection of DNA blood samples robs police of data that have proved to be effective in solving serious crimes."[27] Similarly, in the debate in Florida over a proposed law that would include burglars in Florida's DNA database, "The FDLE [Florida Department of Law Enforcement] cites statistics showing a correlation between burglars and rapists. It says more than half of the state's rapists started out as burglars. Collecting the DNA of burglars could lead them to current or future rapists."[28] However, the editors of the *St. Petersburg Times* write: "But that justification applies just as easily to a host of other types of crimes. If a large percentage of rapists received speeding tickets, would that justify expanding the DNA database to include those with moving violations?"[29]

When the communitarian principle is applied, it may, at first, seem that if a high percentage of non-violent offenders go on to commit violent crimes, then their DNA should be collected and banked, and if the percentage is a lower number, then their DNA should not be collected and banked. If the correlation is low between non-violent offenders and past or future violent crime, then collecting their DNA serves the public interest relatively little, while, if it is high, the service is considerable. But more is at stake here. Even if there is only a low correlation between a particular type of non-violent crime and violent crime, collecting the DNA of convicted non-violent felons may still be justified because they have significantly lowered rights. The final ruling as to how low such a figure may end up must be weighed in reference to the kind of crime at issue. For instance, society may deem that welshing on child support offends its values more (or less) than embezzling, and thereby decide that one category of offenders is entitled to fewer rights than another. It may take such a ranking of non-violent crimes into account when judging whether DNA should be collected from any category of offenders, which is a separate consideration than the question of how likely it is that those who committed one of these crimes will also commit a violent one.

While civil libertarians strongly oppose the testing of non-violent offenders, they are even more vehement in their opposition to testing suspects (including arrestees) and above all innocent people, even if people consent.

To lay out my position it is necessary to define the term "suspect." When the term is used loosely, practically anyone can be considered a suspect, as in the phrase "I think he did it." This broad sense of "suspect" is the one used when, for instance, people suggest, as Troy Duster did during a DNA conference, that we must be wary of the danger that police might treat whole populations as suspects, as is the case for African-Americans when the police engage in racial profiling.[30]

As I use the term here, it is much more narrowly defined. A suspect for the purposes of this discussion is a person who has undergone some kind of legal process that makes it clear that he or she is suspected of having committed a crime. The best-known mechanism for making innocent people into suspects, and the one that is relatively less contested than others, is seeking a warrant from a judge to search a person's home or body. (Others include arresting a person, and stopping and detaining someone who is running from a crime scene.) These mechanisms make people legally suspect, even if they are eventually released or acquitted, as long as there was evidence to detain or search them. As I will discuss briefly later, there are mechanisms that should protect people from being arrested or detained without such evidence.

Once a person is defined as suspect through a legal process, his or her rights are diminished in comparison to innocent people, although not as much as those of convicted fellows. Suspects' homes and cars – and persons – may be legally searched; they may be brought to a police station for questioning, and even arrested and held in prison for defined periods of time; and their passports may be suspended.[31] Above all, they may be fingerprinted, whether or not they consent, which is of special importance given that there are certain similarities between fingerprinting and DNA testing and databases, as both serve to identify a person and tie him or her to a crime. None of these measures can be legally taken against innocent people.

There is a tendency to lump together all people who have not been convicted of a crime because of a very widely held belief that our justice system presumes people to be innocent until proven guilty. While this is of course true, the fact is that suspects in free societies are treated rather differently from both innocent people and convicted criminals. If one prefers, one may wish to talk about innocent-innocent (or fully innocent) people and innocent-suspects (out of respect for the norm that no one is guilty until they are convicted). But such wording is not merely awkward but conceals the fact that, whatever suspects are called, they are treated neither as innocent people nor as convicted criminals.

Given that suspects have diminished rights, including much lower rights to privacy, than innocent people, and given (as we shall see), that DNA tests can be made to be minimally intrusive, there is, on the face of it, no obvious reason why suspects should not be tested and their DNA included in databases. Indeed, in several states DNA profiles that are coded for suspects from one case are run against the DNA profiles from unsolved cases to see if the suspect from the one case might have committed a different crime.

Unfortunately, in accordance with the DNA Identification Act of 1994, CODIS cannot run broad searches in which DNA profiles from suspects are compared to the bank of DNA from unresolved cases. The states that do this can draw only on data in their own banks. (CODIS allows such broad searches only after suspects have been convicted.)

A subsidiary question is whether the results of the tests should be kept. If a suspect is not convicted, his DNA, like other evidence, should be kept in a searchable DNA databank for a certain period of time, and then expunged or sequestered (kept in a non-searchable location) if the suspect has not had any other problems with the law. If sequestered, the evidence would no longer be available to police in their searches regarding unsolved crimes, but would be available if the person were to be convicted of a new crime – for sentencing purposes, for instance. We have already seen that testing suspects seems very much in the public interest.

In short, public authorities cannot indiscriminately declare as a suspect anyone they wish to test. There are relatively clear markers that protect the innocent, and mechanisms to protect these markers. If these mechanisms are too weak, and make it too easy to turn innocent people into suspects, then they should be strengthened – whether or not DNA tests are performed. But, if they work properly, then there is no obvious reason to refrain from collecting DNA from suspects and storing it in databanks.

Civil libertarians are especially aghast at the thought of DNA being collected from innocent people. They are not only worried that DNA may be mandatorily collected from all people, but also hold that, if people are asked by the authorities to consent to DNA testing, their consent is likely not to be truly voluntary.[32] Coerced (mandatory) collection of DNA from innocent people for law-enforcement purposes is indeed abhorrent. (If collected for other purposes, such as for identification of infants or military personnel, penalties should be imposed if it is used for other purposes and the material should be carefully safeguarded.) To collect DNA from all people would treat all members of a free society as if they were suspects, if not criminals. And there is minimal public interest in such a measure (which will decrease even further as more and more criminals and suspects are included in databases). In short, the situation of non-suspect citizens is the opposite of the situation of criminals:

full rights and little public interest versus diminished rights and high public interest.

However, the police must be allowed to ask for DNA samples from people not considered suspects, even though the collection of DNA should not be a mandatory requirement for all citizens. Philip Bereano, a communications professor as the University of Washington and a member of the national board of the American Civil Liberties Union, argues that if the police ask for a DNA sample, "It's situationally coercive." He paints the following picture: "A policeman appears on your doorstep, and he's an authority figure. He says, or at least seems to say, 'Come on, everybody's doing it,' and you feel pressured."[33] A Portland lawyer raises a different concern: "You know that if you say no, you're making yourself a suspect."[34] However, the same argument could be made when people are asked to answer police questions, or when they are asked to open their suitcase or the trunk of their car (and, in fact, has been made). If we accept the argument that people cannot truly consent to a request by authorities, then we must prohibit not only the collection of voluntary DNA samples, but many other law-enforcement activities that are essential for public safety.

At the same time, if there is evidence that undue pressure has been applied, DNA evidence – like all other evidence – should be dismissed. However, the mere fact that the police requested a DNA sample should not be construed as undue pressure. Such requests can be essential in a whole set of situations for effective law enforcement (including speedy clearing of suspects) and, if consent is freely given, entail no diminution of rights.

Privacy violation

DNA testing is said to be particularly intrusive for two reasons. First, critics argue that blood testing is especially intrusive because it involves entering the body. Eric T. Juengst, an Associate Professor of Biomedical Ethics, notes that DNA collection is not the same as photography and manual fingerprinting because it actually involves "taking bits of people's bodies from them."[35] It is an invasion not simply of privacy, but an intrusion into our self-possession of our bodies. In *Jones* v. *Murray*, the inmates recognized that their rights were more limited than ordinary citizens because of their convictions, but "the prisoners defined their right to bodily integrity in a distinctive category."[36] Second, DNA testing is said to be particularly intrusive because it reveals much more information about the person tested than, for instance, fingerprinting does. The question then arises, as Juengst puts it, "What should society be allowed to learn about its citizens in the course of attempting to identify them?"[37]

The first concern is less weighty than the second one, even if one does not agree with the ruling in *People* v. *Wealer* in which the Illinois Court of Appeals upheld the constitutionality of an Illinois DNA databank statute on the grounds that blood testing is minimally intrusive[38] (or with the *Jones* court, which cited *Skinner* to establish that blood testing is a "not significant" intrusion. Indeed, the courts have even authorized drawing blood from a sitting president in order to determine if the semen found on a blue dress was his.)

DNA tests can be performed with a lower degree of bodily intrusion. New York City, for instance, plans to base its bank on saliva taken from people at the same time they are fingerprinted. In fact, DNA can be collected from not only blood, but also from skin cells and dandruff, as well as the cells contained in saliva, sweat, or urine, or attached to strands of hair.[39] Thus, samples other than blood can reliably be used, and collecting them is much less intrusive than collecting blood (or even urine, which often must be provided under supervised conditions).

The second concern, that DNA testing poses a threat to informational privacy, is less easily dealt with. Juengst states:

> [M]any have pointed out that, if the DNA sequences used as the components of iDNAfication profile are taken from the regions of the human genome that code for proteins, important biological information about their sources could be revealed, including information about their paternity, current health status, and potential health risks. Any risk of disclosing sensitive personal information of these sorts would clearly increase the intrusiveness of iDNAfication beyond that of traditional fingerprinting and photography.[40]

There are several other considerations that apply here, which all suggest that the threat to privacy is much lower than some have suggested. First, unless one simply views the government as some kind of ruthless enemy, there is no reason to believe that it will use DNA that is collected for criminal identification purposes to find out about people's family history, illnesses, etc. In addition, bans on such research and disclosure of such information have been introduced. So far there has not been a single reported violation of these restrictions. And even if a few did occur, this might lead to tightening security and raising penalties, but still would not justify preventing the storage of the proper information. After all, we do not shut down other basically beneficial systems, from airline traffic to courts, because some mistakes occur. Making policy by horror stories is a horrible idea.

Second, DNA tests that are done on blood stains, semen, saliva, and biological tissue found at crime scenes are not a violation of privacy. Courts ruled (in line with *Katz* v. *United States*) that there is no privacy violation in places where a reasonable person would have no expectation of privacy, and when society does not presume that one exists. This makes sense. If a man walks down Main Street wearing only his birth suit, he has little reason to complain if people see his private parts. It seems reasonable to assume that criminals who leave behind these samples have no more expectation of privacy than if they leave behind fingerprints.

If a DNA sample is taken from a criminal or suspect under court orders, this does constitute a diminution of their privacy. But, as already indicated, this intrusion can be minimized by collecting hair or saliva rather than blood, and by limiting access to the test results. And, to reiterate, criminals and suspects have diminished privacy rights in general. Even for innocent people, privacy has never been considered an absolute right.

Slippery slope and racial discrimination

Critics employ two other arguments against DNA usages: the slippery slope argument, and the argument that there is a danger of racial and other forms of discrimination. The first argument is exemplified by a Boston public defender who, in response to the collection of DNA from inmates, probationers, and parolees, asked rhetorically, "Why not round up poor people?"[41] Paul E. Tracy and Vincent Morgan write:

> These various scenarios follow a clear-cut progression. A sex-offender-only database seems virtually unobjectionable. The conviction-based databases seem a little more expansive, but still they do not seem particularly troubling. After all, a judge or a jury found the accused guilty. That should be enough. The arrest-based systems are the current thresholds, but here, we have no assurance of guilt, only suspicion. With the total population database, even if one takes cost out of the equation, it still seems a little too futuristic. Something about it just

seems contrary to our notions of individual autonomy, and our sense of personal privacy.[42]

Others argue that DNA tests do or will lead to racial and other forms of discrimination. Peter Neufeld, Barry Steinhardt, and Troy Duster are among those who fear that DNA tests would lead to discrimination because studies might show that people of a given social group that commits more crimes than others share some DNA markers and hence all those with these attributes would be discriminated against.[43]

Both arguments deserve attention, but the main question is where they take us. If the conclusion is that DNA tests and banks should not be used, these arguments must be set aside for reasons already discussed. If they are meant to suggest that we must carefully notch the slippery slope, set clear markers for what is allowed and not allowed, and establish penalties for the abuse of genetic information, they deserve our full support.[44] Thus, just as no responsible person would argue that we should stop enforcing traffic laws and conducting sobriety tests merely because, in some places, racial profiling has been used, DNA banks should not be closed simply because some civil libertarians fear that one day they may be used to discriminate against some people.

DNA adds to the surveillance society

Another major source of the opposition to usages is derived from the concern that DNA databases would significantly add to the capacity of the government to track its citizens. One critic fears that DNA fingerprinting will "usher in a high-tech Orwellian police state."[45] Another, that information-gathering technologies "are rendering individuals more and more transparent, and relentlessly reducing the private spaces into which people have traditionally been able to retreat for refuge and self-definition."[46]

These claims are not without merit. Technological developments make it possible to trace the place from which a person is placing a cell phone call (or using a wireless device to access the internet), to find unlisted phone numbers, to "read" another person's financial records, and generally to gain extensive profiles of people's behavior and, indirectly, even their thoughts. There can be no doubt that genetic testing in general and DNA databanks in particular will significantly deepen and expand the capacity to track people.

Civil libertarians have historically focused their attention on the government, on Big Brother. However, since the 1990s almost all of the new surveillance techniques and databases, including genetic tests, have been developed by the private sector, by Big Bucks. Private corporations have introduced technology that locates where cell phone calls and wireless messages come from in order to advertise nearby restaurants and shops and, they report, to help people who are being attacked, experience car breakdowns, or have lost their way. (The FBI is struggling to gain the changes in the laws that are required to give them the authority to use the same technology.) Tracing who visits which website and what people examine (through "cookies" and "web bugs") and keeping detailed profiles on people's behavior and preferences (even reading drafts of messages that have never left their computers), collecting and selling personal medical and financial information, and shadowing children – these are all done by private companies on a very large scale. (When the FBI introduced the computer program Carnivore, which is able to detect the email messages of those suspected of committing a crime, this became the source of much concern.)

Moreover, private companies are developing and marketing new ways of identifying people that are extremely reliable and that are able to track one and all, without their knowledge or consent. One example of this is biometrics. Biometric technology is defined as technology that "analyses and measures unique physiological or biological characteristics that can be stored electronically and retrieved for positive identification."[47] Various cardless biometric identification technologies are in advanced stages of development, including voice recognition, hand geometry, facial recognition, and retina and iris scans ("eye prints").[48]

While the government's feared abuse of these new capabilities is almost completely hypothetical – "one day, a future government might..." – abuses of surveillance technologies by the private sector are well documented. These include the violation of commitments not to collect information about children 13 or younger without the consent of their parents, and violations of the privacy policies corporations posted for those who frequent their sites.[49]

DNA tests and databases may at first seem to be an exception. They have been largely introduced by the government. However, the largest force driving the use of DNA tests and databases for purposes other than criminal justice is private biotech firms. Here, too, while fears of government abuses have concerned hypothetical futuristic scenarios, this is not the case for DNA use in the private sector.

So far, the main abuses have been by employers, who have used the results of genetic tests to eliminate job applicants from contention, or to ease genetically undesirable people out of jobs. As early as 1996 a study documented 206 cases of genetic discrimination against asymptomatic individuals.[50] Richard Sobel and Harold J. Bursztain report that, "In fact, a recent survey of employers by the American Management Association finds that 30 percent ask for genetic information about employees and 7 percent admit to using the information for hiring and promotion decisions."[51] And there must be more unknown cases of the abuse of genetic information, as people often are not told why they have not been hired, not promoted, or let go, or are given vague or inaccurate explanations.

There are already reports of funeral parlor directors who have collected DNA for private purposes.[52] Hospitals often retain blood samples taken from patients and use these samples in ways unrelated to the patients' own care. Currently, "Only 13 states ban the testing of someone's DNA without that person's permission."[53] In short, practically all the instances of inappropriate and exploitative DNA usages so far in the US have come from the private sector. We are just at the very beginning of this trend. I predict that by 2010 this form of abuse will become much more common and serious.

Confronted with the reality of the surveillance society, we can move in one of two basic directions. We can accept as a fact of life that new technologies, especially biometric ones (DNA tests and banks included), make a very high level of surveillance a fact of life that cannot be avoided and we must learn to live with it. Indeed, several books recently have suggested that "privacy is dead."[54] The head of Sun Microsystems stated, "You already have zero privacy; get over it."[55]

The other response to the expanding surveillance society is to greatly restrict surveillance capabilities, as many civil liberations demand. In this case, though, civil libertarians must recognize that the main source of this new protection must be the government they so mistrust. New laws will have to be enacted and the main actors that will need to be restrained will be private ones. Merely limiting the databases the government may maintain would be like curbing gun violence by prohibiting police departments from selling hand guns they have confiscated – a good idea, but one that deals with only a tiny fraction of the market. And merely limiting the government's ability to use privately maintained databases would mean that these databases could be used for *de facto* discrimination regarding employment, credit, and housing, but could not be used for law enforcement and other common-good purposes.

Currently, laws reflect an earlier view of the surveillance society: they greatly limit what the government can legally do with the information it collects, and impose penalties for government abuses, but impose relatively few restraints on private actors. (The main exception to this generalization is medical information. Reference is to the United States; the situation in the EU is quite different.) There are few limitations on what private companies, including labs, can do with blood and other samples that contain DNA, or what they can do with the results of DNA tests they have already conducted. And, of course, anything that is so freely available in the private sector is at least potentially available to the government.

Because this point is so pivotal, an additional illustration is provided: critics often rail against the abuse of Social Security numbers. They correctly point out that when these numbers were introduced the government promised that they would not be made available for any purposes other than Social Security – and now they are very widely used, and almost serve as a national identification number. What these critics ignore is that it is not the government that put these numbers into almost universal use; they are demanded by mortgage lenders, employers, health insurers, and many other private companies, and are provided by their consumers.

To argue that the government should be the main protector against DNA abuses is not to suggest that it is not to be limited by law and scrutinized. It is like hiring guards who need to be supervised and whose scope of duties needs to be circumscribed. The government still needs to be monitored to ensure that public usages of DNA will be proper. This observation leads to the question: what usages are proper? What should be included in databases, and who should have access to them?

Data-Collection and Access

Civil libertarians argue that the data collected should be greatly limited in content and that the samples themselves should be destroyed and only limited profiles (electronic records of the information needed to identify and match a person) kept.[56] The FBI already limits the extent of the informational privacy invasion involved in DNA profiling. The DNA markers used in CODIS "were specifically selected as law enforcement identification markers because they were not directly linked to any genetic code for a medical condition."[57]

Keeping the samples found at crime scenes and those taken from arrestees and criminals is justified for now on the ground that DNA tests are still rapidly developing. If the samples are destroyed, any new information they may yield as better technology is developed will not be available if future criminals and suspects need it to prove their innocence, nor will it be available to the government for solving crimes. "The main uncertainties now are introduced by 'human frailty at the laboratory level,' says geneticist James Crow of the University of Wisconsin, Madison – so *the best protection for a suspect is to preserve samples for retesting.*"[58] It is enough to imagine if samples were destroyed but a few years back, when DNA tests were less accurate, how much damage would have been done to both rights and the common good. Someone might argue that, at this point, DNA tests are so reliable that no additional gains can be expected. However, new improvements do occur, such as in terms of how little material one needs to extract DNA.[59] In Arizona, a man was exonerated regarding the sodomizing of a young boy, a crime for which he had been convicted a decade earlier. While the small amount of semen that was found was insufficient for reliable testing at the time, new testing procedures showed conclusively that the police had the wrong man.[60] Surely additional improvements that cannot now be anticipated can be expected. The samples should be kept for at least five more years, to see whether or not they are needed.

Second, the use of criminal justice DNA databases for non-forensic usages should be banned, and the use of non-criminal justice databases (e.g., medical research databases) for forensic purposes should be prohibited. The reasons for this position range from principled to prudential ones. In principle, while the government can justify (for the categories of persons discussed, under the conditions discussed) collecting DNA samples without consent for criminal justice purposes, it cannot justify collecting DNA for other purposes, such as producing income (hence the legitimate criticisms of state governments when they sold driver's license information). More difficult are those cases in which the government might make the data from forensic DNA databases available for other public purposes such as medical research and the determination of paternity (as Ohio allows). These require a whole separate discussion. This is not the case for the opposite trend. Information collected for medical purposes should not be used for forensic purposes, for many obvious reasons.

New inmate right

Numerous inmates have asked to be tested to prove their innocence. From their viewpoint, there is nothing to be lost. Many states have been resisting these requests in accordance with finality doctrines that set time limits for the introduction of new evidence after sentencing. They argue that there must be some limit or else cases could be strung along endlessly by frivolous appeals.[61] However, given the high regard we all hold for protecting innocent people, and given the considerable number of cases in which such tests have exonerated people, such a right should be provided, at least for one test per inmate.

One can also readily agree with Barry Scheck, who proposed a duty to preserve biological evidence while an inmate is incarcerated. In proposing this, he noted that, "In 75% of our Innocence Project cases, where we have already determined that a DNA test would demonstrate innocence if it were favorable to the inmate, the evidence is lost or destroyed."[62]

Another suggestion is that DNA testing should be done within 7–14 days of a crime to help ensure that innocent suspects are not incarcerated. At the same time, we should not allow DNA tests to be turned by inmates into a new tactic for delaying their sentences from being carried out, and for imposing costs on the government by demanding test after test, arguing that the previous one has not been carried out quite properly or that it may have been misinterpreted and so on. Under normal circumstances, one test per inmate should be the limit. Otherwise, the ability of the criminal justice system to carry out its duties could be unduly limited.[63]

In Conclusion

The fear that DNA tests and databases will usher in eugenics is unfounded. Governments that introduce eugenics are those that greatly violate a wide range of human rights and abolish democracy, and hence must be fought whether or not there are DNA tests. And such tests contribute significantly to the ability to maintain the conditions under which such governments are unlikely to arise.

The starting point of a communitarian approach to the issue at hand is that both rights and the common good lay major moral claims on us (as the Fourth Amendment suggests), rather than that ours is a rights-centered society and that if rights are to be limited in any way, the burden of proof is on the advocates of the common good.

In this context, one should note that, often, DNA usages can serve both to protect the rights of innocent people and to enhance public safety. However, when the two do conflict, one should take into consideration the very high value of DNA for public safety. Moreover, as we have seen, our right not to be subject to unreasonable search and seizure, our right to privacy, and our right to be generally let alone are not infringed upon (or only minimally so) by DNA tests and databases that encompass criminals and suspects. Innocent people, though, should not be tested for criminal justice purposes, unless they truly volunteer to do so. Other parties should not have access to criminal justice databases, and public authorities should not have access to DNA tests and databases produced for private purposes (such as medical and military ones), although the relationship among such databases are beyond the purview of this study.

Most important, the traditional distrust of the government by civil libertarians is misplaced, because, in contemporary USA, the main violation of rights in this area is, currently, by private corporations. The government will have to play a major role in protecting citizens from such abuses.

6

What is Political?

There is no widely agreed upon definition of what is political. A definition that seems fruitful is to hold that political processes concern bridging power differences with in society with those within the state, bridges that carry inputs both from society to the state (e.g., the results of elections) and from the state to society (e.g., presidential speeches; legislation). The political realm also includes intrastate – but not intra-societal – processes concerning the application, reallocation, and legitimation of power. Hence, if one adopts the suggested definition, one can speak about "politics" within a voluntary association or on a private college board only by the way of vague analogues, because such talk confounds society and the state to the detriment of sound analysis and normative judgment. Indeed, one of the main merits of the suggested definition is that it calls attention to an often overlooked cardinal distinction between the state and society. Note also that only once society and state are systematically separated can one analyze the relationship between the two realms. Let us now examine key attributes of the political realm, including its limits.

The Political is Not the Social

Ever since Aristotle advanced the thesis that human beings are by nature political animals, there has been a tendency to fold the social into the political. The meaning of Aristotle's dictum has been subject to a considerable body of scholarship, but there is a wide consensus that whether it is narrowly or broadly understood, it does mean that people are *social* in nature, that they cooperate and have shared meanings and purposes, and not that the essence of their being is state related or mitigated.[1]

Moreover, when considering a small polis, one could readily collapse state and society and cause relatively limited damage to political and social analysis. However, such a reduction of two essential concepts to one is much more troublesome when one deals with much larger and more complex societies. Nevertheless, there is a common tendency to confound state and society by folding into the "political" numerous processes and actions and institutions that are inherently social. This is evident, for instance, when citizenship (a legal status that defines one's legal obligations to the state and one's legal rights the state is expected to protect and honor) is equated with membership (a social status that defines one's membership in one or more communities or associations, the moral responsibilities one has toward other members of one's community and the common good, and the moral claims that others have over him). Paying taxes, serving in the armed forces (when there is a draft), and – in some countries – voting are the obligations of citizens. The constitution or basic laws enumerate rights citizens have vis-à-vis the state. In contrast, donating to charity, volunteering, caring for one's friends and family (above and beyond one's legal obligations), collaborating with neighbors, being tolerant of people of different background and habits (above and beyond what the law prescribes), pursuing social justice, volunteering to work to protect the environment – these are all matters that concern membership, not citizenship.

The temptation to blur the line between the political and the social is particularly high when one studies nationalism, a phenomenon in which the state acquires some of the attributes of communities. And, atavism is not merely a regrettable social phenomenon but also a conceptual impairment. In countries where civil society is thin, has low visibility, or is merely conceptually unacknowledged, one often hears a tell-tale line from its citizens: "I paid my taxes; now it is up to the government to take care of . . . " – whatever needs attention.

The distinction between citizenship and membership is especially important if one recognizes that the relationship between the state and society is somewhat akin to that between the state and the individual. The more the state takes over functions once discharged by communities, voluntary associations, and families, the weaker society will become. In contrast, the more the state generates opportunities for social actors to initiate and sustain their own action, the more viable the society will become. But, if, for instance, the government starts sending professional grief counselors, licenced and trained by the state, to the homes of people who have lost a loved one, this is likely to weaken friendship ties: those of neighbors, of religious groups, and of extended families. In contrast, public policies that recognize both the need for the state to attend to numerous social as well as personal needs (especially those of the more vulnerable members of society or to vulnerable phases in the lives of all citizens) but also the need not to undermine social actors, are those that build on rather than ignore and undermine the difference between the political and the social. To put it differently, one reason to cherish the distinction between the social and the political is to ensure that the social will not become the political.

The Good Society versus the "Good" State

Social conservatives maintain that it is the role of the state (the core and focus of the political realm) to promote not merely citizenship but also the good person, not only skills needed to participate in the polity but also *social* virtues – those that make the society a good one. *Washington Post* columnist George Will, for instance, argues that people are self-indulgent by nature: left to their own devices, they will abuse their liberties, becoming profligate and indolent.[2] The state needs to restrain them. Other conservatives assert that in the name of "national greatness," people need a "strong national government" that will be a "shaper" of citizens and help them cope with the weaker angles of their nature.[3] Religious social conservatives have long been willing to rely on the state to foster behavior they consider virtuous. They favor banning abortion and pornography, making divorce more difficult, and outlawing homosexual activities.

Additionally, both religious and secular social conservatives have strongly advocated longer, more arduous prison terms for more individuals and more kinds of crime, especially favoring life sentences without the possibility of parole and death sentences. Harsh penalties are often applied to people of whose consumption and business the state disapproves (a large proportion of those in jail in the United States are there for non-violent, drug-related offenses) rather than for endangering public safety or failing to discharge their duties as citizens. These are not good-citizen issues but good-person issues.

The term "the good state" appropriately summarizes the social conservative position because the state here is not viewed as an institution that threatens to debase people or undermine liberty, and hence must be constantly contained – the liberal position – but as an institution that can be entrusted with making people good. That is, although social conservatives do not suggest that the state is inherently good, they do hold that it – and hence the political – can do good by fostering virtue.

Addressing the same socio-historical conditions that led to the rise of the contemporary social conservative position, responsive (or new) communitarians have advocated a fundamentally different approach.[4] It rejects state regulation of most moral behavior, under most circumstances. Communitarians advocate state restraint because they believe that the society should be the main agent responsible for promoting moral behavior, relying on education, persuasion, and leadership rather than the law.

Granted, developing and sustaining a good society does require reaching into what is considered the private realm, shaping behavior that does not directly relate to the state or to the state-mediated relationships with one's fellow citizens. A good society, for instance, fosters trust among its members not solely or even primarily to enhance their trust in the government but to cultivate a better society, one in which certain types of conduct are preferred over others by the community, rather than leaving it to each individual to judge what is good behavior.

Similarly, a good society fosters substantive values other than trust such as stewardship toward the environment, charity for those who are vulnerable, marriage over singlehood, having children, and showing special consideration to the young and elderly. These are all specific goods with regard to which the society, through its various social mechanisms, prefers *one* basic form of conduct over all others, and all concern the private realm.

None of this, however, means that all or even most private matters need to be subject to societal scrutiny and normative suasion. One major way the communitarian position differs from the totalitarian, authoritarian, theocratic, and social conservative ones is that although the good society reaches into the private realm, it seeks to cultivate only a limited set of *core* virtues rather than have an expansive or holistic normative agenda. For example, American society favors being religious over being atheist but is rather "neutral" with regard to which religion a person should follow. There are no prescribed dress codes (e.g., no Spartan Mao shirts), correct number of children to have, places one is expected to live, and so forth. In short, a key defining characteristic of the good society is that, in contrast to the liberal state, it formulates shared formulations of the good, but the scope of the good is much smaller than that advanced by government-centered societies, either of the secular (Soviet style) or religious kind (Iran, Taliban), or by social conservatives. To put it differently, the relationship between the political and the values of the society is deeply affected not merely whether or not there are shared formulations of the good, but also how encompassing these formulations are.

The Political is Moral

One main reason a line should be drawn between the social and the political is that there are no political deliberations, decisions, or actions that do not contain a moral dimension. Even seemingly merely technical decisions on closer examination very often turn out to have significant moral content or implications. For instance, considerations of whether to promote the use of coal or oil, not to mention nuclear sources of energy, affect our commitment to future generations and our stewardship of the environment. The same, of course, holds for economic decisions, from the rate of unemployment a nation decides to tolerate to the amount it plans to spend on armaments versus health care. (The term "moral" is used here to refer to a broad range of moral-social values – to normative or "should" considerations, including justice and equality, not merely to more personal values such as veracity and honor, a more personal and limited set of values. In addition, numerous political deliberations and decisions deal on the face of it with moral issues, although they may also have other implications. For instance, whether or not to recognize gay marriages as legally binding or whether to pay reparations to slave labor.)

Liberals (in the political theory sense of the term) maintain that moral deliberations should be confined to the private realm – outside of the public, political one – and that they should be "braked" when one enters the public (political included) realm.[5] Liberals tend to fear that culture wars – if not civil wars – may arise if values are introduced into the public arena. Even if consensus is reached without undue strife, the state's promotion of the resulting shared values would entail coercion as the public realm is that of the state, thus violating the supreme value – that of autonomy (or liberty). The state, and hence politics, should basically remain "neutral."

I write "basically" because there are some significant differences among liberals as to exactly how completely neutral the state can or ought to be. Some see the merit of the state fostering those virtues that a liberal state requires – critical thinking, for instance.[6] (Note that these are individual virtues and not social obligations.) Others, following Isaiah Berlin, are willing to accept a limited set of values as shared and as guiding public deliberations, those values that define a thin list of actions – say, rape – as unacceptable. Still, on most issues the state is not to take a moral position.

Liberals do not fear public strife or political deadlock if various segments of the society subscribe to divergent and even irreconcilable values. They contend that the representatives of such segments can formulate shared public policies; for instance, both pro-life and pro-choice groups may support better schooling for children, without engaging their value differences.

Communitarians have long argued that politics is and ought to be engaged in the formulation and fostering of a core of shared values. An even cursory review of the politics of free, democratic societies shows that this empirical claim is a valid one. Such deliberations as a rule do not lead to cultural or civil wars. On the contrary, the absence of a broad array of shared values – for instance, between Jewish and Arabic citizens of Israel – is one key reason that such groups find it particularly difficult to resolve conflicts that arise for other reasons. Moreover, the law, never morally neutral, is at its best when it reflects widely shared moral values rather than imposes the values of one group (the majority included) on the general populous.

Value Promotion: The Moral Voice versus Coercion

Another major difference between the good society and the "good" state, other than the scope of values enforced, is found in the ways values are fostered. A major instrument of the good society is the moral voice, which urges people to behave in pro-social ways. Although some tend to stress the importance of the inner voice, and hence good parenting and moral or character education,[7] responsive communitarians recognize the basic fact that without continual external reinforcement, the conscience tends to deteriorate. The validations by fellow human beings, especially of those to whom a person is attached through familial or communal bonds, carry a considerable weight because of a profound human need to win and sustain the approval of others.[8]

One may wonder whether compliance with the moral voice is compatible with free choice, whether one's right to be let alone includes a right to be free not only from state controls but also social pressures. This issue is highlighted by the conflicting interpretations of an often-cited line by John Stuart Mill. In *On Liberty*, Mill writes, "The object of this Essay is to assert one very simple principle, as entitled to govern absolutely the dealings of society with the individual in the way of compulsion and control, whether the means used be physical force in the form of legal penalties, or the moral coercion of public opinion."[9] Some have interpreted this statement to mean that the moral voice is as coercive as the government. Similarly, Alexis de Tocqueville wrote: "The multitude require no laws to coerce those who do not think like themselves: public disapprobation is enough; a sense of their loneliness and impotence overtakes them and drives them to despair."[10] If one takes these lines as written, the difference between reinforcement by the community and that by the state becomes a distinction without a difference.

One should note, though, that Mill has also been understood to suggest that while public opinion written large is coercive, local communal pressures are not. And de Tocqueville is, of course, known for having highlighted the importance of communal associations in holding the state at bay. Indeed, as I see it, it is essential to recognize that there is a profound difference between the moral voice of the community and coercion, and that the moral voice is the best antidote to an oppressive state.

Above all, the moral voice is much more compatible with free choice than with state coercion. The internal moral voice is as much a part of the person's self as are the other parts of the self that are the result of that person's choices. The external moral voice, that of the community, leaves final judgments to the acting person – an element that is notably absent when coercion is applied. Society may persuade, cajole, censure, and educate, but always leaves the final decision to the actor. The state may also persuade, cajole, and censure, but actors realize a priori that if at the end of the day the state is not heeded, it can force the actors to comply.

Some have questioned whether or not the moral voice is ever coercive. In part, this is a definitional matter. When the moral voice is backed up by legal or economic sanctions, one must take care to note that it is not the moral voice per se but rather these *added* elements that are coercive. Also, it is true that in earlier historical periods in the West, and still in some other parts of the world, when people were confined to a single village and the community voice was all-powerful, a unified chorus of moral voices could be quite overwhelming, even if it is not technically coercive, as physical force was not used or threatened. However, most people in contemporary free societies are able to choose, to a significant extent, the communities in which they live or are to become psychologically involved, and can often draw on one to limit the persuasive power of another. Most important, contemporary moral voices are far from monolithic. Indeed, it is a principal communitarian thesis that, in Western societies, moral voices often are, by and large, quite weak.[11] In fact, more often than not, they are too conflicted, hesitant, and weak to provide for a good society.[12] In short, highly powerful moral voices exist largely in other places and eras.

A comparison of the way the United States government fights the use of controlled substances and the way American society fosters parents' responsibilities for their children serves to elucidate this issue. The war against drugs depends heavily upon coercive agents; the treatment of children, by contrast, relies primarily upon the moral voice of members of the immediate and extended family, friends, neighbors, and others in the community. Occasionally, the state does step in. Yet most parents discharge their responsibilities not because they fear jail but because they believe this to be the right way to conduct themselves – a notion that is reinforced by social pressures.

The difference between the ways in which societies and states foster values is further highlighted by comparing the transfer of wealth via charity to a system of taxes; the difference between volunteering to serve one's country and being drafted; and the contrast between attending Alcoholics Anonymous meetings and being jailed for alcohol abuse.

The basically voluntaristic nature of the moral voice is the reason the good society can, to a large extent, be reconciled with liberty, while a state that fosters good on a wide front cannot. It is the reason the good society requires a clear moral voice that speaks for a set of shared core values – something lacking in the very conception of both a liberal state and a society that is merely civil.[13]

Social institutions are important for the characterization of the difference between the good society and state-promoting good, because most institutions are neither merely procedural nor value-neutral; in effect, most are the embodiment of particular values. For instance, the family's definition and structure always reflect a particular set of values, a fact recently highlighted by the debate about gay marriages. The same holds for other social institutions, including schools, voluntary associations, and communal ones. The freer these institutions are from state controls, the more they can serve as the mainstays of a good society rather than politicized agents of state-promoting goods.

Deliberations versus Moral Dialogues

At the heart of the political – whether there is a quest for new public policies, regulations, or laws – are deliberations through which people or factions that have divergent interests are said to arrive at shared resolutions. Deliberations are often depicted as if an aggregate of individuals assemble and discuss dispassionately the facts of the situation, their logical implications, and the available policy alternatives, and then choose the most empirically valid and logical one.[14] Miriam Galston writes:

> Most contemporary legal theorists addressing republican concerns advocate some form of deliberative democracy. The heart of their recommendations for making political life more deliberative is the establishment of certain procedures in the decision making process designed to enhance, if not ensure, a rational or reasoned basis for legislative, judicial, and other determinations.[15]

Jack Knight and James Johnson state: "We view deliberation as an idealized process consisting of fair procedures within which political actors engage in reasoned argument for the purpose of resolving political conflict."[16]

Deliberation and democratic polity are often closely associated. A civil society is said to be one that deals with its problems in a deliberative manner. Kuklinski and his associates sum up this view:

> In a democratic society, reasonable decisions are preferable to unreasonable ones; considered thought leads to the former, emotions to the latter ... citizens are to approach the subject of politics with temperate consideration and objective analysis, that is, to use their heads when making judgments about public affairs.[17]

Somewhat like those economists who build models of prefect competition and then draw conclusions from them about the real world, some political theorists build models of the way politics ought to be – and tend to disregard the fact that this is not the way it is actually practiced, even in the best democracies. Actually resolutions in the political realm are much driven by moral dialogues, although these occur largely in the social realm.

Moral dialogues are processes in which the values of the participants are engaged and shared moral formulations may be worked out. They are substantive and not merely or firstly procedural. When they successfully mature, they lead to a change of values among some of the participants, an essential precondition for reaching newly shared understandings about social policies based on a truly shared consensus rather on merely overlapping ones. Among the moral dialogues that had such effects are those about the environment, civil rights and women's rights, and sexual harassment. None led to a full-fledged, detailed, new shared understanding, but all have moved the societies involved in important ways to change their values and consensus – which then was reflected in various political acts and new legislation.

One may tend to think that moral dialogues occur in families or small communities but wonder how a society could possibly come together to affirm a new, renewed, or some other set of values. I suggest that they occur at the societal levels as well.

Whole societies, even if their population counts in the hundreds of millions, do engage in moral dialogues that lead to changes in widely shared values. The process occurs by linking millions of local conversations (between couples, in neighborhood bars or pubs, in coffee or tea houses, next to water coolers at work) into society-wide networks and shared public focal points. The networking takes place during regional and national meetings of many thousands of voluntary associations in which local representatives dialogue; in state, regional, and national conventions; and increasingly via electronic links (such as groups that meet on the internet). Public focal points occur around call-in shows, debates on network television, and nationally circulated newspapers and magazines. Several voluntary associations are explicitly dedicated to nourishing both local and society-wide (some even cross national) moral dialogues.

Moral dialogues are often extensive, disorderly (in the sense that there is no clear pattern to them), have an unclear beginning, and no clear or decisive conclusion. Nevertheless, they lead to significant changes in core values. One brief illustration follows.

Until 1970, the environment was not considered a shared core value in Western societies (nor in many others). This does not mean that there were not some studies, articles, and individuals who saw great value in it. But society as a whole paid little systematic heed, and the environment was not listed among America's core values.[18]

As is often the case, a book – *Silent Spring*, by Rachel Carson, which was very widely read and discussed – triggered a nationwide megalogue. A massive oil spill and the ensuing protests in Santa Barbara, California and the Three-Mile Island incident further impressed the subject on the national normative agenda. Thousands of people gathered in New York City to listen to pro-environment speeches and to pick up garbage along Fifth Avenue. Two hundred thousand people gathered on Washington DC's Mall in 1970 to demonstrate concern for the environment on "Earth Day."[19] As a result, concern for the environment became a shared core value. (There continue to be disagreements about the level of commitment to this cause and the best ways to proceed, but not about the basic value. A conservative president, Richard Nixon, founded the Environmental Protection Agency, and during his presidency many environmentalist policies, such as recycling, were introduced. The extent to which this value sharing was breached in the mid-1990s is not yet clear, but it held for 25 years and is now found in many other societies.)

After all is said and done, there can be little doubt that (a) aside from rational deliberations, said to take place within legislative bodies and courts and town meetings, in political bodies, there are significant distinct social processes – moral dialogues – that lead to new or reformulated shared moral understandings; (b) these processes are often best advanced in the social realm, although they can also occur within the political one, and their conclusions often have profound political implications.

The Law as Social Change Agent

As already indicated, although moral dialogues also occur within the political realm, this is not the place where they are typically initiated or mature. This is of pivotal importance when one explores the relative role of the law, a core product of political processes, in attaining societal change.

Volumes have been written on this subject that cannot and need not be reviewed here. One notes merely that some argue that the law reflects (or ought to reflect) the society's avant-garde; it should lead social change. An oft-cited example is the base commander in the South who simply ordered desegregation as early as 1943.[20]

Others, especially from the Marxist Left, have maintained that the law serves as a rear guard, that it lags behind societal change, reflects the outgoing regime, is anachronistic. As I see it, *law in a good society is first and foremost the continuation of morality by other means.* The law may sometimes lead to some measure of social change, but if it is not in accordance with the moral culture (shared values and the commitment to them), the social order will not be voluntarily heeded and the society will be pushed toward the edge of the communitarian pattern, and ultimately beyond its limits of toler-ance, transforming it into an authoritarian – if not a totalitarian or theocratic – society.

The limited ability to rely on introducing social changes through the law not backed up by values, and the severe distorting effects that result if this is tried, are highlighted by the failure of many prison authorities to prevent inmates from dealing drugs in jails. If authorities cannot enforce a law here, when they have the perpetra-tors locked up 24 hours a day, seven days a week, under constant and close supervision with next to no autonomy, how can one expect to enforce a law on which there is little assent in a much larger free society? Prohibition is an often cited case in which laws could not be enforced without the support of a strong moral voice.

Recently, some historians have suggested that Prohibition may have had some positive outcomes after all: while it did cause massive corruption, it may have reduced alcohol consumption to some extent. Even if Prohibition-like legislation is somewhat successful in reducing an undesired behavior, the greatly increased levels of cor-ruption and police action are incompatible with a free society. Above all, note that Prohibition self-destructed; it is the only constitutional amendment that was ever repealed. Laws without a firm moral undergirding, what might be called "bare laws," tend to harm the community more than serve it, and tend either not to be enforced or set aside. "Backed laws," those well-undergirded by shared moral understandings, are the best agents of change.

Does this mean that if a community becomes aware of a serious flaw, say segregation, it can never act by mainly relying on the law without first laying moral foundations (assuming that none or rather weak ones are in place)? If the evil that needs to be overcome is great enough, combating it may outweigh the undesirable side-effects and render tolerable the resulting low compliance rate and high costs of enforcement. But these exceptions do not invalidate the rule: enacting laws bereft of moral underpinning tends to be both an un-communitarian and ineffectual exercise. Although a good society can tolerate a few such bare laws, it cannot make them its mainstay of social order. The political must be preceded and undergirded by the social.

In conclusion, it is essential to avoid collapsing or confusing the political and the social realm. Although formation and reformation of power relations are at the core of the political, most of its decisions have a moral dimension. Hence the cardinal importance of moral dialogues that help form these decisions and the difference between laws backed not simply by majority vote but also by profoundly shared moral understanding, the outcome of moral dialogues that have matured.

7

On Ending Nationalism

National*ism* must be ended. It is a creed that has come to burden the expansion of globalism (as evident for instance in the demonstrations against the WTO); hobbles the growth of the European Community (as seen in the votes against the euro in Denmark); stands in the way of resolving violent conflicts (for instance, over the fate of Jerusalem); complicates the resolution of differences within existing nation-states (for example, in Corsica); and turns refugees and immigrants into a threat to the receiving countries. Its ill effects are evident from Kosovo to East Timor, from Chechnya, to Cyprus, to Bolivia.

These are, of course, enormously distinct phenomena, involving very distinguishable issues. Other factors – economic for instance – also play a significant role in their dynamics. My only thesis is that nationalism importantly hinders progress toward solutions in all of these international and domestic situations, as it does in many other ones.

Nationalism is a creed that extols the nation, and regards it as an ultimate value. It deeply affects citizens' sense of self, psychological well-being, and identity; it makes them treat their nation-state as their primary community. The "ism" comes to indicate that reference here is *not* to moderate commitments to one's nation as one source of affiliation and loyalty, but to a highly intensive and nearly exclusive investment of one's collective identity in the national state. (In this sense nationalism differs from reasonable national commitments the way moralism differs from morality.) When in full bloom, people view the state as semi-sacred – or even as directly in the service of their God. As it is written in Romans 13:1: "Let every person be subject to the governing authorities, for there is no authority except from God, and those authorities that exist have been instituted by God."

People imbued with nationalism believe that their independence, ability to control their fate as a collective, and cultural distinctiveness and self-determination are all dependent on their nation. (To save breath, such commitments will be referred to from here on as defining involvements.) Often, at least some sense of superiority over other nations is involved as well as at least some measure of xenophobia. Nationalism tends to be most in evidence when a nation is at war.

While nationalism is often most intense in totalitarian and authoritarian societies, some elements of it, at least in a dormant form, can also be found among the citizens of free democratic countries. The nation, a seemingly remote and abstract social entity, is one for which these citizens – many otherwise quite moderate and self-restrained – are willing to sacrifice their lives and kill others, not merely to defend the nation's existence and integrity but also to redeem its honor. Attacks by foreigners, even on minor and remote outposts, are framed as profound personal insults, followed by popular calls for revenge.

Major reactions to the increasingly distorting effects of nationalism include the suggestion that the nation-state itself is obsolete; the very concept of national sovereignty is depicted as old fashioned,[1] the free flow of trade and capital (and to somewhat lesser extent that of people) is strongly championed across national borders, and the development of numerous supranational bodies is supported.[2] These bodies include the European Commission and Parliament, the international criminal court, committees set up by NAFTA and the WTO among others, and the view that the UN Declaration of Human Rights justifies the intervention of foreign powers in the internal affairs of nations that violate these rights. Further expanding the sovereignty of these supranational bodies is viewed as one major antidote to nationalism. Others have called for the absorption of national states in regional bodies, for instance in a United States of Europe. On the domestic front, nations are chided for clinging to nationalistic, old homogenous cultures and identities, and are urged to embrace diversity and multiculturalism.

Ending Nationalism, Not the Nation-State

The argument advanced here presumes that it is neither necessary nor prudent to attempt to end nationalism by head-on attacks on the legitimacy of the nation-state or by favoring its demise.[3] The vision of replacing the nation-state by regional governments and ultimately by a world government (as UN enthusiasts dream), or of a state that acts as a mere framework for the interactions of groups of people of different cultures but commands no loyalty and involvement of its own, is normatively dubious and unnecessarily threatening. Nationalism can be and is best ended by a much more moderate approach.

To highlight the line between nationalism and moderate, reasoned national involvement, it might be useful to provide an example of a nation-state that is fully intact but harbors little nationalism. Germany, which used to be an extremely nationalistic country, stood out during the last two decades of the twentieth century as a country in which national involvement of most of its citizens was moderate. Indeed, one of its core shared values in this period was a rejection of nationalism.[4] One can also find low-key national involvement in Canada, Costa Rica, and Holland, among other nations.

It should be further noted, very much in line with the thesis that the desired development is not ending involvement in the nation-state but merely ending an immoderate, nationalistic one, that in some states, commitments to the nation are too weak. Such countries have already experienced or stand the danger of being torn apart by secessions or civil wars, when member communities that command strong involvements, such as ethnic and tribal ones, are not bound together by an overarching national commitment. Such countries include Rwanda, the former Yugoslavia, Northern Ireland, Nigeria, and Somalia. (In short, national involvement is what social scientists call a variable, that can be both too high and too low.)

The Role of the Public

The approach outlined below draws on one additional sociological observation and normative position: it presumes that ending nationalism and overcoming the various challenges it has engendered cannot and should not be carried out via secret or closed negotiations among national representatives (the way the Oslo Agreement was reached or even the way the Maastricht Treaty was hammered out) or by arrangements worked out by international lawyers and select civil servants of supranational bodies (such as the EU commission or WTO committees). Nor can the needed changes be successfully introduced if defining down national involvements is presented as relevant merely to technical or economic matters (e.g. the way

Tony Blair has framed the adoption of the euro by the UK). While it is true that foreign policy can often be advanced a great deal with little public involvement, ending nationalism is an important and powerful exception. Because of the strong and widely held support for nationalistic defining involvements, any efforts to redirect and attenuate them must be similarly popular. The public will have to be engaged because the change entails modification, and hence a profound sense of what millions of people consider right, believe in, and identify with. One of the reasons Yasser Arafat had great difficulties in completing the 2000 Camp David negotiations was that they entailed making concessions his people were not prepared to accept. (The same may have been true for Ehud Barak). One key reason WTO expansion was followed by street demonstrations was that important and politically active segments of the public were not convinced of the legitimacy of the WTO's authority over member nations. One major reason opposition to the euro succeeded in Denmark – and threatened the participation of other countries – is that large segments of the public realized that much more than a monetary issue was at stake, and they had not been won over to the large-scale reduction of national autonomy that was likely to follow.

A Communitarian Approach

The main approach outlined here favors shifting much of the defining involvements of citizens in those countries that are inflicted with nationalism from the nation-state to the body society, specifically to communities (not to be confused with local governments), the community of these communities, and to a "thick" civic fabric. It entails developing and championing public policies, institutions, symbols, and belief systems that help people realize that they can maintain their sense of self, identity, and social and cultural distinctiveness, as well as a good part of their control over their individual and collective fate – all through involvement in a variety of communities.[5] Millions already draw on such commitments, and these commitments can be extended and expanded to a point that will significantly reduce the involvement in the nation-state and thus enhance the ability of treating the various problems that must be faced – without abolishing the nation-state or eradicating commitments to it. To put it in different terms: the reference is to shifting a good part of the legitimacy now associated with particular states to societies and their component units. This approach is not without risks of its own, which we will explore after the approach itself has been spelled out.

Limited Historical Precedents

Those who wonder whether the suggested shift of defining involvements to some other body than the nation can actually be achieved may wish to note that such a condition was crudely approximated before the onset of nationalism. After all, both the mere existence of the nation-state and its elevation to a semi-sacred status by nationalism are of a relatively recent vintage.[6] Neither existed before the eighteenth century and, for a good part of the nineteenth century the nation-state was the project of narrow elites and later small classes.[7]

In earlier generations, people's involvements were largely focused on their extended family, clan, and village. (This is still the case in some of the less developed countries, among the less educated, especially if they are not exposed to mass media.) Further, for those in power and for the educated, the defining involvements were often divided between religious and secular bodies, and not all centered in one centrally controlled territorial entity. (The line, "Give to Caesar what is Caesar's and give to God what is God's," captures this point.) People did not see themselves mainly just as members of this or that territorial group (say, a given fiefdom), but also as members of a church, and their secular involvements were also split between their local commitments and those to other social groups. (For instance, many Russian aristocrats identified with and shared a culture with their French counterparts more than they did with the Russian peasantry.) The well-known conflicts between the Catholic Church and the British monarchy – and those loyal to each – further illustrate strong involvement in a religious and non-statist social corpus.

In this limited sense, the pre-nationalistic world provides a precedent for the post-nationalistic one. The precedent is, of course, limited, because defining involvements in earlier ages were largely a matter for a thin layer of the educated and active, and not for the much larger numbers of other people.

An Intra-Domestic Development

Most discussions on ending nationalism focus on international developments, such as the increasing role of international NGOs,[8] international law and courts and regulatory bodies, and the UN and other international organizations. These are often valuable but may not develop much further unless accompanied by domestic developments because the main roots of nationalism are domestic. Hence, the discussion here focuses on the needed intra-national changes, especially that of involving definitions. My thesis is that only as such involvements are shifted away from the nation-state not merely to supranational bodies but also to sub-national ones can the difficulties posed by nationalism and the efforts by nation-states to monopolize sovereignty be significantly rearranged. To reiterate, reference is to a partial shift, resulting in split involvements between the state and various social bodies, rather than expunging all national involvements.

Criss-Crossing and Thick Communities

For enhanced involvement in communities to help end nationalism, the social bonds and loyalties entailed must criss-cross rather than run parallel to and thus enforce the nationalistic ones. This means that membership in such groups cannot be coextensive with citizenship (which would make the nation into the relevant community) and the groups' loyalty itself cannot be centered around extolling the nation. Thus when Hitler championed Germany as one *volksgemeinschaft*, he was promoting a community that was coextensive with the nation, precisely in order to absorb the communal defining involvement into the nation, as a way to further fuel nationalism.

Aside from criss-crossing memberships and loyalties, communities must also be "thick." It has been shown that their scope of activities must be extensive enough to provide significant involvement of the kind not found in thin groups such as chess clubs, bird-watching societies, and bowling leagues.[9] Increasing people's involvement in religious or secular communities or voluntary associations (communitarian bodies for short) can all serve to dampen nationalism but only when they meet the said conditions. Indeed, when these groups are coextensive with the nation, or when involvement in them entails extolling the nation, they can act to further strengthen nationalism.

Religious communities

All major religions can provide for the needed involvements when they satisfy the said prerequisites: when they criss-cross and are thick.

Thus, the Catholic Church provides many millions of people with a source of involvement and community in American society and in other societies with a Protestant majority and a secular state; in numerous Asian and African societies; in former communist countries; and in countries in which Catholics are the majority but where the national government is largely secular (e.g., Italy). The same holds for Protestant groups in China and the USSR.

Similarly, Islam has provided for defining involvement in communities in nations in which the government has been largely secular (e.g., Turkey) or the established religion has been a different one (e.g. in the UK or in Israel). Judaism arguably provides the strongest example of a people able to maintain their culture and identity separate from a nation-state over long periods of time (some 2,000 years).

Religious involvement is more effective as an antidote to nationalism when it entails more than mere attendance – when, for instance, children attend a religious school, or when members of a religious group socialize mainly with other members or take part in voluntary associations that involve only fellow church members (e.g. Catholic teacher associations) so that social bonds are shared. Some religious groups may also provide their own dispute-resolution institutions, such as Qadis and rabbinical courts.

All these religious bodies show that it is possible in principle to nurture a sense of self, identity, and independence not associated with the state or any other specific territory. (Members of religious communities are often dispersed among members of other communities.)

It is true that, like all cures, shifting the defining involvement can be excessive. This would not be suitable for societies in which national involvement is low to begin with, for example. And this is the reason I stated from the onset that nationalism should be ended by a partial rather than a holistic shift of involvement from the nation to member communities.

An indication of the strength of the separate loyalty involvement religious groups provide, and its dampening effect on nationalism, can be seen in cases where secular totalitarian regimes (such as the USSR and Nazi Germany) made strenuous efforts to suppress religious groups. Further indication of this strength can be gleaned from the fact that when Catholics or Jews have run for public office in the United States, their national loyalty has sometimes been questioned.

In contrast, when membership in a religious community and a nation-state are coextensive and the values extolled by these communities are national ones, the opposite effect results: nationalism is intensified. This is evident in theocracies such as Afghanistan and Iran; in those religious Jewish groups that embrace the ideas of a Greater Israel as part of their core values; and in those situations where the Church has supported nationalism (for instance, the generals in Argentina in order to eradicate the "cancer of communism").

"Charitable choice" in the US is a major example of how religious-based involvement may be enhanced (at least in the American context), while the role of the state is curtailed. Charitable choice, enacted in the US in 1996 under the Welfare Reform Act, encourages the state to provide funds for the provision of social services by religious groups rather than using the same funds for delivery of those services by government agencies. (References are mainly to welfare and health services.[10]) While theoretically such provisions are not supposed to entail any religious proselytizing, even if this regulation is well maintained, the very fact that numerous people would regularly attend and participate in the social activities of religious groups is likely to enhance their involvement in these bodies.

Separation of church and state – which, all other things being equal, helped dampen involvement in the nation-state – is a rather American idea. However, such separation may be embraced by more societies as they become increasingly diverse, because their ageing societies require large-scale immigration and the immigrants tend to be from different religious and cultural backgrounds. Thus, Germany is moving toward having Muslim as well as Jewish schools and it considered stopping the collection of dues via the state to pay for the clergy. In Israel there is a strong demand to turn what has been conceived as a Jewish state into a secular one. Sweden is making considerable progress in this direction.[11] Other societies may have to separate church and state if the distinct social fabric of religious communities is to develop into one able to provide non-nationalist sources of involvements.

The civil (secular) society

The other main basis for non-nationalistic involvement is the civil society, including voluntary associations and secular communities. It is telling that totalitarian states tend to ban voluntary associations and work to absorb the functions of the civil society into the state, to ensure that people's involvement is focused on the state. The opposite development occurs when there is a rich fabric of voluntary associations, which can provide a major source of non-statist involvements which in turn can moderate nationalism. Thus, the fewer individuals there are who see themselves merely or even primarily as "good" Singaporeans, Frenchmen, and so on, and the more there are who consider themselves to be dedicated environmentalists, feminists, or members of professional communities, the less nationalistic they will tend to be.

There is a secular version of the grand exception which parallels the religious one: nationalism is intensive rather than demoted when the core values of a given voluntary association are nationalistic, as in the case of many veteran organizations. The same holds for many secular right-wing groups.

I cannot stress enough that the thesis presented here about the transition away from a nationalistic state to a communitarian society is not retracing oft-made arguments in favor of a strong civil society, although there are some parallels. The standard arguments about the merit of civil society center around its primary aims of sustaining liberty, respect for individual rights, and for the democratic regime. The main thesis advanced here is that a civil society can also provide a major source for communitarian defining involvements and thus moderate nationalism. Moreover, while almost any civil society can advance liberty (indeed, some hold that a "thin" society can best so serve), only rather "thick" civil societies can provide for satisfactory opportunities for defining involvements. Thickness in this context entails providing a substantive (as distinct from merely procedural) and considerable set of values, as well as social bonds that encompass significant relations rather than trivial ones. Voting, for instance, is thin; serving in the Peace Corps is thick. Serving as an observer at a polling station is thin; serving as a deacon at one's church is thick.

The crucial significance of thickness for the purpose at hand leads to the important observation that from this viewpoint not all voluntary associations are created equal. The defining involvement these associations are able to provide range from socially and normatively trivial to rather powerful. Those voluntary associations that are often mentioned and studied and hence jump to mind – especially following the important work of Robert Putnam[12] – such as bowling leagues, provide a rather thin scope of social activities and values and hence rather meager involvement. With the exception of a few, such as activists or diehards, people do not define themselves as bowlers or bird-watchers or derive their norms from such activities.

Moreover, the much celebrated NGOs tend to provide involvement for their cadres but not for most of their members, who often feel rather detached, if not excluded and alienated. Consider, for instance, the typical members of the league of women voters or the PTA.

Much more consequential for the building up of non-nationalistic, communitarian involvements are thicker voluntary associations that have more of a normative content and/or are socially more encompassing. Among the first kind are ideological associations such as the Sierra Club. Among the second kind are those labor unions in which the members share a social life, hang around a hiring hall, frequent the same bars and so on. These associations almost make communities.

Communities (which are often excluded from discussion of civil society, among other reasons because they are in part ascribed, not voluntarily chosen or constructed; they are, for instance, excluded from Putnam's calculations) are multifaceted and hence socially thick. They tend to encompass numerous different activities of their members rather than merely one (e.g. the PTA's focus on schooling of children). Indeed, communities often contain several voluntary associations. Numerous policies to strengthen communities that are advanced for other reasons can also help build up non-nationalistic involvements. In the US these include community policing, crime watch, mutual saving societies, self-help groups, block parties, safer public spaces, and much more.

More generally, the thicker the civil society (beyond the mere existence of a rich and varied body of thick voluntary associations and communities), the more opportunities there are for non-nationalistic involvements to evolve and to be nurtured. The more civil society is extolled in culture and mores, the stronger the social norms that limit conflict among citizens and among political parties and public leaders and the stronger opportunities and encouragements for community service in schools and otherwise.

Note that the thickness of the civil society that is relevant to the issue at hand is not measured by the extent of participation in politics or public affairs (e.g. the proportion of the public conversant with public affairs, or those who vote, or the trust people put in the government) but by the richness of informal social norms and controls, the trust people place in one another, the extent to which they are tolerant and civil to one another.

While one should readily acknowledge that if the various communitarian bodies make extolling the nation their core value, they will tend to reinforce nationalism, one should also note that these bodies provide a grand potential: communitarian bodies can – and often do – form bonds and build loyalties and social norms that cut across national borders and thus dampen nationalism. At the least, they are *capable* of so doing, which is not the case if the involvement is the nation itself. Among the thinner examples are public policy networks and groups of civil servants committed to the same cause, e.g. the stewardship of the environment. Thicker examples include the feminist movement, anti-war movements, and Amnesty International.

The Community of Communities and its State

When the strengthening of communities is advocated – especially when reference is made not merely to their social fabric, but also to loyalties to them and to their particularistic values – a legitimate concern arises: that communities will engage in cultural wars with each other and that these may turn into civil wars.[13] Furthermore, there is a fear that if ever more social diversity and multiculturalism is allowed, a nation may lose its identity, shared culture, and history. This fear is evoked by large-scale immigrations (especially if the immigrant's cultural traditions are substantially different from those of the host country). Such fears are reinforced when communities seek exceptions from nationwide laws (e.g. to use narcotics during religious services) or practices in public schools (Muslim girls wearing scarfs in French schools – or not wearing swimsuits in Germany). To put it in more general terms, particularism, diversity, and multiculturalism, or more generally community separation, can undermine the integrity of the nation and lead to its destruction.[14]

It should, though, be noted that such developments mainly threaten a nation that has rather meager involvements in its state to begin with, rather than one that is infected with nationalism. For this reason, as already indicated, such shifting of involvement from the state to communities is not recommended under these circumstances.

In this matter, American society – which is often criticized by members of other societies as being violent, materialistic, and excessively individualistic (all criticisms that contain some merit) – provides an important sociological design that allows for less national involvement but still provides for maintaining the integrity of the nation. American society is basically organized as a community of communities in which the member communities are free to follow their own subcultures in numerous matters ranging from religious practices to second languages, from involvement in their countries of origin to tastes in music and cuisine. These particularistic involvements are not viewed as threatening to the nation at large.

At the same time a set of values exists to which all are expected to adhere, shared values that serve as a sort of framework and glue that keeps the rich and colorful mosaic from falling apart. These include commitment to the Constitution and its Bill of Rights, the democratic form of government, command of the English language, mutual tolerance, and what Sandy Levinson called the constitutional faith.[15] Moreover, to sustain unity, the loyalty to the community of communities is expected to take precedence over that to member communities if and when these two loyalties come into conflict.

Seeking neither assimilation (in which member communities would be stripped of their particularistic values and involving powers) nor separatism, American society as a community of communities draws on a concept that is missing in many others: hyphenation. Much more is at stake here than referring to people on the basis of their ethnic origins, not simply as Polish or Irish or Mexican, but as Polish-Americans, Irish-Americans, or Mexican-Americans. Hyphenation is an expression of the legitimization of their distinct subcultural status, of their non-state-driven particularism – but also of their being contained by a shared American creed and a set of related institutions. It speaks of pluralism within unity, not sheer pluralism as American diversity is often mistakenly depicted. This model allows for much more socially based defining involvements than one in which the only sanctioned sets of values and involvements are nationally shared ones.

All this is not to suggest that the state plays no role in a society that is based on the community of communities model. Ending nationalism does not entail shutting down the nation-state. The state helps to sustain the shared part, the frame, that keeps communities as members of one overarching community. For instance, the nation-state upholds rights defined in the Constitution that might clash with the particularistic values of some member communities, and helps ensure that differences among communities will not turn violent.

While all states can help to ensure that the increase in community involvement will not undermine the society of which they are members, some formats serve this purpose better than others. All other things being equal, as has been often noted, unitary states (France) are less accommodating than federations (Germany). Higher levels of devolution (and subsidiarity) tend to be more favorable to the community of communities than to lower levels. It should, though, be recognized that devolution does not automatically provide the preferred context. If devolution merely shifts functions and control from the national level to large subentities (e.g. of the size of Scotland), it is much more likely to feed separatist nationalism than if devolution reaches into much smaller local units. Nationalism is not needed for a nation to be able to modify the balance between the central government and local ones to work out modifications in the relationship that provide more autonomy to the member communities without breaking the frame. The US's increased recognition of states' rights in recent years and the shifting of funds and missions and controls from Washington, DC to the states reflect such an accommodation. Even China's incorporation of Hong Kong, under the "one nation, two systems" model, has this format. In contrast, the clashes between Spain and the Basques, France and Corsica, Turkey and Iraq and the Kurds in their respective countries, Sri Lanka and the Tamil all reflect clashes of strong nationalism of both the country and those who seek full-fledged self-determination.

Most importantly for the purposes at hand, the model of a community of communities points to the possibility of adding supranational layers of loyalty and state power – without threatening particularistic involvements. One may come to think about regional communities, such as the EU, as second-order communities; as communities whose members are nations (which already contain communities).[16] Regional communities could apply the ideas behind the model of community of communities, of pluralism within unity, allowing for considerable continued national variations. The more this model is embraced and legitimated, the less resistance there will be to the development of supranational institutions and an additional layer of loyalty (as compared to the simple concept of community, which evokes an image of a much greater measure of blending). The model can serve to reassure people that if Germany, France, or the UK were integrated into a United States of Europe, such action would not lead to loss of identity, culture, or state rights by these nations.

To put it differently, the community of communities provides a sociological model and lends legitimacy for divided and layered sovereignty. It indicates that sovereignty, as legal scholars and historians have long established, is never an absolute concept, and can be shared and redefined without loss of control and self-determination for those who agree to delegate some of their decision-making power and judiciary rights to a more encompassing level.[17]

A Cultural Exception

A policy issue that by itself is not of the highest importance illustrates the approach that combines building up additional layers of communities of communities (or, say, communities of the third order) while respecting the member communities' particular values. The issue concerns cultural exceptions to various international agreements.[18] The question is whether cultural products (such as magazines and movies) should be treated in the same manner as other goods and services or accorded an exception for trade freed from national borders within whatever supra-community is being constructed. It is a complex subject, as some might wish to see such an approach extended to the internet, where it might well be overridden by technological devices.

For the purpose at hand, it suffices to note that to the extent that some of these cultural products are of special import for sustaining the member communities involving powers, they should be exempt from some parts of free trade agreements (which of course would involve renegotiating them). The underlying reason is that defining involvements are nourished by cultural products. If these are undermined, nationalism is likely to grow more rampant. This will not necessarily occur if widgets, cranes, and ball bearings are imported. While any product, from airlines to sports cars, can be turned into a matter of national pride, cultural products are much more likely to carry a richer and more authentic symbolic content. Numerous images and word choices indicate the culture of origin, which can hardly be said about the pieces used to make a plane or car, whose origin is likely to be mixed and multinational to begin with and often not visible from the outset.

Providing cultural exceptions need not be all-encompassing. For instance, they may tolerate subsidies for local film-makers and the productions of plays of the kind banned for non-cultural products (as a way of supporting the local culture), but not encompass import controls on magazines and films (i.e. excluding other cultures).

Similarly, there seems to be no reason to oppose academies of languages trying to come up with national terms for new objects from computers to satellites, rather than relying on English words. Language is a major center of a culture and people are correctly concerned about protecting it from excessive absorption of foreign terms (although this has occurred throughout history). However, to the extent that these efforts attack the rapid development of English as a *second* language – a language that more and more people of the world use for instrumental purposes such as trade and coordination – they are not justified by the criteria applied here. English is on its way to becoming the language of the third layer community, the lingua franca. To nurture one's national language should not be combined with attacks on English as long as it is a second (or third) language.

One can combine protecting national culture with openness to the world. This is evident when one witnesses the significant cultural differences that exist between communities within the same nation – for instance, between Bavaria and north-west Germany, Sicily and Milan, Manhattan and Louisiana.

Must Supranational Bodies be Democratic?

A major objection to shifting more involvement to communitarian bodies (whether domestic or cross-national) and to supranational bodies is that the latter are not democratically governed.[19] Indeed, we have known since Robert Michels's *Political Parties* that these associations tend to become oligarchic, and that in effect they are governed by small elites, whether or not they have elections (as in evident in many labor unions).[20] Discussions of the increased supra-national role of NGOs has led some to fear the rise of a world government of a syndicalist or corporate nature, in which various interests gain ever more decision-making power. The same fear of lack of accountability to elected bodies has been raised against the NAFTA and WTO committees and the European Commission.

Several considerations come into play. Domestically, the shift of involvement from the state to communitarian bodies does not mean that citizens give up their rights to vote for local and national governments. These in turn set limits on the action of these social bodies, and can serve to ensure that individual rights will not be violated and that the laws of the land will be abided by. Also, many of these bodies do adhere to democratic procedures, and if these are not honored steps can be taken to ensure that they are, as was done in the case of the Teamsters Union. And people who are disaffected by the way one voluntary association is conducted can readily join another, as happened with the Parent Teachers Associations, leading people to join Parent Teacher Organizations.

Internationally, at issue is the scope of the function and power of the new supranational bodies. NGOs, with very few exceptions, have rather limited scope and power. Hence the ways they are controlled matter relatively little. The same is true so far about the NAFTA and WTO committees. However, the European Commission has reached a level of scope and power which ought to be, and is becoming, more accountable to the European Parliament. In short, there seems here to be no principled objection to the development of social involvements and supranational ones.

In Conclusion

Our generation is challenged by the fact that globalization so far has been largely economic and technological, and not social, political, and moral.[21] As a result, the ability of the people of the world to control their fate has been diminished. A national government may enact laws banning the distribution of designs to make bombs or of *Mein Kampf*, create legislation to protect children from pedophiles or to safeguard the privacy of medical records, but these will be of little viability in the age of the internet. A bioethics commission may curb certain experiments conducted in one nation; however, in the absence of supranational bodies to agree and enforce such bans, these experiments may easily be conducted in some other country. Crime and pollution know no borders, and are increasingly internationalized.

The gap between that which needs to be guided and those who seek to guide cannot be closed, as some hope, by restoring national controls. With few exceptions, in the longer run, in order for mankind to gain control, to direct these processes to its benefit and curb excesses or anti-human developments, it will require social, political, and moral institutions whose reach is as global as the challenges are. Nationalism stands in the way of the development of these institutions.

8

Cyberspace and Democracy

This chapter asks whether communities and democracy can thrive in the new world – in cyberspace. This requires a two-step examination. First, can there be virtual communities? Second, can these – and other (including offline) communities – govern themselves in a democratic way by drawing on new developments in cyberspace?

Communities On and Off

Communities defined

The very term "community" has often been criticized as a concept that is vague and elusive, as a term that either has not been defined or cannot be defined, and as one that is used because of its political appeal rather than its scholarly merit.[1] In response, one should note, first of all, that terms commonly used in social science often resist precise definition, as in the case of such widely used concepts as rationality and class. And while "community" has often been used without an explicit definition, I have previously suggested the following definition: communities are social entities that have two elements. One, a web of affect-laden relationships among a group of individuals, relationships that often criss-cross and reinforce one another (rather than merely one-on-one or chain-like individual relationships). The other, a measure of commitment to a set of shared values, norms, and meanings, and a shared history and identity – in short, to a particular culture.[2]

Among those who have responded to this definition of community, Benjamin Zablocki noted that while the definition is quite clear, few communities left in modern societies meet its requirements.[3] This is a common concern that has been with us since Emile Durkheim and Ferdinand Tönnies suggested that modern history is marked by a transition from *Gemeinschaft* to *Gesellschaft*. Others have viewed our society as a "mass" society composed of individuals without shared bonds or values. Actually, while there has been a decline in community, many social entities that fit the definition provided above abound even in large metropolitan areas. These communities are often ethnicity-based. In the US, communities are found in Little Havana, Chinatowns, Koreatown, Spanish Harlem, on the south shore of Boston, and in Williamsburg, NY, among many others. Others are composed of people who share a sexual orientation (for instance gay communities) or an occupation (for instance, the medical staff of some hospitals).

Important for the discussion that follows is that communities, as defined, need not be local or residential. The faculty of a small college might make up one community even if its members do not live next door to one another or on the campus. The same holds for the members of a labor union.

The definition excludes interest groups. Groups of people who merely share an interest in lower tariffs, in gaining a tax deduction, and so on, as a rule do not constitute a community. They share neither affective bonds nor a moral culture. (Of course, some social entities can both be a community and share some interests, but this does not negate the difference between these two concepts.) In short, communities can be defined and are far from defunct.

Are there virtual communities?

Many of those who argue that there can be no true communities in cyberspace implicitly follow a different notion as to what a community is from the one relied upon here (which, in my judgment, is quite close to what most people mean when they employ the term.) These critics of virtual communities have in mind numerous accidental rather than essential features of offline communities, such as face-to-face meetings. One should grant that online communities do not have all the features of offline ones (nor do offline communities have all the features of online ones). But the question is, can cyberspace meet the basic prerequisites of communities?[4]

The answer is in the affirmative, although one must grant that the needed prerequisites are not often provided, at least not in full. Indeed, there is a distinct inclination by commercial sites to pretend that community exists (because such claims bring "eyeballs" to one's site) where there is none. To provide but one example, GeoCities purports to provide "neighborhoods" and "neighborhood clubs" within their "community," but these neighborhoods simply amount to collections of home pages and chat rooms that are about the same topic. (For instance, "Sunset Strip" is a "neighborhood" of home pages and chat rooms devoted to the discussion of rock and punk rock.)

More generally, a very large part of the communications and transactions on the internet either are not interactive at all (e.g., placing an order for a consumer product) or are only point to point (e.g., exchange of email messages), which by themselves do not make communities. In 1998, according to a survey conducted by the Pew Center for the People and the Press, the following percentages of online users engaged in the following activities at least once a week: 72 percent sent email, 47 percent did research for work, and 38 percent got news on current events, public issues, and politics. Far fewer users participated in online group activities. Only 22 percent engaged in online forums or chat groups, and only 4 percent engaged in online political discussions.[5] A recent Gallup poll provided similar results, reporting that 95 percent of people use the internet to obtain information, 85 percent to send or receive email, and 45 percent use it for shopping, while only 21 percent visit chat rooms.[6]

But all that these facts show is that, just like offline interactions, the greater part of online interactions is not community-focused. They do not indicate that communities cannot be formed on the internet.

There are numerous informal accounts of strong affective bonds – the first element of communities – that have been formed via the internet as people who did not previously know one another "meet" and form intense relationships. There are a fair number of reports of people who abandon their spouses on the basis of liaisons they have formed online, and some of singles who first met in cyberspace and then married.

The second element of communities – forming a shared moral culture – is much less often met. At first, it may seem that chat rooms could provide opportunities for developing such a culture (as well as affective bonds) because at first glance they bear some resemblance to communities: groups of people meet and interact. The main reason, in my judgment, that the hundreds of thousands of chat rooms that exist do not, as a rule, provide for shared cultures (or affective bonds) is the way they are set up. Typically, chat room participants use aliases, and are keen to maintain their anonymity. Exchanges are very brief and intersected by other exchanges that occur in the same "space." Participants tend to partake in very limited exchanges and often engage in a false presentation of self.[7] As a result, piecing together a picture of the person one deals with, which may well be a prerequisite for forming shared values (as well as affective relationships), is hampered. The situation is akin to meeting someone for the first time on a bar stool or on an airplane flight. Conversation tends to be superficial and no relationship develops.[8]

The conditions under which virtual communities would thrive are, in effect, the mirror opposite of chat rooms: membership would be limited in number and relatively stable; members would have to disclose their true identity, and it would be verified. In addition, the subjects explored would cover a broad range rather than be limited to a few such as stock tips or dating-related banter. The fact that so far these conditions are infrequently satisfied should not be viewed as suggesting that they cannot be met; it merely suggests that they do not readily lend themselves to profit-making (and hence are of little interest to those who run chat rooms on the internet), and that they conflict with the individualistic ideologies of those who originally shaped the internet.

While the said conditions for successful community-building are rarely satisfied in full by such chat rooms, some are met via thousands of so-called clubs run by, for example, Yahoo!, Excite, and eCircles. Membership in these clubs is limited to a given number (say, 2,000). In some, one needs to apply to become a member. While many of these clubs are listed in indexes maintained on the respective websites, one can refuse to list a club in order to protect it from open-ended participation.

At the same time, these clubs do not provide for disclosure of self or verified identity. In addition, the topics they specialize in are often quite narrow and limited (for example, examples of Excite clubs include "Amateur Astronomers" (1,159 members), "Amateur Models of Virginia" (1,046 members), and "The Homebrewing Club" (340 members).

ECircles has a more personal focus than do other online club sites. It provides families and friends with private areas within cyberspace to meet and exchange messages, and is less interest- or issue-based.

H-net runs some 80 "clubs" that fully meet the said conditions: not only is participation limited, but identities are disclosed. (Albeit the subjects under discussion are rather specialized, such as French literature in one club and certain periods of German history in another.) So far there are no studies of the community-building effects of these clubs, although personal observation suggests that they are considerably stronger than those of the typical chat rooms.

MediaMOO has occasionally been referred to as a true online community, although the extent to which it lives up to this description is at least unclear.[9] Howard Rheingold's accounts of online communities are often cited as examples of how it is possible to develop close relationships and a rich emotional life online. For instance, he describes an online funeral he attended as a "rite of passage for all of [the virtual community] CIX, a time when the original members of the group felt closest to each other."[10] According to Rheingold, there were strong affective bonds among group members and there was a shared group history and culture (i.e. the group he describes qualifies as a real community according to the definition of community I proposed above).

Finally, one should also not overlook that some online communities work to complement and reinforce existing offline communities. (I refer to these as hybrid communities.) There is something artificial about the very way the question is typically posed, comparing virtual to other communities. After all, nobody lives in cyberspace; even the avatars in Neal Stephenson's *Snow Crash* are put on by three-dimensional people. The more realistic questions that arise concern community (and democracy) in a new world in which there are both on- and offline group relationships. (Rheingold, who is a firm believer in the depth of online relationships and community, nevertheless describes how his online relationships often led to face-to-face meetings and friendships.)

Among the reports of neighborhood communities significantly reinforced by virtual links is the often-cited example of Blacksburg, Virginia. Around 87 percent of Blacksburg's residents are online,[11] and the town has an online community called Blacksburg Electronic Village (<www.bev.net>). Both the town and the various groups and neighborhoods in it benefit from their ability to post meetings, share information, and interact via the shared site.

When all is said and done, there are very few reports of full-fledged, purely online communities. It is rather difficult to establish whether the reason for this finding is that the internet has not been set up to facilitate community-building despite the fact that this could be quite readily done, or (as several have argued) that there is something in its structure that inherently prevents true community-formation. I personally hold that communities would thrive if stable and disclosed membership were to be made relatively easy to attain, but this remains to be demonstrated. There is, though, little doubt that online communities can significantly reinforce offline ones.

Quantitative data

The discussion so far has focused on so-called qualitative observations, one case at a time. There is, though, considerable quantitative data concerning the ability to form and to sustain social relations on the internet. Because these data concern not merely friendships (which can just be between two people, and are hence point to point) but also families (which contain community-like web relationships), they speak to the question of whether one of the key prerequisites of community-building can be met online.

The question of whether cyberspace agitates against social bonds or enriches them has been recently examined in several studies. One study, by Norman H. Nie and Lutz Erbring, has claimed to find that the internet is detrimental to such bonding. According to them, "the more hours people use the Internet, the less time they spend in contact with real human beings."[12]

Nie and Erbring say: "Internet time is coming out of time viewing television but also out at the expense of time people spend on the phone gabbing with family and friends or having a conversation with people in the room with them." They acknowledge that most internet users use email, which increases their "conversations" with family and friends via this medium, "but you can't share a coffee or a beer with somebody on e-mail or give them a hug."[13] In short: "The Internet could be the ultimate isolating technology that further reduces our participation in communities even more than did automobiles and television before it."[14]

Nie and Erbring's study found that, as they spend more time online, 13 percent of people spend less time with family and friends and 8 percent attend fewer social events. Furthermore, 34 percent spend less time reading the newspaper, while 59 percent spend less time watching television and 25 percent spend less time shopping in stores. Finally, 25 percent of people are working more hours at home, yet there has not been a decline in work at the office.[15]

What do Nie and Erbring's figures actually show? In discussing the findings, one must note that they concern two groups of people: those who are not connected to the internet (N = 2,078) and those who are connected (N = 2,035). The latter are further divided into light users (fewer than 5 hours per week; 64 percent of the "connected" sample) and heavy users (more than 5 hours per week; 36 percent of the "connected" sample).

Of all users, only 9 percent said that they spend less time with their family, and 9 percent said they spend less time with their friends, while nearly ten times more people – 86 percent and 87 percent respectively – said that they spend the same amount of time with family and friends as before! Moreover, quite a few (6 percent and 4 percent respectively) reported that they spend more time with family and friends.

The picture does not change much even if one focuses on the heavy users. Only 10 percent of those who spend 5–10 hours online per week reported that they spend less time with family and friends. Of those who spend 10 or more hours per week online, only 15 percent made the same report.

The finding that some internet users spend more time with family and friends may at first seem unlikely, but it is hardly so. The study itself shows that by far the largest effect of internet activity for all users is to reduce the amount of time spent watching TV (46 percent of users) and shopping (19 percent). For heavy users, 59 percent spend less time watching TV and 25 percent spend less time shopping. (Obviously it takes less time to order things from eToys or Amazon than to go to a mall or store.) The study did not inquire into how the time saved in these ways is used and whether or not some of it is allocated to increasing social life.

Along the same lines, the study found – as is widely known – that people's most common use of the internet is communicating via email. This, too, is a time-saving device compared to letter-writing and even phone calls. Ergo, the internet readily allows people to spend both more time online and more time socializing. In effect, the fact that people use the internet largely for communication (90 percent use email) and not shopping (36 percent buy products online) or banking (12 percent), and that most of this communication is with people they are familiar with rather than with strangers, strongly suggests that they relate to one another more rather than less as a result.

A study on technology by the Kaiser Family Foundation, National Public Radio, and Harvard's Kennedy School of Government reported the following findings:

Despite their overall positive attitudes, Americans do see some problems with computers and technology....More than half say computers have led people to spend less time with their families and friends (58 percent). Furthermore, slightly fewer than half (46 percent) of Americans say that computers have given people less free time, although 24 percent say computers have given people more free time and 28 percent say computers haven't made much of a difference.[16]

Note, though, that people were asked about computer use, not their internet connections. The question people were asked was, "Do you think the use of computers has given people more free time, less free time, or hasn't made much difference?" This kind of question makes people think about non-interactive uses of their computers, especially word-processing, preparing documents, number-crunching, and so on. Questions about use of the internet, which is merely one function of computers, are more revealing.

A study released in May 2000 by the Pew Internet and American Life Project found

clear evidence that email and the Web have enhanced users' relationships with their family and friends – results that challenge the notion that the Internet contributes to isolation. Significant majorities of online Americans say their use of email has increased the amount of contact they have with key family members and friends. Fifty-nine percent of those who exchange email with a family member say they are in contact with that relative more often thanks to email. Only 2 percent say they are in contact less often with this family member since they struck up their e-correspondence. Email users say virtually the same thing about the frequency of their contact with close friends via e-letters. Sixty percent of those who email friends say they communicate more often with a key friend now that they use email and 2 percent say they do so less often.

Additional Pew findings make an even stronger case:

As a group, Internet users are more likely than nonusers to have a robust social world. The use of email seems to encourage deeper social connectedness. The longer users have been online, the more likely it is that they feel that email has improved their ties to their families and friends. Forty percent of Internet veterans – those who have been online for at least three years – say there has been a lot of improvement in their connections with family and friends because of email, compared with just over a quarter of Internet newcomers (those online for six months or less) who report that.

Even more impressive are the Pew findings that

> More than those who have no Internet access, Internet users say they
> have a significant network of helpful relatives and friends. Some 48
> percent of Internet users say they can turn to many people for support
> in a time of need, while just 38 percent of nonusers report they have a
> large social network. Furthermore, only 8 percent of Internet users
> indicate they are socially isolated – that is, they say they have no one
> or hardly anyone they can turn to for support. In contrast, 18 percent
> of nonusers say they have no one or hardly anyone to turn to.[17]

Finally, a Harris poll found:

> [B]ecause people are online, they tend to communicate more often
> with their friends and family. Almost half (48 percent) of all adults
> who are online at home say they communicate more often with friends
> and family than they did before they could use email. Only 3 percent
> say they communicate less.
>   Perhaps the most interesting finding is that many more people say
> that they meet and socialize with friends and family more often be-
> cause of the Internet than do so less often (27 percent v. 9 percent).
> This debunks the theory that Internet users cut themselves off physic-
> ally from social interaction.[18]

When all is said and done, meaningful and reinforcing interactions
seem to be quite common in the online world. Under what conditions these suffice to satisfy the first prerequisite for community
remains to be established. As I argued in the previous section, the
conditions for forming shared cultures are possible to create online,
but they are not often provided. Call me moderately optimistic on
this account. As I see it, the evidence suggests that if the internet
were to be made more community-friendly along the lines discussed
at the start of this chapter, online communities might be much more
common.

Communities' Cyberspace Democracy

The same question can be applied to online, offline, and hybrid communities: can they be democratically governed by drawing on the
internet? In order for democracy to thrive, at least four prerequisites
must be satisfied. Numerous studies show that two key prerequisites,
sharing information and voting, are quite feasible on the internet.

The third element, that of deliberation, has been much less often explored, but I shall attempt to show below that it seems to pose no insurmountable difficulties once internet designers put their mind to fashioning the software needed for deliberation in cyberspace. The same holds for the fourth element, that of representation.

Sharing information

Much has been made – in several writings on the subject, and even more in numerous projects dedicated to the subject – of the fact that information can be distributed, stored, retrieved, duplicated, and illustrated with much greater ease and at much lower costs on the internet than in the offline world. This is undoubtedly true. One should not, however, accord too much importance to information-sharing as an element of democratic governance. True, providing voters with all the speeches made by all the politicians, a full catalogue of all the positions they have taken in the past and every vote they have cast, is helpful. The same is true of having websites chock-full of information about the issues of the day.

However, at the end of the day, voters can cast only one vote per election. For instance, in a presidential election they cannot vote for the environmental policies of a given candidate but against his foreign policy, for his position on choice but against his ideas about health insurance, and so on. Hence, detailed information about these issues and the positions of the candidate are not particularly useful in their decisions as to whom to vote for.

Those who suggest that people's decisions take the form of an index, in which they would inform themselves about numerous issues and then vote for the candidate who gets the highest score, do not take into account that, in actuality, decisions typically seem to be made in a lexographic form: two or three considerations (for instance, the state of the economy and whether or not the country is involved in a war) make up most of the "index" for most voters.

More important, for numerous voters the process is much less information-driven than is quite often assumed. Values, party affiliations, and loyalties and community pressures play a very important role in determining the one choice they can make.

In short, the fabulous information features of the internet are pro-democratic, but they surely add much less to existing democratic institutions than the more dedicated information enthusiasts presume.[19]

E-voting

Initially, there was great concern that voting on the internet would lead to large-scale ballot-box stuffing, fraud, and other forms of electoral abuse. However, as new encryption techniques have developed and procedures for recognizing e-signatures have been approved, these concerns have subsided. It seems that in the future, with proper procedures in place, e-voting could be made at least as secure as off-line voting which, after all, has never been perfectly authenticated.

The main difficulty in this area lies elsewhere, namely in access. Democracy, of course, requires that all those who have reached a given age are citizens of a given polity, and, if they have not been convicted of a crime, will be allowed to vote. At the moment, significant parts of the population, especially the poorer and otherwise disadvantaged ones, do not have personal computers and hence cannot vote electronically. However, this defect is rapidly being corrected as the cost of computers and other devices that allow access to the internet are plunging. Providing the rest of the population with a device needed to vote could be easily contemplated.

France long ago provided all citizens with devices resembling personal computers to provide them with access to Minitel, France's pre-internet public electronic system. While Minitel is not used for voting, the distribution of the terminals to private citizens and their placement throughout France in public kiosks demonstrate the possibility of providing widespread access to an electronic network.

Deliberation

Deliberation, an important prerequisite for sound democratic processes, is much less often discussed than information-sharing or voting, because of a tendency to view democracy in a simple way, as one in which people vote and the majority rules. Ross Perot, for instance, proposed that leaders and experts could present Americans with a set of options, and then the people themselves could vote for their preferred one, skipping the deliberative step.[20]

It is, however, widely recognized that if a proposition is put before the voters, and they are allowed to immediately click their responses (say in some kind of electronic form of the kind of initiatives many states offer their voters), the result would reflect the worst impulses of the people, their raw emotions, readily wiped up by demagogues.

Democratic polities provide two antidotes to this danger: delay loops and opportunities for interaction among the voters. First, they allow time for voters to examine the issues and discuss them with other community members – in town meetings, over their fences, in bars, and so on – before votes are taken. For e-democracy not to turn demagogic, it will have to provide such delay loops – in other words, time for deliberation – and opportunities for interaction among the voters in between the time a proposition or a slate of candidates is put before the voters and the time the votes are cast. Delay per se provides no difficulties. There is no reason votes have to follow immediately, or even very closely, the presentation of a choice to an electorate.

The second antidote, interaction, provides more difficulties. As we have seen in the discussion of communities, chat rooms' composition and rules of access and anonymity do not provide sound conditions for meaningful interaction, let alone democratic deliberation. If democracy is to thrive on the internet, provisions will have to be made to provide for, indeed foster, the kinds of interaction deliberation requires. Deliberation is most fruitful among people who know one another and in small numbered groups with low turnover – the same conditions that nurture communities.

The difficulties here are not inherent in the technology; there seem to be no obvious reasons these conditions could not be readily met online, but so far they have not been – largely, it seems, because they may not be profitable and because of ideological objections to any setting aside of online anonymity.

Representation

Democracy works best, as has been well and long established, when the voters do not directly decide which policies they favor (as they do in plebiscites and in initiatives), but instruct their elected representatives as to what their basic preferences are, and then allow them to work out the remaining differences. (The more limiting the mandate the voters provide for their representatives and the stricter the instructions, the more difficulties representatives have in working out the inevitable compromises that democracy entails, as people of different values and interests must find a shared course.) This is, of course, the way parliaments work, as well as state assemblies and most city councils.

The internet, which has not yet been groomed to serve democratic processes, has no established procedures for representation. However, there are on the face of it no special difficulties in providing for representation. Indeed, some years ago I conducted an experiment on this matter, using a much more "primitive" technology than the internet. The experiment was conducted with the help of the League of Women Voters at a statewide level. The League's New Jersey chapter was attempting to decide, as it does once a year, which issues deserved priority. We organized the League's members into groups of ten, and they conducted "town meetings" by means of conference calls. Each group chose its own priorities and selected a representative to take these preferences to the next level for discussion. We then held conference calls with groups of ten representatives, who decided among themselves which views and preferences to carry to the third and final level, at which statewide policy decisions were made.

A survey established that the League's members, who participated in the decision and representation process, were highly satisfied with the results. The experiment allowed all the members of the League to participate in the decision-making process, and yet the elected representatives were free, within an area indicated by those who elected them, to work out a league-wide consensus.[21]

There is little reason to doubt that such a multilayered, representative model can be applied to online communities; but can it serve nationwide democracy, in which many millions of individuals are involved? Can there be a representative nationwide democratic process that relies at least in part upon online devices?

I suggest that the answer is in the affirmative, drawing on the magical power of exponential curves: if representatives were layered in the suggested manner, millions of participants could quite readily be included. Suppose that various experts addressed the country on Sunday from 10.00 to 11.00 a.m. about whether the United States should cut back the military by 50 percent over five years. The conference buzz would start with groups of 14 citizens, each having an hour to discuss and vote. Each group would elect one representative to participate in conference call discussions with 13 representatives of other groups. Each group of representatives would in turn elect an individual to speak for them, and so on in a rising pyramid. If this process occurred seven times, by six o'clock in the evening 105 million adults could be reached, which is more than the 91 million who voted in the 1988 presidential election.

The same basic approach could be readily applied to the internet. Voters could convene in, say, 25-person online town meetings. Their discussion would be much more productive than those of chat rooms because the number of participants would be limited, they would already have some shared attributes (all from the same area?), and they would realize that at the end of a given time period they would have to provide their elected representative with a mandate on the next level of this town hall pyramid. Then the representatives of the separate 25-member groups would be convened, and so on.

Participants would soon learn that the views of those groups that provide their representatives with very detailed instructions and leave them with little room to negotiate would, as a rule, be more likely to be left out of the final consensus-making process than would those that provide their representatives with relatively broad mandates. Moreover, members would realize that if many groups were to provide their representative with narrow and strict instructions, national politics would tend to be confrontational and unproductive.

A major issue is left unaddressed here. Multilayered or representative democracy conducted by the use of the internet could vary a great deal in terms of two variables. One is the scope of issues submitted to a full court multilevel deliberative process of the kind depicted above. For instance, is the public at large going to be invited to deliberate and instruct its representatives only on a few issues every umpteen years – or much more often? Second, are the representatives chosen in the "lower" levels going to change with each issue, or will they serve set terms? And are any of the modifications suggested in the preceding discussion going to make virtual democracy more democratic or more populist?

In short, the internet could not only fully duplicate offline democratic procedures and outcome, but it could also improve upon them. It would be much easier online than offline for millions not merely to gain information and to vote, but also to participate in deliberations and in instructing their chosen representatives.

In Conclusion

The chapter argues that some qualitative accounts and quantitative data suggest that communities can be formed on the internet. They are much more likely to thrive in "clubs" in which membership is relatively stable, participants disclose their identity, and the subjects under discussion are significant and encompassing rather than narrow and specialized. Furthermore, it is important to recognize that because people live both on and offline, online communities can reinforce offline ones.

Regarding the use of the internet for democratic processes for on- or offline communities – small or large ones – we agree with those who suggest that information-sharing and voting can be quite readily accommodated. However, I stress the importance of providing for deliberations and representation, the software for which is, as a rule, not available.

All that has been argued so far is that virtual democracy is quite feasible. It remains to be discussed at a future date whether or not greater reliance on virtual politics would make the joint on- and off-line polity more or less democratic than it currently is.

Notes

INTRODUCTION

1 For more discussion see Amitai Etzioni, *The New Golden Rule: Community and Morality in a Democratic Society* (New York: Basic Books, 1997).

2 Robert Bellah, Richard Madsen, William M. Sullivan, Ann Swidler, and Steven M. Tipton, *Habits of the Heart* (Berkeley: University of California Press, 1985).

3 See the Responsive Communitarian Platform at <www.communitarian network.org>.

4 For more information, see Amitai Etzioni, *My Brother's Keeper: A Memoir and a Message* (New York: Rowman & Littlefield, 2003).

5 See Michael Elliot, "What's Left?," *Newsweek International*, 10 October 1994, 13.

6 For more on the relationship between privacy and the common good, see Amitai Etzioni, *The Limits of Privacy* (New York: Basic Books, 1999), especially pp. 3–10.

CHAPTER 1 ARE PARTICULARISTIC OBLIGATIONS JUSTIFIED?

1 A similar point was made by Adam Smith in *The Theory of Moral Sentiments*, although Smith refers to the difference between a man's reaction to his own problems and a disaster far away; Adam Smith, *The Essential Adam Smith*, ed. Robert L. Heilbroner (New York: W.W. Norton, 1986), p. 106.

2 I would have preferred the term "moral claims" to obligations, because obligations, like duties, imply imposition from the outside, while using "moral claims" may help to remind us that reference is made to claims

whose innate merit we recognize. They are, at least in part, internally motivated.

3 Jeremy Bentham, *An Introduction to the Principles of Morals and Legislation* (New York: Doubleday, 1935), p. 8.

4 For more discussion of this concept, see Amitai Etzioni, *The New Golden Rule* (New York: Basic Books, 1996), especially ch. 7.

5 John Rawls, *Political Liberalism* (New York: Columbia Univ. Press, 1993), p. 243.

6 John Stuart Mill, *On Liberty*, ed. David Spitz (New York: W.W. Norton, 1975), p. 71: "But neither one person, nor any number of persons, is warranted in saying to another human creature ... that he shall not do with his life for his benefit what he chooses to do with it." In developing a principle for dealing with "compulsion and control," Mill explicitly says this applies "whether the means used be physical force in the form of legal penalties, or the moral coercion of public opinion." For Mill, neither community nor state ought to tell people how to live their lives. For a discussion of the difference between social pressure and censorship, see Jean Bethke Elshtain, "On Moral Outrage, Boycotts, and Real Censorship," *The Responsive Community* 2:2 (Spring 1992).

7 Amy Gutmann, "Communitarian Critics of Liberalism," *Philosophy and Public Affairs* 14 (1985): 319.

8 See Marilyn Friedman, "The Practice of Partiality," *Ethics* 101 (1991): 818–35; Bernard Gert, "Moral Impartiality," *Midwest Studies in Philosophy, Volume XX: Moral Concepts*, ed. Peter A. French, Theodore E. Uehling, Jr., and Howard K. Wettstein (Notre Dame, IN: University of Notre Dame Press, 1996); Thomas Nagel, *Equality and Partiality* (New York: Oxford University Press, 1991).

9 Lawrence A. Blum, "Vocation, Friendship, and Community: Limitations of the Personal–Impersonal Framework," in *Identity, Character, Morality: Essays in Moral Psychology*, ed. Owen Flanagan and Amelie Oksenberg Rorty (Cambridge, MA: MIT Press, 1990), p. 173.

10 Marcia W. Baron, "Impartiality and Friendship," *Ethics* 101 (1991).

11 See, for instance, Martha Nussbaum with Respondents, *For Love of Country: Debating the Limits of Patriotism*, ed. Joshua Cohen (Boston: Beacon Press, 1996); Seyla Benhabib, "Dismantling the Leviathan: Citizen and State in a Global World," *The Responsive Community* 11 (2001): 14–27; Michael Walzer, "In Response: Support for Modesty and the Nation-State," *The Responsive Community* 11 (2001): 28–31; Henry Shue, "Mediating Duties," *Ethics* 98 (1988): 687–704.

12 I am indebted to David Archard for this point.

13 An anonymous commentator on an earlier draft made this argument.

14 Anemona Hartocollis, "Chancellor to Keep Teacher in Her Job in Parents' Victory," *New York Times* (September 26, 1997), p. A1.

15 See mention of Queens School in Romesh Ratnesar, "Class-Size Warfare," *Time* (October 6, 1997).

16 Hartocollis, "Chancellor to Keep Teacher."

17 For example: "The practice of PTAs and other parent groups hiring supplemental teaching staff has been banned in Washington's suburbs and other parts of the country because of concerns that it could lead to inequalities among schools and create a have/have not educational environment. Opponents say allowing PTAs to pay for extra teachers challenges the concept that a strong public education should be available to all students – not just those who live in affluent communities" (Justin Blum, "PTAs Give Some D.C. Schools an Edge; Affluent Parents Providing Extras that Poorer Neighbors Can't," *Washington Post* (April 17, 2000), p. B1.)

18 James Q. Wilson, *The Moral Sense* (New York: Free Press, 1993); see also Amitai Etzioni, "Basic Human Needs, Alienation and Inauthenticity," *American Sociological Review* 33 (1968): 870–84.

19 J. L. Mackie, *Ethics: Inventing Right and Wrong* (Harmondsworth, Middlesex: Penguin Books, 1977), pp. 131–2. For additional discussion of human nature in this context, see Derek Parfit, *Reasons and Persons* (Oxford: Oxford University Press, 1984), p. 34; Keith Horton, "The Limits of Human Nature," *Philosophical Quarterly* 49 (1999): 452–70.

20 Discussed by Bernard Williams, "Persons, Character and Morality," *Moral Luck: Philosophical Papers 1973–1980* (Cambridge: Cambridge University Press, 1981); Williams takes the example from Charles Fried, *An Anatomy of Values: Problems of Personal and Social Choice* (Cambridge, MA: Harvard University Press, 1970).

21 The most often discussed example of this is William Godwin's suggestion that a person should not save a loved one before a person of greater societal worth, in *Enquiry Concerning Political Justice*, 1st edn, ed. Raymond A. Preston (New York: Knopf, 1926). Godwin is discussed in, among other works, Marcia W. Baron, *Kantian Ethics without Apology* (Ithaca, NY: Cornell University Press, 1995); Alasdair MacIntyre, "The Magic in the Pronoun 'My'" (review of Williams's *Moral Luck*), *Ethics* 94 (1983): 113–25; and Marilyn Friedman, "The Practice of Partiality," *Ethics* 101 (1991): 818–35. For a criticism of Williams's analysis of the example (and the suggestion that the man in the example has "one thought too many"), see Baron, *Kantian Ethics*.

22 Many of the authors who address this oft-discussed case analyze it from a different perspective, suggesting that the person in the case should not think of his wife in the same way he thinks of the stranger (this is Bernard Williams's point in raising the case in his essay "Persons, Character and Morality," p. 18). Here, the case is used to illustrate a different point, that the person in the case will not treat his wife in the same way as the stranger (or think of her in the same way) because it is not human nature to do so.

23 J. O. Urmson, in his classic essay "Saints and Heroes," writes: "There is, indeed, a place for ideals that are practically unworkable in human

affairs, as there is a place for the blueprint of a machine that will never go into production;... there are ample grounds why our code should distinguish between basic rules, summarily set forth in simple rules and binding on all, and the higher flights of morality of which saintliness and heroism are outstanding examples" (in *Essays in Moral Philosophy*, ed. A. I. Melden (Seattle: University of Washington Press, 1958), p. 211). And: "To take a parallel from positive law, the prohibition laws asked too much of 1958, and the American people were consequently broken systematically; and as people got used to breaking the law a general lowering of respect for the law naturally followed; it no longer seemed that a law was something that everybody could be expected to obey. Similarly in Britain the gambling laws, some of which are utterly unpractical, have fallen into contempt as a body" (p. 212).

24 Ibid., p. 202.
25 For more on supererogation, see Shelly Kagan, *Normative Ethics* (Boulder, CO: Westview Press, 1997); David Heyd, *Supererogation: Its Status in Ethical Theory* (Cambridge: Cambridge University Press, 1982).
26 Urmson "Saints and Heroes," p. 202.
27 Kagan, *Normative Ethics*, pp. 154–5.
28 Ibid., p. 155.
29 Heyd, *Supererogation: Its Status in Ethical Theory*, p. 166. Heyd's points are summaries of Urmson's grounds in "Saints and Heroes."
30 There is a considerable literature that is critical of functional explanations that cannot be reviewed here.
31 Philosophers sometimes make similar assumptions about our self-interested nature (recall J. L. Mackie, *Ethics: Inventing Right and Wrong*). In establishing claims about our fundamentally self-interested nature, some authors invoke the insights of evolutionary biology (see James Griffin, "Review of *The Limits of Morality* by Shelly Kagan," *Mind* 99 (1990): 129–30).
32 Edmund S. Phelps, *Altruism, Morality, and Economic Theory* (New York: Russell Sage Foundation, 1975).
33 Emile Durkheim, *The Division of Labor in Society* (New York: The Free Press, 1997).
34 One may argue that reciprocity is, actually, a universal principle: Whoever does X for me I will do X for them, regardless of who or where they are (as long as they have basically the same attributes). Without going here into ways of challenging this interpretation, it suffices to note that even if it is fully endorsed, it amounts to a universal dictate to honor particularistic obligations. Even if one holds that I owe a ride to anyone who gives me a ride (although people outside my social range hardly can do so), the obligation is always to specific people who accorded me a ride in the past.
35 See Amitai Etzioni, *An Immodest Agenda: Rebuilding America Before the 21st Century* (New York: McGraw-Hill, 1983).

36 Talcott Parsons, *The Structure of Social Action* (Glencoe, IL: Free Press, 1937).

37 On gift relations, see *International Encyclopedia of the Social Sciences*, s.v. "interaction: social exchange" and "exchange and display."

38 For criticism of the use of the term "community," see Colin Bell and Howard Newby, *Community Studies: An Introduction to the Sociology of the Local Community* (New York: Praeger, 1973), 15; *The Sociology of Community: A Selection of Readings* (London: Frank Cass, 1974), p. xliii.

39 Robert Putnam, *Bowling Alone: The Collapse and Revival of American Community* (New York: Simon & Schuster, 2000), pp. 326–35.

40 Francis Fukuyama, *The Great Disruption: Human Nature and the Reconstitution of Social Order* (New York: Touchstone, 1999).

41 Robert N. Bellah, Richard Madsen, William M. Sullivan, Ann Swidler, and Steven M. Tipton, *Habits of the Heart* (Berkeley: University of California Press, 1985).

42 Putnam, *Bowling Alone*, pp. 326, 329.

43 Ibid., pp. 331–3. See also Leo Srole, Thomas S. Langner, Stanley T. Michael, Marvin K. Opter, and Thomas A. C. Rennie, *Mental Health in the Metropolis: The Midtown Manhattan Study* (New York: McGraw-Hill, 1962).

44 Sigmund Freud, *Civilization and Its Discontents*, ed. and trans. James Strachey (New York: W. W. Norton, 1989); Christopher Lasch, *The Culture of Narcissism: American Life in an Age of Diminishing Expectations* (New York: W. W. Norton, 1979).

45 Quoted in Isaiah Berlin, *The Crooked Timber of Humanity: Chapters in the History of Ideas*, ed. Henry Hardy (New York: Alfred A. Knopf, 1991), p. 100.

46 The mirror opposite of this argument is to point to the loss of identity in the mass society, the ill effects of atomization, the resulting alienation. See William Kornhauser, *The Politics of Mass Society* (Glencoe, IL: Free Press, 1959).

47 Michael Sandel, *Liberalism and the Limits of Justice*, 2nd edn (New York: Cambridge University Press, 1998), p. 179.

48 Charles Taylor, *Sources of the Self: The Making of Modern Identity* (Cambridge, MA: Harvard University Press, 1989), p. 27.

49 Letter to author, September 29, 2001.

50 Ibid.

51 Michael Walzer, *Spheres of Justice: A Defense of Pluralism and Equality* (New York: Basic Books, 1983), pp. 312–16; see also *Thick and Thin: Moral Arguments at Home and Abroad* (Notre Dame, IN: University of Notre Dame Press, 1994), pp. 7–8.

52 See my *The New Golden Rule*, ch. 8.

53 Erich Fromm, *Escape from Freedom* (New York: Rinehart, 1941); Gustave Le Bon, *The Crowd: A Study of the Popular Mind* (London: T. Fisher Unwin, 1908). See also Srole, *Mental Health in the Metropolis*.

54 See, for instance, the vast body of literature examining the fall of the Weimar Republic and the rise of Nazism, especially Sheri Berman, "Civil Society and the Collapse of the Weimar Republic," *World Politics* 43 (1997): 401–29.

55 David B. Wong, "On Flourishing and Finding One's Identity in Community," *Midwest Studies in Philosophy, Vol. XIII: Ethical Theory: Character and Virtue*, ed. Peter A. French, et al. (Notre Dame, IN: University of Notre Dame Press, 1988), p. 333.

56 This is not some Hobbesian heuristic, but a statement based on empirical studies: see Susan Curtiss, *Genie: A Psycholinguistic Study of a Modern-Day "Wild Child"* (New York: Academic Press, 1977); Jean-Marc Gaspard Itard, *The Wild Boy of Aveyron*, trans. George and Muriel Humphrey (New York: Appleton-Century-Crofts, 1962); Harlan Lane and Richard Pillard, *The Wild Boy of Berundi: A Study of an Outcast Child* (New York: Random House, 1978); J. A. L. Singh and R. M. Zingg, *Wolf-Children and Feral Man* (London: Harper, 1942); Douglas Candland, *Feral Children and Clever Animals* (New York: Oxford University Press, 1993).

57 I am not arguing that universal commitments' moral standing is based on their introduction and re-enforcement by particularistic relations, but that without these relations people will not acquire or sustain them, whatever their intrinsic merit.

58 Dennis Wrong, *The Problem of Order* (New York: Free Press, 1994).

59 Robert J. Sampson, et al., "Neighborhoods and Violent Crime: A Multilevel Study of Collective Efficacy," *Science* (15 August 1997): 918–24.

60 On this issue, see Philip Selznick, *The Moral Commonwealth* (Berkeley: University of California Press, 1992) and David Archard, "Moral Partiality," *Midwest Studies in Philosophy, Volume XX: Moral Concepts*, ed. Peter A. French, Theodore E. Uehling, Jr., and Howard K. Wettstein (Notre Dame, IN: University of Notre Dame Press, 1996).

61 Philip Selznick, *The Moral Commonwealth*, pp. 196–7.

62 Ibid., p. 197.

63 John Cottingham, "Partiality, Favouritism and Morality," *Philosophical Quarterly* 36 (1986): 363.

64 Ibid., p. 369; emphasis in original.

CHAPTER 2   PRIVACY AS AN OBLIGATION

1 Amitai Etzioni, *The Limits of Privacy* (New York: Basic Books, 1999), p. 197.

2 The term "obligation" implies imposition, while the term "social responsibility" implies voluntary compliance with social mores. It might therefore be best to associate privacy obligations with mandated priv-

acy and privacy as a social responsibility with expected privacy. However, introducing such conceptual distinctions would only complicate the vocabulary and is not essential for this first cut at the subject.

3 Geraldine Brooks, *Nine Parts of Desire* (New York: Anchor Books, 1996), pp. 21–2.

4 Hanna Papanek, "Purdah: Separate Worlds and Symbolic Shelter," *Comparative Studies in Society and History* 3 (1973): 294.

5 Brooks, *Nine Parts of Desire*, pp. 26, 162.

6 Igor S. Kon, *The Sexual Revolution in Russia*, trans. James Riordan (New York: The Free Press, 1995), pp. 67–84, 135–6.

7 Jeffrey Rosen, *The Unwanted Gaze* (New York: Knopf, 2001), pp. 18–19.

8 Menachem Elon, *Jewish Law: History, Sources, Principles* (Jerusalem: The Hebrew University, 1994), p. 943.

9 Eugene B. Borowitz and Frances Wienman Schwartz, *The Jewish Moral Virtues* (Philadelphia, PA: The Jewish Publication Society, 1999), pp. 150, 252.

10 Anita Allen, "The Wanted Gaze," 89 *Georgetown Law Journal* 2013 (June 2001): 2015.

11 Laurel Thatcher Ulrich, *Good Wives* (New York: Knopf, 1980), pp. 95, 108–9.

12 For further discussion of the republican and individualist strains in American culture, see Robert Bellah, Richard Madsen, William M. Sullivan, Ann Swidler, and Steven M. Tipton, *Habits of the Heart* (Berkeley: University of Californial Press, 1985), pp. 27–39.

13 *Griswold* v. *Connecticut*, 381 US 479 (1965); *Eisenstadt* v. *Baird*, 405 US 438, 439 (1972); *Roe* v. *Wade*, 410 US 113 (1973).

14 Samuel Warren and Louis Brandeis, "The Right to Privacy," 4 *Harvard Law Review* 193 (1890).

15 Mary Ann Glendon, *Rights Talk* (New York: The Free Press, 1991), pp. 1–18.

16 See Bellah et al., *Habits of the Heart*.

17 Amitai Etzioni, *The New Golden Rule: Community and Morality in a Democratic Society* (New York: Basic Books, 1996), pp. 64–71, 102–10.

18 See, e.g., Ala. Code section 13A-6-68 (1994); Alaska Stat. section 11.41.460 (1989); Ariz. Rev. Stat. Ann. section 13-1402 (1989); Colo. Rev. Stat. Ann. section 18-7-302 (West 1990 & Supp. 1994); Del. Code Ann. tit. 11, sections 764–5 (Supp. 1994); Fla. Stat. Ann. section 800.03 (West Supp. 1995); Haw. Rev. Stat. sections 707–34 (1994); Ind. Code Ann. section 35-45-4-1 (Burns 1994); Iowa Code Ann. section 709.9 (West 1993); Kan. Stat. Ann. section 21-3508 (Supp. 1994); Ky. Rev. Stat. Ann. section 510.150 (Michie/Bobbs-Merrill 1990); La. Rev. Stat. Ann. section 14:106(A)(1) (West 1986); Me. Rev. Stat. Ann. tit. 17-A, section 854 (West Supp. 1994); Mont. Code Ann. section 45-5-504 (1993); Neb. Rev. Stat. section 28-806 (1989); N.H. Rev. Stat. Ann.

section 645: 1 (Supp. 1994); N.J. Stat. Ann. section 2C:14-4 (West Supp. 1995); N.M. Stat. Ann. section 30-9-14 (Michie 1994); N.D. Cent. Code section 12.1-20-12.1 (1985); Okla. Stat. tit. 21, section 1021 (West Supp. 1995); Or. Rev. Stat. section 163.465 (1990); 18 Pa. Cons. Stat. section 3127 (1983); R.I. Gen. Laws section 11-45-1(7) (1994); S.D. Codified Laws Ann. section 22-24-1 (Supp. 1995); Tenn. Code Ann. section 39-13-511 (Supp. 1994); Tex. Penal Code Ann. section 21.08 (West 1994); Utah Code Ann. section 76-9-702 (1995); W. Va. Code section 61-8-9 (1992); Wis. Stat. section 944.20 (Supp. 1994).

19 For discussion of the societal trends the communitarian movement helped to foster, see Amitai Etzioni, *My Brother's Keeper: A Memoir and a Message* (New York: Rowman & Littlefield, 2003), ch. 16.

20 *Miriam Webster's Collegiate Dictionary*, 10th edn.

21 Based on results of search conducted on March 20, 2002.

22 See, e.g., ABC News/Washington Post poll asking "What do you think is more important right now – for the FBI (Federal Bureau of Investigation) to investigate possible terrorist threats, even if that intrudes on personal privacy, or for the FBI not to intrude on personal privacy, even if that limits its ability to investigate possible terrorist threats?" June 7–9, 2002; CBS News poll asking "Government agencies have said they are going to install video surveillance cameras in public places such as national monuments and sights that are important symbols of our county's history. Do you consider this an invasion of people's privacy?" (If the response is "yes," ask:) "Is it a major invasion of privacy or a minor invasion of privacy?" April 15–18, 2002.

23 David Brin, *The Transparent Society* (New York: Perseus Publishing, 1999); Rosen, *The Unwanted Gaze*; Ellen Alderman and Caroline Kennedy, *Right to Privacy* (New York: Knopf, 1995); Charles J. Sykes, *The End of Privacy* (New York: Saint Martin's Press, 1999).

24 Etzioni, *The Limits of Privacy*, pp. 196–7.

25 Based on results of a Lexis-Nexus search conducted on February 25, 2002 of articles that appeared between January 1, 2000 and January 31, 2000.

26 *Barnes* v. *Glen Theater, Inc.*, 501 US 560 (1991); *City of Erie* v. *Pap's A.M.*, 529 US 277 (2000).

27 See, e.g., David Cole, "Playing by Pornography's Rules," 143 *University of Pennsylvania Law Review* 111 (November 1994): 176.

28 Ibid.

29 Timothy M. Tesluk, "*Barnes* v. *Glen Theater*: Censorship? So What?," 42 *Case Western Reserve Law Review* 1103 (1992): 1126–7.

30 David Kushner, "Property Rights in Nude Sunbathing," 18 *Whittier Law Review* 261 (Winter 1997); Cole, "Playing by Pornography's Rules."

31 *Williams* v. *Hathaway*, 400 F. Supp. (D. Mass. 1975): 126, 127.

32 See, e.g., *Chapin* v. *Town of Southampton*, 457 F. Supp. 1170, 1174–5 (EDNY 1978).

33 *Cohen* v. *California*, 403 US 15 (1971): 21.
34 1 Cal. App. 3d 94, 97–8, 81 Cal. Rptr. 503, 505 (1969).
35 *Cohen* v. *California*, 403 US 15 (1971): 21, 25.
36 Hadley Arkes, *The Philosopher in the City* (Princeton, NJ: Princeton University Press, 1981), pp. 65–6.
37 Priscilla Regan, *Legislating Privacy* (Chapel Hill, NC: University of North Carolina Press, 1995), pp. 24–5.
38 Cited in ibid., p. 27.
39 Ibid., pp. 220–30.
40 Anita L. Allen, "Coercing Privacy," 40 *William and Mary Law Review* 723 (1999): 726–7.
41 Allen "The Wanted Gaze,", p. 2014.
42 Ibid., p. 2016.
43 Allen, "Coercing Privacy," p. 735.
44 Ibid., p. 747.
45 Some do refer to civic virtues such as voting and following public affairs, but these do not qualify by the definition of virtues here followed, namely moral excellence and doing good.
46 For additional discussion, see Etzioni, *The New Golden Rule* and Philip Selznick, *The Communitarian Persuasion* (Washington, DC: Woodrow Wilson Center Press, 2002).
47 See *The American Heritage Dictionary*, 3rd edn (1996), p. 1442, defining privacy as "The quality or condition of being secluded from the presence of view of others."
48 For additional criticism of the simplistic distinction between private and public space, see Jeff Weintraub and Krishan Kumar (eds.), *Public and Private in Thought and Practice: Perspectives on a Grand Dichotomy* (Chicago, IL: University of Chicago Press, 1997).
49 Felicity Barringer, "CBS News Criticized for Showing Part of Video of Slain Reporter," *New York Times*, May 16, 2002, p. A10.
50 *Ashcroft* v. *Free Speech Coalition*, No. 00–795, argued October 30, 2001, decided April 16, 2001. Available at <http://a257.g.akamaitech.net/7/257/2422/16apr20021045/www.supremecourtus.gov/opinions/01pdf/00 795.pd> (last visited July 31, 2002).
51 See *City of Renton* v. *Playtime Theaters, Inc.*, 475 US 41, 48 (1986).
52 See *Ginsberg* v. *New York*, 390 US 629 (1968).
53 See e.g., Judd Zulgad and Kevin Seifert, "Vikings Announcer Quits After One Game," *Star Tribune*, April 16, 2001, p. A1; Liz Clarke, "Packers' White Stands by Remarks," *Washington Post*, March 27, 1998, p. D01; Benjamin Pimentel, "KFRC Fires DJ Who Insulted Gays, Asians," *San Francisco Chronicle*, December 8, 1994, p. A21; and Paul D. Colford, "ABC Axe Chops Bob Grant After Ron Brown Remarks," *Newsday*, April 19, 1996, p. A05.
54 See, e.g., "Fundamental Standard Interpretation: Free Expression and Discriminatory Harassment," adopted by Stanford University, June

1990; *Doe* v. *University of Michigan*, 721 F. Supp. 852 (E.D. Mich. 1989); Report of President's Ad Hoc Committee on Racial Harassment, University of Texas at Austin 17 (November 27, 1989); University of Wisconsin Board of Regents, UWS 17.06(2)(a)(2) (effective September 1, 1990).

55 Criminal Code of Canada, Part VIII, §319; Kathleen E. Mahoney, "Hate Speech: Affirmation or Contradiction of Freedom of Expression," *University of Illinois Law Review* 789 (1966): 803.

56 See, e.g., Leonard Eron, et al., "Does Television Violence Cause Aggression?" 27 *American Psychologist* 4 (April 1972): 253–63; F. Scott Andison, "TV Violence and Viewer Aggression: A Cumulation of Study Results 1956–1976," 41 *Public Opinion Quarterly* 3 (Autumn 1977): 314–31; David Pearl, Lorraine Bouthilet, and Joyce B. Lazar (eds.), *Television and Behavior: Ten Years of Scientific Progress and Implications for the Eighties* (Rockville, MD: US Department of Health and Human Services, Public Health Service, Alcohol, Drug Abuse, and Mental Health Administration, National Institute of Health, 1982); L. Rowell Huesmann, Kirsti Lagerspetz, and Leonard D. Eron, "Intervening Variables in the TV Violence-Aggression Relation: Evidence from Two Countries," 20 *Developmental Psychology* 5 (September 1984): 746–75; Chris Boyatzis, Gina M. Matillo, and Kristen M. Nesbitt, "Effects of 'The Mighty Morphin Power Rangers' on Children's Aggression with Peers," 25 *Child Study Journal* 1 (1995): 45–55; Eric Dubow and Laurie S. Miller, "Television Viewing and Aggressive Behavior," in Tannis M. MacBeth (ed.), *Tuning into Young Viewers: Social Science Perspectives on Television* (Thousand Oaks, CA: Sage, 1996), pp. 117–47; Richard B. Felson, "Mass Media Effects on Violent Behavior," *Annual Review of Sociology* 22 (1996): 103–28; Stacy L. Smith and Edward Donnerstein, "Harmful Effects of Exposure to Media Violence: Learning of Aggression, Emotional Desensitization, and Fear," in Russell G. Geen and Edward Donnerstein (eds.), *Human Aggression: Theories, Research and Implications for Social Policy* (San Diego, CA: Academic Press, 1998), pp. 167–202; John Sherry, "The Effects of Violent Video Games on Aggression: A Meta-Analysis," 27 *Human Communication Research* 3 (July 2001): 409–31; Brad J. Bushman and Craig Anderson, "Media Violence and the American Public: Scientific Facts Versus Media Misinformation," 56 *American Psychologist* 6/7 (June/July 2001): 477–89.

57 See, e.g., Catharine A. MacKinnon, *Feminism Unmodified* (Cambridge, MA: Harvard University Press, 1987), pp. 127–62; Andrea Dworkin, *Pornography: Men Possessing Women* (New York: Plume, 1981).

58 Elizabeth Oddone-Paolucci, Mark Genius, and Claudio Violato, "A Meta-Analysis of the Published Research on the Effects of Pornography," in Claudio Violato, Elizabeth Oddone-Paolucci, and Mark Genius (eds.), *The Changing Family and Child Development* (Aldershot, UK: Ashgate Publishing, 2000), pp. 49, 51–3.

59 Mike Allen, Dave D'Alessio, and Keri Brezgel, "A Meta-Analysis Summarizing the Effects of Pornography: II. Aggression After Exposure," 22 *Human Communications Research* 2 (December 1995): 258–83.

60 Louis P. Masur, *Rites of Execution: Capital Punishment and The Transformation of American Culture, 1776–1865* (New York: Oxford University Press, 1989, p. 108.

61 See, e.g., "Witness to an Execution," *New York Times*, April 13, 2001, p. A16; Jonathan Kellerman, "Don't – It's Bloodlust," *USA Today*, July 11, 2001, p. 13A; Debra J. Saunders, "Executions Are Not for Prime Time," *San Francisco Chronicle*, April 29, 2001, p. D6; and Paul Finkelman, "Execution as Carnival," *Baltimore Sun*, April 22, 2001, p. 1C.

62 Anthony Lewis, "Their Brutal Mirth," *New York Times*, May 20, 1991, p. A15.

63 R. M. Hare, "Arguing About Rights," 33 *Emory Law Journal* 631 (Summer 1984): 641.

64 Though *Ginsberg* v. *New York* recognizes in general the duty of legislators in "safeguarding minors from harm," it discusses only the availability and possible harm of "sex material." *Ginsberg* v. *United States*, 390 US 629, 630 (1968). Similarly, the current California Penal Code defines "harmful material" as matter that "appeals to the prurient interest" and "depicts or describes in a patently offensive way sexual conduct": California Penal Code §313(a).

65 MO. Rev. Stat. §573.090 (Supp. 1992); Tenn. Code Ann. §39-17-911 (1993); and Colo. Rev. Stat. Ann. §18-7-601 (West 1992). For further discussion, see Jassalyn Hershinger, "State Restrictions on Violent Expression: The Impropriety of Extending an Obscenity Analysis," 46 *Vanderbilt University Law Review* 473 (1993). For further discussion of this issue, see Kevin W. Saunders, "Media Violence and the Obscenity Exception to the First Amendment," 3 *William and Mary Bill of Rights Journal* 107 (Summer 1994).

66 Mo. Rev. Stat. §573.090 (Supp. 1993) provides: "Video cassettes, morbid violence, to be kept in separate area – sale or rental to persons under seventeen prohibited, penalties 1. Video cassettes or other video reproduction devices, or the jackets, cases or coverings of such video reproduction devices shall be displayed or maintained in a separate area if the same are pornographic for minors as defined in section 573.010, or if: (1) Taken as a whole and applying contemporary community standards, the average person would find that it has a tendency to cater or appeal to morbid interest in violence for persons under the age of seventeen; and (2) It depicts violence in a way which is patently offensive to the average person applying contemporary adult community standards with respect to what is suitable for persons under the age of seventeen; and (3) Taken as a whole, it lacks serious literary, artistic, political, or scientific value for persons under the age of seventeen. 2. Any video cassettes or other video reproduction devices meeting the description in

subsection 1 of this section shall not be rented or sold to a person under the age of seventeen years. 3. Any violation of the provisions of subsection 1 or 2 of this section shall be punishable as an infraction, unless such violation constitutes furnishing pornographic materials to minors as defined in section 573.040, in which case it shall be punishable as a class A misdemeanor or class D felony as prescribed in section 573.040, or unless such violation constitutes promoting obscenity in the second degree as defined in section 573.030, in which case it shall be punishable as a class A misdemeanor or class D felony as prescribed in section 573.030."

67 *Video Software Dealers Association* v. *Webster*: 773 F. Supp. 1275 (W.D. Mo. 1991), aff'd, 968 F.2d 684 (8th Cir. 1992), p. 1278.

68 In the past, many EU member states have been able to protect minors from harmful material through a public monopoly on broadcasting that allowed them to keep certain materials off the air and sequester others to late-night hours. Recently, new technologies, such as the internet and satellite broadcasting, combined with an increase in the channels available, have required new means of regulating harmful content. Though so far most EU member countries have relied on self-regulation to protect children from harmful content in the media, the European Parliament found that government–industry cooperation in this matter has been quite productive. The European Parliament has recommended that member states take a more active role in regulating broadcasting, the internet, and video games, while continuing to build partnerships with industry and engaging in public campaigns to increase parental awareness and involvement. See Christopher J. P. Beazley, "Report on the Evaluation Report of the Commission to the Council and the European Parliament on the Application of the Council Recommendations of 24 September 1998 Concerning the Protection of Minors and Human Dignity," February 20, 2002 (European Parliament session document A5-0037/2002).

69 John Copeland Nagle, "Moral Nuisances," 50 *Emory Law Journal* 265 (Winter 2001): 265.

70 For further discussion, see Denise E. Antolini, "Modernizing Public Nuisance: Solving the Paradox of the Special Injury Rule," 28 *Ecology Law Quarterly* 755 (2001).

71 See, e.g., *Mark* v. *Oregon State Department of Fish and Wildlife*, 974 P. 2nd 716 (Or. Ct. App. 1999) (in which homeowners claimed that a nude beach adjacent to their property constituted a moral nuisance); Omar Saleem, "Killing the Proverbial Two Birds with One Stone: Using Environmental Statutes and Nuisance to Combat the Crime of Illegal Drug Trafficking," 100 *Dickinson Law Review* 685, 708–28 (1996) (describing the use of nuisance claims to shut down drug activity).

72 Nagle, "Moral Nuisances."

73 See, e.g., Ala. Code section 13A-6-68 (1994); Alaska Stat. section 11.41. 460 (1989); Ariz. Rev. Stat. Ann. section 13-1402 (1989); Colo. Rev. Stat.

Ann. section 18-7-302 (West 1990 & Supp. 1994); Del. Code Ann. tit. 11, sections 764–5 (Supp. 1994); Fla. Stat. Ann. section 800.03 (West Supp. 1995); Haw. Rev. Stat. sections 707–34 (1994); Ind. Code Ann. section 35-45-4-1 (Burns 1994); Iowa Code Ann. section 709.9 (West 1993); Kan. Stat. Ann. section 21-3508 (Supp. 1994); Ky. Rev. Stat. Ann. section 510. 150 (Michie/ Bobbs-Merrill 1990); La. Rev. Stat. Ann. section 14:106 (A)(1) (West 1986); Me. Rev. Stat. Ann. tit. 17-A, section 854 (West Supp. 1994); Mont. Code Ann. section 45-5-504 (1993); Neb. Rev. Stat. section 28-806 (1989); N.H. Rev. Stat. Ann. section 645:1 (Supp. 1994); N.J. Stat. Ann. section 2C:14-4 (West Supp. 1995); N.M. Stat. Ann. section 30-9-14 (Michie 1994); N.D. Cent. Code section 12.1-20-12.1 (1985); Okla. Stat. tit. 21, section 1021 (West Supp. 1995); Or. Rev. Stat. section 163.465 (1990); 18 Pa. Cons. Stat. section 3127 (1983); R.I. Gen. Laws section 11-45-1(7) (1994); S.D. Codified Laws Ann. section 22-24-1 (Supp. 1995); Tenn. Code Ann. section 39-13-511 (Supp. 1994); Tex. Penal Code Ann. section 21.08 (West 1994); Utah Code Ann. section 76-9-702 (1995); W. Va. Code section 61-8-9 (1992); Wis. Stat. section 944.20 (Supp. 1994).

74 *Barnes* v. *Glen Theater, Inc.*, 501 US 560 (1991), citing *Winters* v. *New York*, 333 US 507, 515 (1948): "Acts of gross and open indecency or obscenity, injurious to public morals, are indictable at common law, as violative of the public policy that requires from the offender retribution for acts that flaunt accepted standards of conduct. When a legislative body concludes that the mores of the community call for an extension of the impermissible limits, an enactment aimed at the evil is plainly within its power, if it does not transgress the boundaries fixed by the Constitution for freedom of expression" (citations omitted); *Le Roy* v. *Sidley*, 1 Sid. 168, 82 Eng. Rep. 1036 (K.B. 1664).

75 Jeffrey Narvil, "Revealing the Bare Uncertainties of Indecent Exposure," 29 *Columbia Journal of Law and Social Problems* 85 (Fall 1995).

76 Ibid.

77 See, e.g., Wash. Rev. Code Ann. 9A 88.010 (West) (amended by Laws 1987, ch. 277, 1): "(1) A person is guilty of indecent exposure if he intentionally makes any open and obscene exposure of his person or the person of another knowing that such conduct is likely to cause reasonable affront or alarm ..."

See also Haw. Rev. Stat. 707–38 (1985): "(1) A person commits the offense of indecent exposure if, with intent to arouse or gratify sexual desire of himself or of any person, he exposes his genitals to a person to whom he is not married under circumstances in which his conduct is likely to cause affront or alarm."

78 *Redrup* v. *New York*, 386 US 767, 769 (1967).

79 *Barnes* v. *Glen Theater, Inc.*, 501 US 560 (1991): 575.

80 "Contemporary public concern for protecting nature's ecological equilibrium should lead to the conferral of standing upon environmental objects to sue for their own preservation." *Sierra Club* v. *Morton*, 405

US 727 (1972), p. 741 (Douglas, J. dissenting; citations omitted). For further discussion of this argument, see Christopher D. Stone, "Should Trees Have Standing? Toward Legal Rights for Natural Objects," 45 *S. California Law Review* 450 (1972).

81 The extent to which moral culture is shared with other societies, and the place which universal truth holds in it, are subjects beyond the scope of this essay. See, e.g., Etzioni, *The New Golden Rule*, pp. 217–37.

82 For further explication of this approach, see James Q. Wilson and George L. Kelling, "Broken Windows," *The Atlantic Monthly* (March 1982): 29–38.

83 For further discussion, see George L. Kelling and Catherine M. Coles, *Fixing Broken Windows: Restoring Order and Reducing Crime in Our Communities* (New York: Martin Kessler Books, 1996). For a critique of "broken window" theory and its effectiveness, see Bernard E. Harcourt, "Reflecting on the Subject: A Critique of the Social Influence Conception of Deterrence, the Broken Windows Theory, and Order-Maintenance Policing in New York City," 97 *Michigan Law Review* 291 (November 1998).

84 Robert J. Sampson, Stephen W. Raudenbush, and Felton Earls, "Neighborhoods and Violent Crime: A Multilevel Study of Collective Efficacy," *Science* (August 1997): 918–24.

85 Sissela Bok, *Lying: Moral Choice in Public and Private Life* (New York: Pantheon Books, 1978), pp. 26–7.

86 Barrington Moore, *Privacy* (Armonk, NY: M.E. Sharpe, 1984), pp. 59–60, 66–71.

87 Warren and Brandeis, "The Right to Privacy" (italics added).

88 It is purported that Mrs Samuel Warren's concern over gossip and the voyeuristic nature of media reporting prompted her to encourage her husband to defend the right to privacy. Richard A. Prosser, "The Right of Privacy," 12 *Georgia Law Review* (1978): 383.

89 Harry M. Clor, "The Death of Public Morality?" 45 *American Journal of Jurisprudence*. 33 (2000): 33, 34, 36, 37, 44–5.

90 Nagle, "Moral Nuisances," p. 304.

91 *United States* v. *O'Brien*, 391 US 367 (1968), p. 376.

92 *Barnes* v. *Glen Theater, Inc.*, 501 US 560 (1991).

93 *City of Erie* v. *Pap's A.M.*, 529 US 277 (2000).

94 553 Pa. 348, 719 A 2d, p. 273.

95 Ibid., p. 279.

96 *Barnes* v. *Glen Theater, Inc.*, 501 US 560 (1991), p. 568.

97 Ibid., citing *Roth* v. *United States*, 354 US 476 (1957), pp. 485, 575.

98 Brooks, *Nine Parts of Desire*, pp. 17, 21.

99 Hilary Von Rohr, "Lactation Litigation and the ADA Solution: A Response to *Martinez* v. *NBC*," 4 *Washington University Journal of Law and Policy* 341 (2000); Kushner, "Property Rights in Nude Sunbathing," p. 273.

100 Narvil, "Revealing the Bare Uncertainties," pp. 90, 111.
101 Alexis de Tocqueville, *Democracy in America* (New York: Harper, 1966), vol. 1, pp. 290–4; cited in Clor, "The Death of Public Morality?" p. 33.
102 Clor, "The Death of Public Morality?" p. 33.
103 *Sexuality Information and Education Council of the United States, Guidelines for Comprehensive Sexuality Education*, 2nd edn (Sexuality Information and Education Council, 1996), p. 7; Mirian Ehrenberg and Otto Ehrenberg, *The Intimate Circle* (New York: Simon & Schuster, 1988), pp. 40–58.
104 Sigmund Freud, *Civilization and its Discontents*, ed. and trans. James Strachey (Norton & Company, 1961; orig. pub. 1930), pp. 22–36.
105 Moore, *Privacy*, p. 71.
106 The violent crime rate was 160 offenses per 100,000 inhabitants in 1960 and 732 offenses per 100,000 inhabitants in 1990. US Department of Justice, *Uniform Crime Reports for the United States: 1993* (Washington, DC: GPO, 1993), table 1; and US Department of Commerce, *Historical Statistics of the United States: Colonial Times to 1970, Part I* (Washington, DC: GPO, 1975) H952-61. For further evidence of antisocial developments, see William J. Bennett, *The Index of Leading Cultural Indicators: American Society at the End of the Twentieth Century* (New York: Simon & Schuster, 1999).
107 Etzioni, *The New Golden Rule*, pp. 3–33.
108 For further discussion of moral dialogues, see ibid., ch. 4.

CHAPTER 3 CHILDREN AND FREE SPEECH

1 See Combined Proposed Findings of Fact of the ACLU and ALA Plaintiffs in the cases of *ACLU* v. *Reno* and *ALA* v. *Reno*, April 29, 1996. Available at <http://www.aclu.org/issues/cyber/trial/finding. htm> (last visited June 18, 2002). Civil libertarians find very little speech they would agree to bar. For instance, they hold that using children to make child pornography is indeed a crime because children are abused, but once a tape is made, it should not be suppressed since the children were already harmed and suppressing the tape would create a precedent for limiting speech. Thus, when the Supreme Court upheld a New York State statute making the sale of child pornography illegal, the ACLU's Jack Novik denounced child pornography as "ugly, vicious stuff" that should be fought through stronger laws against exploitation of minors, but denounced the Court's decision, saying: "Government intrusion into freedom of speech is expanded." "Impact of Court's Child Pornography Ruling Assessed," *Christian Science Monitor*, July 7, 1982, p. 3.
2 See, e.g., David Burt (ed.), *Dangerous Access: Uncovering Internet Pornography in America's Libraries* (Family Research Council, 2000).

3 This idea is developed in Amitai Etzioni, *The New Golden Rule: Community and Morality in a Democratic Society* (New York: Basic Books, 1996).
4 The choice of the term "value" rather than "right" is deliberate here; rights imply things much less given to balancing with other considerations than values, for which one recognizes possible conflicts that will have to be worked out.
5 Communications Decency Act of 1996, Pub. L. No. 104–104, 110 Stat. 133 (1996); Child Online Protection Act, Pub. L. No. 105–277, 112 Stat. 2681–736 (1998); Children's Internet Protection Act, P.L. No. 106–554, tit. xii, 114 Stat. 2763, 2763A-335 (2001), codified at 20 USC §9134 and 47 USC §254(h).
6 *Prince* v. *Massachusetts*, 321 US 158, 170 (1944) (upholding the "interests of society to protect the welfare of children, and the state's assertion of authority to that end").
7 *Ginsberg* v. *New York*, 390 US 629, 630 (1968).
8 Ibid., pp. 629–30.
9 *FCC* v. *Pacifica Foundation*, 438 US 726 (1978), pp. 733, 757, 758.
10 See *Chaplinsky* v. *New Hampshire*, 315 US 568, 572 (1942). For discussion of the fighting words doctrine and its application, see also Note "The Demise of the Chaplinsky Fighting Words Doctrine: An Argument for its Interment," 106 *Harvard Law Reveiw* 1129 (March 1993); Michael J. Mannheimer, "The Fighting Words Doctrine," 93 *Columbia Law Review* 1527 (October 1993); and Melody L. Hurdle, "*R.A.V.* v. *City of St. Paul*: The Continuing Confusion of the Fighting Words Doctrine," 47 *Vanderbilt Law Review* 1143 (May 1994).
11 *Reno* v. *ACLU*, 521 US 844, 882 (1997), pp. 1, 39, 48, 39–43.
12 *ACLU* v. *Reno*, 31 F. Supp. 2d 473, 476 (E.D. Pa. 1999); *ACLU* v. *Reno*, 217 F.3d 162, 173 (2000).
13 *Roth* vs. *United States*, 354 US 476 (1957).
14 Warren Richey, "Porn Cases Exacerbate Divide on High Court," *Christian Science Monitor*, May 15, 2002, p. 2.
15 Charles Lane, "Justices Partially Back Cyber Pornography Law," *Washington Post*, May 14, 2002, p. A03.
16 Linda Greenhouse, "Justices Give Reprieve to an Internet Pornography Statute," *New York Times*, May 14, 2002, p. A17.
17 Cited in ibid.
18 For a full discussion of this concept, see Eugene Volokh, "Speech and Spillover," posted July 19, 1996. Available at <http://slate.msn.com/default.aspx?id=2371> (last visited May 15, 2002).
19 The United States Code makes it a crime not only to produce child pornography, which constitutes the sexual exploitation of minors (18 USC 2151), but also to distribute or possess child pornography (18 USC 2252). The justification for prohibiting the possession of child pornography as well as the production was laid out in *New York* v.

Ferber, 458 US 747 (1982), which states that "the distribution network for child pornography must be closed if the production of material which requires the sexual exploitation of children is to be effectively controlled."

20 Justin Blum, "For Black, Core Support Was the Difference," *Washington Post*, February 8, 1998, p. V01; Victoria Benning, "Two Conservatives to Leave Library Board," *Washington Post*, June 13, 1996, p. V01; Peter Pae, "Abortion Rights Group Opens Office in 'Conservative Country'," *Washington Post*, June 20, 1994, p. B1; "Virginia Library Board Adopts Internet Restrictions," *ACLU News Wire* (ACLU, New York, NY), August 5, 1997.

21 "Virginia County Restricts Net Access in Libraries," *ACLU News Wire* (ACLU, New York, NY), October 24, 1997.

22 *Mainstream Loudoun* v. *Board of Trustees of the Loudoun County Library*, 24 F. Supp. 2d 552 (E.D. Va., 1998).

23 "Loudoun Country Public Library, Policy on Internet Sexual Harassment" (October 20, 1997). Available at <http://www.loudoun.net/ mainstream/ Library/summintpol.htm> (last visited May 13, 2002).

24 *Mainstream Loudoun*, 24 F. Supp. 2d., at 4.

25 Ibid., pp. 45, 18, 24, 28.

26 Ibid., p. 30 (referring to *Turner Systems, Inc.* v. *FCC*, 512 US 622, 664, and *Johnson* v. *Los Angeles Fire Department*, 865 F. Supp. 1430, 1439 (C.D. Cal. 1994)).

27 Ibid., pp. 36, 30.

28 Ibid., p. 40.

29 Ibid., pp. 41–2.

30 Kern County Board of Supervisors, Resolution 96–341 (July 30, 1996) (available at <http://www.kerncountylibrary.org/resolution.html>).

31 Letter from Ann Beeson, ACLU National Legal Department, to Bernard C. Barmann, Kern County Counsel (January 21, 1998). Available at <http://www.aclu.org/issues/cyber/kerncodemand.html> (last visited May 14, 2002).

32 Ibid.

33 Ibid.

34 The ALA has released a statement that "The use in libraries of software filters to block constitutionally protected speech is inconsistent with the United States Constitution and federal law and may lead to legal exposure for the library and its governing authorities. The American Library Association affirms that the use of filtering software by libraries to block access to constitutionally protected speech violates the Library Bill of Rights." American Library Association Intellectual Freedom Committee, Statement on Library Use of Filtering Software (July 1, 1997; revised November 17, 2000). Available at <http://www. ala.org/alaorg/oif/filt_stm.html> (last accessed July 8, 2002).

35 Ibid.

36 Letter from Bernard C. Barmann, Kern County Counsel, to Ann Beeson, ACLU Foundation (January 27, 1998). Available at <http://www.aclu.org/news/n012898d.html> (last visited July 24, 2001).

37 Memorandum from Marje Rump to All Kern County Library Branches (January 27, 1998). Available at <http://www.aclu.org/news/n012898d.html> (last visited July 24, 2002).

38 Letter from Ann Beeson, ACLU National Legal Department, to Bernard C. Barmann, Kern County Counsel (January 28, 1998). Available at <http://www.aclu.org/news/n01898d.html>.

39 Federal Communications Commission, Report and Order on CIPA (April 5, 2001).

40 Response in Opposition of Plaintiffs Multnomah County Public Library et al. to Defendants' Motion to Dismiss, p. 16; *American Library Association et al.* v. *United States of America, et al.* (No. 01-CV-1303) and *Multnomah County et al.* v. *United States of America et al.* (No. 01-CV-1322).

41 Press Release, Senator John McCain, "Congress Passes Internet Filtering For Schools, Libraries" (December 15, 2000). Available at <http://mccain.senate.gov/intfinal.htm> (last visited May 24, 2002).

42 Children's Internet Protection Act, H.R. 4577, 106th Cong. (2000), §1703(b)(1) (hereinafter CIPA legislation).

43 Ibid., §1703(b)(2).

44 Peg Brickley, "Internet Decency Standards Pose Ethical and Financial Problems for Many Companies, Schools and Libraries," *Corporate Legal Times* (October 2001): 80.

45 CIPA legislation, §1712 (f)(1).

46 *American Library Association et al.* v. *United States of America et al.* and *Multnomah County et al.* v. *United States of America et al.* See also John Schwartz, "Law Limiting Internet in Libraries Challenged," *New York Times*, March 25, 2002, p. A18. Other plaintiffs include the Multnomah (Ore) County Public Library system, librarians, patrons, website providers, and Jeffrey L. Pollock, a Republican candidate for Congress who was a proponent of mandatory filtering software until he learned that his campaign website was blocked by a popular filtering program.

47 Plaintiffs' Joint Pretrial Brief, 3-20-02, p. 8: *American Library Association et al.* v. *United States of America et al.* and *Multnomah County et al.* v. *United States of America et al.* (hereinafter ALA/Multnomah County Joint Pretrial Brief).

48 Ibid., p. 11.

49 Ibid. For example, filters have blocked websites such as <www.the-strippers.com> (wood varnish removal service), <www.muchlove.org> (a non-profit organization dedicated to rescuing animals) and that of House Majority Whip Richard "Dick" Armey.

50 Ibid., pp. 8–9.

51 Ibid., p. 9.

52 Children's Internet Protection Act, P.L. No. 106–554, tit. xii, 114 stat. 2763, 2763A-335 (2001), codified at 20 USC §9134 and 47 USC §254(h).

53 ALA/Multnomah County Joint Pretrial Brief, p. 10. Though CIPA allows a research exemption for all patrons at schools and libraries receiving Museum and Library Services Act funds and Secondary Education Act funds (20 USC 9134(f)(3) and 20 USC 3601 (3))), it allows only exemptions for adults in libraries receiving e-rate funds (47 USC 254(h)(6)(D))).

54 Robert O'Harrow, Jr., "Curbs on Web Access Face Attack; Content Filters for Children Also Restrict Adults, Groups Say," *Washington Post*, March 20, 2001, p. A4.

55 Defendants' Pretrial Brief, p. 2, *American Library Association et al.* v. *United States of America et al.* and *Multnomah County et al.* v. *United States of America et al.* (hereinafter Defendants' Pretrial Brief).

56 Cited in O'Harrow, "Curbs on Web Access Face Attack."

57 Donna Rice Hughes, *Kids Online: Protecting Your Children In Cyberspace* (Old Tappan, NJ: Fleming H. Revell Co., 1998).

58 Cited in John Schwartz, "Internet Filters Used to Shield Minors Censor Speech, Critics Say," *New York Times*, March 19, 2001, p. A15.

59 Defendants' Pretrial Brief, at 2.

60 Cited in Brickley, "Internet Decency Standards Pose Ethical and Financial Problems."

61 Cited by Bob Keveney in *The Daily Record*, March 9, 2002, p. A13.

62 "Should Libraries Pull the Plug on Web Site Obscenity? Kids, Porn and Library Censors," *San Francisco Chronicle*, August 5, 2001 (debate between Judith Krug of the ALA and Mike Millen of the Pacific Justice Institute).

63 Ibid.

64 Ibid.

65 Opinion of the Court, *American Library Association et al.* v. *United States of America et al.* and *Multnomah County et al.* v. *United States of America et al.* (hereinafter *ALA* v. *United States*).

66 Ibid.

67 David Burt, spokesman for the N2H2 Inc. software filtering company, claims that his company's filters have a "99-plus percent accuracy rate." John Schwartz, "Court Overturns Law Mandating Internet Filters for Public Libraries," *New York Times*, June 1, 2002, p. A1.

68 *ALA* v. *United States*.

69 "National Association of Attorneys General, Tobacco Settlement Summary" (November 6, 1998). Available at <http://www.naag.org/tobac/glance.htm> (last visited July 24, 2002). (Hereinafter NAAG tobacco settlement summary.)

70 Ibid.

71 National Youth Tobacco Survey (NYTS), conducted by the American Legacy Foundation and the CDC Foundation, fall 1999. A summary of

this survey is available at <http://www.cdc.gov/mmwr/preview/mmwrhtml/mm4903a1.htm> (last visited April 5, 2002).

72 For a discussion of the importance of the content of peer pressure, see Amitai Etzioni, *A Comparative Analysis of Complex Organizations*, revised edition (New York: The Free Press, 1975), pp. 279–302.

73 61 Fed. Reg. 45239, 45247.

74 *Lorillard Tobacco* v. *Rielly*, 121 S. Ct. 2404, 2432 (2001), citing 60 Fed. Reg. 41332, p. 28.

75 Ibid., citing 61 Fed. Reg. 45246 (Fischer Schwartz & Richards, Brand Logo Recognition by Children Aged 3 to 6 Years, Mickey Mouse and Old Joe the Camel.)

76 Tobacco Information and Prevention Source, "Trends in Smoking Initiation Among Adolescents and Young Adults" (July 21, 1995). Available at <http://ww.cdc.gov/nccdphp/osh/ythstart.htm>.

77 Federal Trade Commission, "Complaint in the Matter of R. J. Reynolds Tobacco Company," May 28, 1997. Available at <http://www.ftc.gov/os/1997/9705/d9285cmp.htm> (last visited April 19, 2002).

78 Paul Farhi, "Push to Ban Joe Camel May Run Out of Breath," *The Washington Post*, December 4, 1993, p. C1.

79 "Justice Department Suing Tobacco Firms," *USA Today*, September 22, 1999. Available at <http://www.usatoday.com/news/smoke/smoke287.htm>.

80 NAAG tobacco settlement summary.

81 ACLU Freedom Network, "Paternalism and the Harkin-Bradley Bill: Proposal on Tobacco Advertising Would Violate the First Amendment," March 21, 1998: available at <http://www.aclu.org/news/n032195.html>. Tobacco Hearing on Advertising Marketing and Labeling Before the Senate Commerce, Science and Transportation Committee, 105th Cong. (1998) (statement of the American Civil Liberties Union): available at <http://www.aclu.org/congres/t030398a.html> (last visited April 19, 2002).

82 Hearing on the Global Tobacco Settlement Before the Senate Committee on the Judiciary, 105th Cong. (1997) (statement of Robert A. Levy, Ph.D., J.D., Senior Fellow in Constitutional Studies, The Cato Institute). Available at <http://www.cato.org/testimony/ct-bl071697.html> (last visited May 20, 2002).

83 Classification and Ratings Administration, "Questions and Answers: Everything You Always Wanted to Know About the Movie Rating System." Available at <http://www.filmratings.com/questons.htm> (last accessed April 22, 2002). (Hereinafter CARA Q&A.)

84 American Civil Liberties Union, "Popular Music Under Siege." Available at <http://www.aclu.org/library/pbr3.html> (last accessed April 22, 2002). (Hereinafter Popular Music Under Siege.)

85 Telecommunications Act of 1996, Public Law 104–104, section 551 (b)(1). (Hereinafter 1996 Telecom Act).

86 Ibid., section 551 (e)(1)(A).
87 Press Release, Federal Communications Commission, ' "Commission Finds Industry Video Programming Rating System Acceptable; Adopts Technical Requirements to Enable Blocking of Video Programming" (March 12, 1998). Available at <http://www.fcc.gov/bureaus/cable/news_releases/1998/nrcb8003.html> (last accessed April 19, 2002).
88 Hearing on the Matter of Industry Proposal for Rating Video Programming Before the Federal Communications Commission, May 8, 1997 (reply comments of the American Civil Liberties Union). Available at <http://www.aclu.org/congress/1050897a.html> (last visited April 22, 2002). (Hereinafter ACLU comments on ratings.)
89 Popular Music Under Siege.
90 Press Release, American Civil Liberties Union, "FCC Gives Final Approval to V-Chip Technology," March 12, 1998. Available at <http://www.aclu.org/news/n031298a.html> (last visited August 22, 2002); Press Release, American Civil Liberties Union, "ACLU Expresses Concerns on TV Rating Scheme; Says 'Voluntary' System is Government-Backed Censorship," February 29, 1996. Available at <http://www.aclu.org/news/n022996b.html> (last accessed August 22, 2002). Aside for the reasons discussed in the text, the ACLU also opposed V-chips as forms of government censorship. Though the government requires that the V-chip be built into televisions, it is voluntarily activated and used.
91 Marjorie Heins, "Screening Out Sex: Kids, Computers, and the New Censors," *The American Prospect* (July/August 1998): 41 (emphasis added). See also Marjorie Heins, "Rejuvenating Free Expression," *Dissent* (Summer 1999).
92 Paul Farhi, "FCC Set to Back V-Chip," *The Washington Post*, March 6, 1998, p. G03.
93 Rhoda Rabkin, "Guarding Children: No Need for Government Censorship," *Current* (May 2002): 19.
94 American Civil Liberties Union, "Fahrenheit 451.2: Is Cyberspace Burning?," August 7, 1997. Available at <http://www.aclu.org/issues/cyber/burning.html> (last accessed April 22, 2002). (Hereinafter Fahrenheit 451.2.)
95 See, e.g., Reno v. ACLU, 521 US 844, 882 (1997); ALA v. Pataki, 969 F. Supp. 160; ACLU v. Johnson, 194 F. 3d 1149 (10th Cir. 1999).
96 Nancy Willard, "The Constitutionality and Advisability of the Use of Commercial Filtering Software in US Public Schools," 2002, p. 7. Available at <http://netizen.uoregon.edu/Constitutionality.pdf> (last visited July 12, 2002).
97 This problem of distinguishing between protected and unprotected speech was discussed eloquently by Justice Brennan in his dissenting opinion in *Paris Adult Theatre I* v. *Slaton* 413 US 49 (1973), pp. 73–7 (Justice Brennan joined by Justices Stewart and Marshall, dissenting).
98 ALA v. United States.

99 Volokh, "Speech and Spillover."
100 Such an assertion is supported by the ruling in *Ginsberg* v. *New York*, 390 US 629, 630 (1968).
101 For an in-depth discussion of the balancing of privacy with various public interests, see Amitai Etzioni, *The Limits of Privacy* (New York: Basic Books, 1999).
102 ACLU Freedom Network, "ACLU Joins Opposition to Tobacco Pact; Says Speech Limits are Unconstitutional," March 24, 1998. Available at <http://www.aclu.org/news/n032498b.html> (last visited July 24, 2002). "Tobacco Hearing on Advertising, Marketing, and Labeling Before the Senate Committee on Commerce, Science, and Transportation," 105th Cong. (1998) (statement of the American Civil Liberties Union). Available at <http://www.aclu.org/congress/t030398a.html> (last visited July 24, 2002).
103 *Butler* v. *Michigan*, 352 US 380 (1957) at 383.
104 See *Virginia State Bd. of Pharmacy* v. *Virginia Citizens' Consumer Council*, 425 US 748, 771–2 (1976).
105 Television Decoder Circuitry Act of 1990, codified at 47 USC 303(u); Telecomm. Act of 1996, sec. 551 (c), codified at 47 USC 303 (x).
106 Information about the V-chip and its use is available at <http://www.fcc.gov/vchip>, but the government is not actively promoting it through such means as advertisements or brochures.
107 In 1999 the FCC established a V-chip Task Force to ensure correct implementation of FCC rules regarding the V-chip and television ratings. The Task Force was also charged with gathering information on the "availability, usage and effectiveness of the V-Chip." Press Release, Federal Communications Commission, "FCC Chairman William E. Kennard Established Task Force to Monitor and Assist in the Roll-out of the V-Chip" (May 10, 1999). Available at <http://www.fcc.gov/Bureaus/Miscellaneous/News_Releases/1999/nrmc9026.html> (last visited June 17, 2002). The Task Force has not yet released a report on the effectiveness of the V-chip or the current ratings system, as I was unable to find any outside report on this matter.
108 Though public school teachers are government actors, meaning the First Amendment does technically apply, there is Supreme Court precedent that allows teachers and administrators to limit a student's speech rights under certain circumstances. In Tinker v. Des Moines Independent Community School District, the Supreme Court held that First Amendment protection does not extend to student speech which "materially disrupts class work or involves substantial disorder or invasion of the rights of others" (393 US 503 (1969), p. 513). Later, in *Bethel School District No. 403* v. *Fraser*, the Court held that a student's right to speech must be "balanced against the society's countervailing interest in teaching students the boundaries of socially appropriate behavior" (478 US 675 (1986), p. 681).

109   *Tinker* v. *Des Moines Independent Community School District*, p. 513;
      Bethel School District No. 403 v. *Fraser*, p. 681.
110   Popular Music Under Siege; ACLU comments on ratings.
111   Brickley, "Internet Decency Standards Pose Ethical and Financial
      Problems."
112   Jim Rutenberg, "Survey Shows Few Parents Use TV V-Chip to Limit
      Children's Viewing," *New York Times*, July 25, 2001, p. E1; Andy
      Seiler, "Movie Theaters Vow to Enforce Ratings," *USA Today*,
      November 7, 2000, p. 1D. According to a Princeton Survey Research
      Associates poll, only 38 percent of the adult parents of children who
      use the internet polled said they had software on their home com-
      puters that prevents users from accessing certain types of material.
      Roper Center at the University of Connecticut, accession number
      0383943, question number 028, July 20, 2001.
113   See *Ginsberg* v. *New York*, 390 US 629 (1968).
114   See *Reno* v. *ACLU*, 521 US 844, 882 (1997).
115   Popular Music Under Siege.
116   ACLU comments on ratings, n. 9.
117   See, e.g., Leonard Eron, et al., "Does Television Violence Cause Ag-
      gression?" 27 *American Psychologist* 4 (1972): 253; F. Scott Andison,
      "TV Violence and Viewer Aggression: A Cumulation of Study Results
      1956–1976," 41 *Public Opinion Quarterly* 3 (Autumn 1977): 314;
      David Pearl, Lorraine Bouthilet, and Joyce B. Lazar (eds.), *National
      Institute of Mental Health, Television and Behavior: Ten Years of Sci-
      entific Progress and Implications for the Eighties* (US Department of
      Health and Human Services, 1982); L. Rowell Huesmann, Kirsti
      Lagerspetz, and Leonard D. Eron, "Intervening Variables in the TV
      Violence–Aggression Relation: Evidence from Two Countries," 20 *De-
      velopmental Psychology* 5 (1984): 746; Eric Dubow and Laurie S.
      Miller, "Television Viewing and Aggressive Behavior," in Tannis M.
      MacBeth (ed.), *Tuning into Young Viewers: Social Science Perspectives
      on Television* ((Thousand Oaks, CA: Sage, 1996), pp. 117–47; Richard
      B. Felson, "Mass Media Effects on Violent Behavior," 22 *Annual
      Review of Sociology* 103 (1996); Stacy L. Smith and Edward Donner-
      stein, "Harmful Effects of Exposure to Media Violence: Learning of
      Aggression, Emotional Desensitization, and Fear," in Russell G. Geen
      and Edward Donnerstein (eds.), *Human Aggression: Theories, Re-
      search and Implications for Social Policy* (San Diego, CA: Academic
      Press, 1998), pp. 167–202; John Sherry, "The Effects of Violent Video
      Games on Aggression: A Meta-Analysis," 27 *Human Communication
      Research* 3 (2001): 409.
118   See above, pp. 72–5.
119   Though *Ginsberg* v. *New York* recognizes in general the duty of legis-
      lators in "safeguarding minors from harm," it discusses only the avail-
      ability and possible harm of "sex material." Similarly, the current

California Penal Code defines "harmful material" as matter that "appeals to the prurient interest" and "depicts or describes in a patently offensive way sexual conduct" (Cal. Penal Code §313(a)).

120 Mo. Rev. Stat. §573.090 (supp. 1992); Tenn. Code Ann. §39-17-911 (1993); and Colo. Rev. Stat. Ann. §18-7-601 (west 1992). For further discussion, see Jassalyn Hershinger, "State Restrictions On Violent Expression: The Impropriety of Extending an Obscenity Analysis," 46 *Vanderbilt Law Review* 473 (1993). For further discussion of this issue, see Kevin W. Saunders, "Media Violence and the Obscenity Exception to the First Amendment," 3 *William and Mary Bill of Rights Journal* 107 (Summer 1994).

121 *Video Software Dealers Association* v. *Webster* 773 F. Supp. 1275 (W.D. Mo. 1991), aff'd, 968 F.2d 684 (8th Cir. 1992), p. 1278. Mo. Rev. Stat. §573.090 (supp. 1992) provides: "Video cassettes, morbid violence, to be kept in separate area – sale or rental to persons under seventeen prohibited, penalties. 1. Video cassettes or other video reproduction devices, or the jackets, cases or coverings of such video reproduction devices shall be displayed or maintained in a separate area if the same are pornographic for minors as defined in section 573.010, or if: (1) Taken as a whole and applying contemporary community standards, the average person would find that it has a tendency to cater or appeal to morbid interest in violence for persons under the age of seventeen; and (2) It depicts violence in a way which is patently offensive to the average person applying contemporary adult community standards with respect to what is suitable for persons under the age of seventeen; and (3) Taken as a whole, it lacks serious literary, artistic, political, or scientific value for persons under the age of seventeen. 2. Any video cassettes or other video reproduction devices meeting the description in subsection 1 of this section shall not be rented or sold to a person under the age of seventeen years. 3. Any violation of the provisions of subsection 1 or 2 of this section shall be punishable as an infraction, unless such violation constitutes furnishing pornographic materials to minors as defined in section 573.040, in which case it shall be punishable as a class A misdemeanor or class D felony as prescribed in section 573.040, or unless such violation constitutes promoting obscenity in the second degree as defined in section 573.030, in which case it shall be punishable as a class A misdemeanor or class D felony as prescribed in section 573.030."

122 See Sissela Bok, *Mayhem: Violence as Public Entertainment* (Reading, MA: Addison-Wesley, 1998), p. 57.

123 Monroe Lefkowitz, Leonard D. Enron, Leopold O. Walder, and L. Rowell Huesmann, *Growing Up to be Violent: A Longitudinal Study of the Development of Aggression* (New York: Pergamon Press, 1977), pp. 115–16 (emphasis in original). L. Rowell Huesmann et al., "Stabil-

ity of Aggression Over Time and Generations," 20 *Developmental Psychology* (1984): 1120. For criticisms of the methods and findings of this study, see Marjorie Heins, *Not in Front of the Children* (New York: Hill and Wang, 2001), pp. 248–50 and Jonathan Freedman, "Effect of Television Violence on Aggressiveness," 96 *Psychology Bulletin* 227 (1984): 241–3.

124 See, e.g., Albert Bandura, "Influence of Model's Reinforcement Contingencies on the Acquisition of Imitative Responses," 1 *Journal of Personality and Social Psychology* 6 (1965): 589; Edward Donnerstein, Ronald Slaby, and Leonard Eron, "The Mass Media and Youth Aggression," in Leonard Eron, Jacquelyn Gentry, and Peggy Schlegel (eds.), *Reason to Hope: A Psychological Perspective on Violence and Youth* (Washington, DC: American Psychological Association, 1994), pp. 219–50. See also Surgeon General's Scientific Advisory Committee on Television and Social Behavior, *Television and Growing Up: The Impact of Televised Violence. Report to the Surgeon General, United State Public Health Service* (National Institute of Mental Health, 1972).

125 Tannis MacBeth Williams, "Background and Overview," in Tannis MacBeth Williams (ed.), *The Impact of Television: A Natural Experiment in Three Communities* (Orlando, Florida: Academic Press, Inc., 1986), p. 4.

126 Lesley A. Joy, Meredith Kimball, and Merle L. Zabrack, "Television and Children's Aggressive Behavior," in Tannis MacBeth Williams (ed.), *The Impact of Television: A Natural Experiment in Three Communities* (Orlando, Florida: Academic Press, Inc., 1986), pp. 334–5, 320–1.

127 Edith Fairman Cooper, "Television Violence: A Survey of Selected Social Science Research Linking Violent Program Viewing With Aggression in Children and Society," CRS Report 95–593, May 17, 1995, p. 2.

128 Hearing on the Effects of Television Violence on Children Before the Senate Committee on Commerce Science and Transportation, 106th Cong. 1999 (statement of Leonard Eron).

129 Rowell Huesmann et al., "Stability of Aggression Over Time and Generations," pp. 1120–34.

130 Jeffrey G. Johnson, Patricia Cohen, Elizabeth M. Smailes, Stephanie Kasen, and Judith S. Brook, "Television Viewing and Aggressive Behavior During Adolescence and Adulthood," *Science* (March 29, 2002): 2470.

131 James P. Steyer, *The Other Parent* (New York: Atria Books, 2002), p. 72.

132 For further discussion of the issues involved in studying the effect of pornography on children, see Dick Thornburgh and Herbert S. Lin, *Youth, Pornography and the Internet, National Academy Press* (Washington, DC: National Academy Press, 2002); and Althea C. Huston, Ellen Wartella, and Edward Donnerstein, "Measuring the Effects of

Sexual Content in the Media, A Report of the Kaiser Family Foundation" (May 1998) (available at <http://www.kff.org/content/archive/
1389/content.pdf> (last accessed July 11, 2002).

133 The lack of social science findings on the matter did not stop the
Supreme Court from issuing their ruling in *Ginsberg* v. *New York*.
They note: "To be sure, there is no lack of 'studies' which purport to
demonstrate that obscenity is or is not 'a basic factor in impairing the
ethical and moral development of . . . youth and a clear and present
danger to the people of the state.' But the growing consensus of
commentators is that 'while these studies all agree that a causal link
has not been demonstrated, they are equally agreed that a causal
link has not been disproved either' " (p. 642).

134 Huston et al., "Measuring the Effects of Sexual Content in the
Media," pp. 13–14.

135 Edward P Mulvey and Jeffrey L. Haugaard, *Report of the Surgeon
General's Workshop on Pornography and Public Health* (Washington,
DC: Office of the Surgeon General, US Public Health Service, 1986),
p. 23.

136 Elizabeth Oddone-Paolucci, Mark Genius, and Claudio Violato,
"A Meta-Analysis of the Published Research on the Effects of Pornography," in Claudio Violato, Elizabeth Oddone-Paolucci, and Mark
Genius (eds.), *The Changing Family and Child* (Aldershot, UK: Ashgate Publishing, 2000), pp. 52–3.

137 For a description of the role of violent content in determining television ratings, see <http://www.mpaa.org/tv>. For the criteria used in
granting film ratings, see <http://www.filmratings.com>.

138 For a further discussion of this balancing and re-balancing, see
Etzioni, *The New Golden Rule*, pp. 58–84.

139 For an excellent discussion, see Mary Ann Glendon, *Rights Talk*
(New York: The Free Press, 1991).

140 For further discussion, see "Implications of Select New Technologies
for Individual Rights and Public Safety," 15 *Harvard Journal of Law
and Technology* 257 (Spring 2002).

141 See Glendon, *Rights Talk*, pp. 1–17, and Amitai Etzioni, *The Spirit of
Community: The Reinvention of American Society* (New York: Touchstone, 1993), pp. 164–6.

142 For further discussion, see Robert Bellah, Richard Madsen, William
M. Sullivan, Ann Swidler, and Steven M. Tipton, *Habits of the Heart*
(Berkeley: University of Californial Press, 1985).

143 Many European nations ban the broadcasting of certain material considered harmful to minors. In addition, associations of Internet Service Providers have established codes of conduct for protecting minors
and have established an Internet Content Rating Association to develop an international ratings system. Christopher J. P. Beazley,
"Report of the Committee on Culture, Youth, Education, the Media,

and Sport to the European Parliament," session document A5-0037/ 2002 (February 20, 2002). For a survey of childcare policies in other nations, see Sheila B. Kamerman and Alfred J. Kahn, *Child Care, Family Benefits, and Working Parents* (New York: Columbia University Press, 1981).

144 Volokh, "Speech and Spillover."

145 See Etzioni, *The New Golden Rule*, pp. 73–7; Amitai Etzioni, *My Brother's Keeper: A Memoir and a Message* (New York: Rowman & Littlefield, 2003), ch. 17.

146 Richard Posner, "The Trust About Our Liberties," *The Responsive Community* (summer 2002): 4.

147 In *Tinker* v. *Des Moines School District*, the Court ruled against a high school's policy of expelling students for wearing black armbands to school in protest at the Vietnam war. The Court stated that "Students in school as well as out of school are 'persons' under our Constitution. They are possessed of fundamental rights which the State must respect just as they themselves must respect their obligations to the State" (p. 511).

148 In his discussion of children's rights, Harry Brighouse considers the types of rights children have, rather than the extent of their rights. He distinguishes between welfare rights (which pertain to the direct well-being of the child) and agency rights (which involve the right to make choices about how to act) of children. He argues that if children do not have the same rational capacity as adults, providing for the welfare rights of children often means curtailing their agency rights. His full discussion of this matter can be found in Harry Brighouse, "What Rights (if any) Do Children Have?" in David Archard and Colin MacLeod (eds.), *The Moral and Political Status of Children* (New York: Oxford University Press, 2002).

149 For an excellent history of how ideas about childhood have evolved, see Phillippe Aries, *Centuries of Childhood* (New York: Knopf, 1962).

150 See, e.g., Heins, "Rejuvenating Free Expression," pp. 43–9.

151 ACLU Freedom Network, "ACLU Hails Victory as California Library Agrees to Remove Internet Filters from Public Computers," January, 28, 1998. Available at <http://www.aclu.org/news> (italics added)

152 American Library Association, "Access to Electronic Information, Services, and Networks: An Interpretation of the Library Bill of Rights." Available at <http://www.ala.org/alaorg/oif/electacc.html>.

153 American Library Association, Library Bill of Rights, section V (adopted June 18, 1948; amended February 2, 1961, and January 23, 1980, inclusion of "age" reaffirmed January 23, 1996, by the ALA Council).

154 The ALA advises its members: "Librarians should not breach a child's confidentiality by giving out information readily available to the parent from the child directly. Libraries should take great care to limit

the extenuating circumstances in which they will release such information." ALA, "Questions and Answers on Privacy and Confidentiality" (drafted May 20, 2002). Available at <http://www.ala.org/alaorg/oif/privacyqanda.html> (last visited June 13, 2002).

155 Fahrenheit 451.2

156 ACLU Freedom Network, "ACLU Enters VA Library Internet Lawsuit on Behalf of Online Speakers," February 6, 1998. Available at <http://www.aclu.org/news/n020698a.html> (italics added)

157 Michael S. Wald, "Children's Rights: A Framework for Analysis," *University of California Davis Law Review* 12 (1979): 274.

158 Archard and MacLeod (eds.), *The Moral and Political Status of Children*, p. 2.

159 *Horton* v. *Goose Creek Elementary School*, 690 F. 2d 470 (5th Cir. 1982), pp. 479, 481–2.

160 John Locke, *Two Treatises of Government*, ed. Peter Laslett (Cambridge: Cambridge University Press, 1960), vol. II sections 55, 57.

161 Nathan Tarcov, *Locke's Education for Liberty* (Lanham, MD: Lexington Books, 1999), pp. 71–3.

162 Locke, *Two Treatises of Government*, vol. II, section 59.

163 John Stuart Mill, *On Liberty*, ed. Alan Ryan (London: Norton & Company, 1997), p. 48.

164 To take just one example from among many, the index to Ronald Dworkin's *Taking Rights Seriously* (Cambridge, MA: Harvard University Press, 1977) includes neither "children" nor "minors."

165 In *New York* v. *Ferber*, the Supreme Court upheld a statute prohibiting not only the production of child pornography, but also the distribution or possession of child pornography. The Court argued that "the distribution network for pornography must be closed if the production of material which requires the sexual exploitation of children is to be effectively controlled" (458 US 747 (1982), p. 759).

166 *Ashcroft* v. *Free Speech Coalition*, 122 S. Ct. 1389 (2002).

167 For an additional discussion, see chapter 2.

168 Jeffrey Narvil, "Revealing the Bare Uncertainties of Indecent Exposure," 29 *Columbia Journal of Law and Social Problems* 85 (Fall 1995): 90, 111.

169 *Roth* v. *United States*, 354 US 476 (1957), p. 489.

170 *Memoirs* v. *Massachusetts*, 383 US 413 (1966); *Miller* v. *California*, 413 US 15 (1972).

171 C. J. Burger, quoting in part *Roth* vs. *United States*, 354 US 476 (1957), p. 489 (citation omitted). See also, e.g., *Jenkins* v. *State of Georgia*, 418 US 153 (1974); *Hamling* v. *United States*, 418 US 87 (1974); *Smith* v. *United States*, 431 US 291 (1977); *Pope* v. *Illinois*, 481 US 497 (1987).

172 *Reno* v. *ACLU*, 000 US 96–511 (1997), p. 44.

173 Popular Music Under Siege.

174 Kelly M. Doherty, "www.obscenity.com: An Analysis of Obscenity and Indecency Regulation on the Internet," 32 *Akron Law Review* 259 (1999): 286.

175 Philip E. Lewis, "A Brief Comment on the Application of the 'Contemporary Community Standard' to the Internet," 22 *Campbell Law Review* 143 (Fall 1999): 166.

176 535 US (2002), pp. 16–20.

177 535 US (2002) (Justice O'Conner concurring), pp. 3–4.

CHAPTER 4 PRIVACY AND SAFETY IN ELECTRONIC COMMUNICATIONS

1 There were 161 separate provisions in the Uniting and Strengthening America by Providing Appropriate Tools Required to Intercept and Obstruct Terrorism Act of 2001, Pub. L. 107–56. (Hereinafter USA Patriot Act.)

2 Senator Hatch, during the discussion of USA Patriot on the Senate floor, warned: "I think of the civil liberties of those approximately 6,000 people who lost their lives, and potentially many others if we don't give law enforcement the tools they need to do the job" (Cong. Rec. S11023–11024; daily ed. October 23, 2001).

3 Nadine Strossen, "Remarks at the Communitarian Dialogue on Privacy v. Public Safety" (November 26, 2001) (transcript available from the Communitarian Network).

4 I refer to a zone because I don't claim that there is a precise point of balance one can identify at which the government tilts clearly in one direction of the other.

5 For further detail on the responsive communitarian position, see the Responsive Communitarian Platform, available at <http://www.communitariannetwork.org/platformtext.htm> (last modified October 1991); Amitai Etzioni, *The New Golden Rule: Community and Morality in a Democratic Society (New York: Basic Books, 1996); Amitai Etzioni, The Limits of Privacy (New York: Basic Books, 1999). For a critical treatment, see Elizabeth Frazer, The Problems of Communitarian Politics (Oxford, UK: Oxford University Press, 1999).*

6 See Etzioni, *The New Golden Rule*, chs. 1 and 2.

7 For additional discussion of such criteria, see Amitai Etzioni, *The Spirit of Community: The Reinvention of American Society* (New York: Touchstone, 1993), pp. 177–90; *The New Golden Rule*, pp. 51–5; and *The Limits of Privacy*, pp. 10–15.

8 Richard A. Posner, "Security versus Civil Liberties," *The Atlantic Monthly*, December 2001, p. 46.

9 For a short overview of FBI abuses during the 1970s and the responses to them, see Cong. Rec. S10992–10994 (daily ed. October 25, 2001; statement by Sen. Leahy).

10 Katharine Q. Seelye, "Draft Rules for Tribunals Ease Worries, But Not All," *New York Times*, December 29, 2001, p. B7.

11 James Murry, *Wireless Nation* (Cambridge, MA: Perseus, 2001), pp. 20, 313. According to Philip C. W. Sih, though early fax technology was developed in the nineteenth century, and the US military began using well-developed fax machines during World War Two, it was not until the 1970s that the integration of new modem, computer, and telephone technologies created the circumstances for a "fax explosion" (see *Fax Power* (New York: Van Nostrand Reinhold, 1993), pp. 1–5.

12 Peter Salus, *Casting the Net* (Reading, MA: Addison-Wesley, 1995), pp. 82–3.

13 The decision in the Supreme Court case of *United States* v. *New York Telephone Company* notes that "a pen register is a mechanical device that records the numbers dialed on a telephone by monitoring the electrical impulses caused when the dial on the telephone is released" (434 US 159, 161 n.1 (1977)). The decision in *United States* v. *Giordano* notes that a pen register is "usually installed at a central telephone facility [and] records on a paper tape all numbers dialed from [the] line" to which it is attached (416 US 505, 549, n. 1 (1974)).

14 Murry, *Wireless Nation*, pp. 20, 313.

15 Nielsen/Net Rating for July 2001, available at <www.nielsennetrating. com> (last visited December 6, 2001).

16 18 USC 3122, 3123, 2518.

17 *Smith* v. *Maryland*, 442 US 735 (1979) established that the use of a pen register to obtain the numbers dialed from a telephone did not constitute a search under the Fourth Amendment, and therefore did not require a warrant. The court held that "it is doubtful that telephone users in general have any expectation of privacy regarding the numbers they dial, since they typically know that they must convey phone numbers to the telephone company and that the company has facilities for recording this information and does in fact record it for various legitimate business purposes."

18 Peter Swire writes: "The term 'pen register' comes from the old style for tracking all of the calls originating from a single telephone. At one point, the surveillance technology for wiretapped phones was based on the fact that rotary clicks would trigger movements of a pen on a piece of paper" ("Administration Wiretap Proposal Hits the Right Issues But Goes Too Far," Brookings Institution Analysis Paper #3, America's Response to Terrorism (The Brookings Institution, Washington, DC) October 3, 2001).

19 Omnibus Crime Control and Safe Streets Act of 1969, Pub. L. No. 90–351, 82 Stat. 197, 211 (1968) codified as amended at 18 USC. §2510–2521 (1982 & Supp. IV 1986). (Hereinafter Title III.)

20 Rep. Nancy Pelosi, on CNN, *Novak, Hunt and Shields*, October 27, 2001. See also "Victoria Toensing Remarks at the Communitarian Dia-

logue on Privacy v. Public Safety" (November 26, 2001) (transcript available from the Communitarian Network). (Hereinafter Toensing remarks.)

21 For a discussion of the various analogies applied, see Lt. Col. Joginder Dhillon and Lt. Col. Robert Smith, "Defensive Information Operations and Domestic Law: Limitations on Government Investigative Techniques," 56 *Air Force Law Review* 135 (2001): 149.

22 The United States Code defines a pen register as a "device which records or decodes electronic or other impulses which identify the numbers dialed or otherwise transmitted on the telephone line to which such device is attached" (18 USC 3127(3) (1994)).

23 Swire, "Administration Wiretap Proposal Hits the Right Issues."

24 Ibid.

25 Field Guide on the New Authorities (Redacted) Enacted in the 2001 Anti-Terrorism Legislation. Available at <http://www.epic.org/privacy/terrorism/DOJ_guidance.pdf> section (last visited January 29, 2002), p. 216A. (Hereinafter DOJ Field Guide.)

26 Electronic Communications Privacy Act (ECPA), Pub. L. 99–508, 100 Stat. 1848 (1986). The ECPA extended the section of the US Code requiring a court order to intercept oral or wire communications to include electronic communications; see 18 USC 2511, as amended by ECPA title I, sections 101(b), (c)(1), (5), (6), (d), (f)[(1)], 102.

27 For further discussion, see Terrence Berg, "www.wildwest.gov: The Impact of the Internet on State Power to Enforce the Law," *Brigham Young University Law Review* 1305 (2000); James X. Dempsey, "Communications Privacy in the Digital Age: Revitalizing the Federal Wiretap Laws to Enhance Privacy," 8 *Albany Law Journal of Science and Technology* 65 (1997); Dhillon and Smith, "Defensive Information Operations and Domestic Law"; Susan Freiwald, "Uncertain Privacy: Communications Attributes Under the Digital Telephony Act," 69 *South California Law Review* 949 (March 1996); and Paul Taylor, "Issues Raised by the Application of the Pen Register Statutes to Authorize Government Collection of Information on Packet-Switched Networks," 6 *Virginia Journal of Law and Technology* 4 (2001).

28 Christian David Hammel Schultz, "Unrestricted Federal Agent: 'Carnivore' and the Need to Revise the Pen Register Statute," 76 *Notre Dame Law Review* 1215 (June 2001): 1221–3. Swire, "Administration Wiretap Proposal Hits the Right Issues."

29 See 18 USC.A. 2703 (West 2000), which reads: "(a) Contents of electronic communications in electronic storage. A governmental entity may require the disclosure by a provider of electronic communication service of the contents of an electronic communication, that is in electronic storage in an electronic communications system for more than 180 days or less, only pursuant to a warrant issued under the Federal Rules of Criminal Procedure or equivalent State warrant."

30 DOJ Field Guide, section 220.
31 An oft-repeated anecdote that illustrates the point: at the launch of Jini, a wireless device that has the potential to track a user's movements, Sun Microsystems CEO Scott McNealy responded to privacy concerns with the declaration that "You have zero privacy now. Get over it!" For a further discussion, see Jeffrey Rosen, *The Unwanted Gaze: The Destruction of Privacy in America* (New York: Knopf, 2000).
32 See Etzioni, *The Limits of Privacy*, ch. 3.
33 Deborah Russell and G. T. Gangemi Sr., "Encryption," in Lance Hoffman (ed.), *Building in Big Brother* (Santa Clara, CA: Springer-Verlag Publishers, 1995), p. 11. Dorothy E. Denning and William E. Baugh Jr., "Encryption and Evolving Technologies as Tools of Organized Crime and Terrorism" (US Working Group on Organized Crime, National Strategy Information Center, 1997).
34 Jonathan Krim, "High-tech RBI Tactics Raise Privacy Questions," *The Washington Post*, August 14, 2001, p. A01.
35 Steven Levy, *Crypto: How the Code Rebels Beat the Government – Saving Privacy in the Digital Age* (New York: Viking, 2001), pp. 310–11.
36 In practice, it is difficult to make the information completely secure, just as it is difficult to completely delete files. For example, if the operating system needs to perform another task while an encryption application is in progress, it will halt the application temporarily and return to it later. Before it halts the program, it writes the encryption application, and its key, to disk as a safety measure. When the application is completed later, many users do not realize that a version of the unencrypted key will remain on the disk until the computer writes it over. Bruce Schneier, *Applied Cryptography* (New York: Wiley, 1994), p. 148.
37 FBI Director Louis J. Freeh stated that: "From 1995 to 1996, there was a two-fold increase (from 5 to 12) in the number of instances where the FBI's court-authorized electronic efforts were frustrated by the use of encryption that did not allow for law enforcement access" ("Hearing on Encryption Before the Senate Committee on the Judiciary," 107th Cong. (2001)). See also, Etzioni, *The Limits of Privacy*, ch. 3.
38 I wrote "seem" because it is not possible to know whether the National Security Agency has found a way to decrypt high-power encryption. However, the great efforts made to gain keys reinforce the view that the NSA has failed in its endeavors to this effect.
39 See John Perry Barlow, "Cyberspace Independence Declaration," issued February 9, 1996. Available at <http://www.eff.org/~barlow/Declaration-Final.html> (last visited January 22, 2002); and Steven Levy, "The Battle of the Clipper Chip," *New York Times*, June 12, 1994.
40 FBI Director Louis J. Freeh testified that: "The looming specter of the widespread use of robust, virtually untraceable encryption is one of the most difficult problems confronting law enforcement as the next century approaches. At stake are some of our most valuable and reliable

investigative techniques, and the public safety of our citizens. We believe that unless a balanced approach to encryption is adopted that includes a viable key management infrastructure, the ability of law enforcement to investigate and sometimes prevent the most serious crimes and terrorism will be severely impaired" ("Hearing on Encryption Before the Senate Committee on the Judiciary," 107th Cong. (2001)).

41 Roving wiretaps were initially introduced in the ECPA.

42 18 USC 2518 (11)(b) (1994 Supp. IV). The addition of this section was part of the ECPA.

43 Ibid.

44 Ibid.

45 Intelligence Authorization Act for Fiscal 1999, Pub. L. No. 105–272, 604, 112 Stat. 2396, 2413 (1998), amending 18 USC 2518 (11)(b)(1994).

46 The most significant case is that of *United States* v. *Petti*, 973 F.2d 1441, 1444–45 (9th Cir. 1992). For further discussion, see also Bryan R. Faller, "The 1998 Amendment to the Roving Wiretap Statute: Congress 'Could Have' Done Better," 60 *Ohio St. Law Journal* 2093 (1999).

47 USA Patriot Act, section 206 (amending 50 USC 1805(c)(2)(B)).

48 "Hearing on the Foreign Intelligence Surveillance Act of 1978 Before the Subcommittee on Criminal Laws and Procedures of the Senate Committee on the Judiciary," 95th Cong. (1977).

49 Tom Ricks, "A Secret US Court Where One Side Always Seems to Win," *Christian Science Monitor*, May 21, 1982.

50 USA Patriot Act, section 218 (amending 50 USC. 1804(a)(7)(B), 1823(a)(7)(B)). See also 147 Cong. Rec. S11004.

51 Department of Justice overview of the USA Patriot Act, as entered into the Cong. Rec. S 11055 (daily ed. October 25, 2001).

52 50 USC 1806.

53 William Carlsen, "Secretive US Court May Add to Power," *San Francisco Chronicle*, October 6, 2001.

54 USA Patriot Act, sections 214, 216 (amending 50 USC 1842, 1843 and 18 USC 3121, 3123, 3127).

55 Ibid., section 216 A. See also DOJ Field Guide, section 216A.

56 The law is worded in a peculiar way, saying that a single order can be used at any carrier's facility, but not explicitly establishing that the order has nationwide scope. USA Patriot Act, section 216A.

57 Ibid., section 220 (amending 18 USC 2703). See also DOJ Field Guide, section 220.

58 See Etzioni, *The Limits of Privacy*, ch. 3; Levy, *Crypto: How the Code Rebels Beat the Government*, pp. 226–8.

59 See, e.g. Bruce W. McConnell and Edward J. Appal, Draft paper, "Enabling Privacy, Commerce, Security and Public Safety in the Global Information Infrastructure," available at <http://www.epic.org/crypto/key_escrow/white_paper.html> (last visited January 29, 2002);

and statement of Robert S. Litt, Principal Associate Deputy-Attorney General, "Hearing on Privacy in a Digital Age: Encryption and Mandatory Access Before the Senate Committee on the Judiciary, Subcommittee on the Constitution, Federalism, and Property Rights," 105th Cong. (1998). For a fuller history of key escrow, see A. Michael Froomkin, "It Came From Planet Clipper: The Battle Over Cryptographic Key 'Escrow,'" *University of Chicago Law Forum* 15 (1996)

60 JEDI Callusing, "White House Yields a Bit on Encryption," *New York Times*, July 8, 1998, p. D1; Lance J. Hoffman, "Encryption Policy for the Global Information Infrastructure," statement at the Eleventh International Conference on Information Security, Cape Town South Africa, May 9–12, 1995.

61 USA Patriot Act, section 412. AG Order No. 2529–2001, 66 Fed. Reg. (October 31, 2001) (to be codified at 28 CAR pt. 500–501). Military Order of November 13, 2001: "Detention, Treatment, and Trial of Certain Non-Citizens in the War Against Terrorism," 66 Fed. Reg. 57831–57836 (November 16, 2001).

62 Senator Patrick Leahy, speaking ABC News, *This Week*, (Burwell's Information Services, November 18, 2001): "We don't protect ourselves by bending or even shredding our Constitution. We protect ourselves by upholding our Constitution and demonstrating to the rest of the world we will defend ourselves, but we will do it by also defending our own core values." Morton Halperin, "Less Secure Less Free," *The American Prospect*, November 19, 2001, p. 10.

63 "Hearing on the Department of Justice and Terrorism Before the Senate Committee on the Judiciary," 107th Cong. (2001) (statement of Senator Hatch).

64 Attorney-General Ashcroft told Congress that tactics of attempting to scare citizens with "phantoms of lost liberty" "only aid terrorists" and "give ammunition to America's enemies" ("Hearing on DOJ Oversight: Preserving Our Freedoms While Defending Against Terrorism Before the Senate Committee on the Judiciary," 107th Cong. (2001)).

65 *Olmstead* v. *United States*, 277 US 438 (1928), p. 466.

66 *Katz* v. *United States*, 389 US 347 (1967), pp. 351, 361.

67 See, e.g., Anthony G. Amsterdam, "Perspectives on the Fourth Amendment," 58 *Minnesota Law Review* 349 (1974): 384–5; Richard S. Julie, "High-tech Surveillance Tools and the Fourth Amendment: Reasonable Expectation of Privacy in the Technological Age," 37 *Crim. Law Review* 127 (2000): 131–3; Jonathan Todd Laba, "If You Can't Stand the Heat, Get Out of the Drug Business: Thermal Imagers, Emerging Technologies, and the Fourth Amendment," 84 *California Law Review* 1437 (1996): 1470–5; Scott E. Sundby, "'Everyman's' Fourth Amendment: Privacy or Mutual Trust Between Government and Citizen?" 94 *Columbia Law Review* 1751 (1994); *State* v. *Reeves*, 427 So. 2nd, p. 425 (Justice Dennis dissenting).

68 *United States* v. *Maxwell*, 45 M.J. 406 (C.A.A.F. 1996); *United States* v. *Charbonneau*, 979 F. Supp. 1177 (SD Ohio 1997).
69 Dhillon and Smith, "Defensive Information Operations and Domestic Law," p. 150.
70 *Smith* v. *Maryland.* For further discussion of the implications of this case for seizure of electronic communications, see the Department of Justice search and seizure manual, "Searching and Seizing Computers and Obtaining Electronic Evidence in Criminal Investigations," Computer Crime and Intellectual Property Section, Criminal Division, United States Department of Justice (January 2001). Available at <http://www.usdoj.gov:80/criminal/cybercrime/searchmanual.wpd> (last visited January 24, 2002).
71 Dhillon and Smith, "Defensive Information Operations and Domestic Law," p. 150.
72 *United States* v. *Petti*, citing *Maryland* v. *Garrison*, 480 US 79, 84, 94 L. Ed. 2d 72, 107 S. Ct. 1013 (1987).
73 Ibid., citing *United States* v. *Turner*, 770 F.2d 1508, 1510 (9th Cir. 1985).
74 The United States code specifies that in the case of a roving intercept "the order authorizing or approving the interception is limited to interception only for such time as it is reasonable to presume that the person identified in the application is or was reasonably proximate to the instrument through which such communication will be or was transmitted" (18 USC 1518 (11)(b)(iv)); and that the interception "shall not begin until the place where the communication is to be intercepted is ascertained by the person implementing the interception order" (18 USC 1518 (12)).
75 Tracey Maclin, "Another Grave Threat to Liberty," *National Law Journal*, November 12, 2001, p. A20. *Steagald* v. *United States*, 451 US 204 (1981).
76 Clifford S. Fishman, "Interception of Communication in Exigent Circumstances: The Fourth Amendment, Federal Legislation, and the United States Department of Justice," 22 *Georgia Law Review* 1 (Fall 1987): 65–9.
77 Solicitor-General Ted Olsen, on CNN, *Larry King Live*, October 24, 2001.
78 Nadine Strossen, on CNN News International, October 30, 2001.
79 Bart Kosko, "Your Privacy is a Disappearing Act," *Los Angeles Times*, December 2, 2001, p. M5
80 Cited in Adam Clymer, "Anti-terrorism Bill Passes, US Gets Expanded Powers," *New York Times*, October 26, 2001, p. A1.
81 Strossen, "Remarks at the Communitarian Dialogue on Privacy v. Public Safety."
82 Alan Dershowitz, on CNN News International, October 30, 2001.
83 "The USA-PATRIOT ACT Boosts Government Powers While Cutting Back on Traditional Checks and Balances" (ACLU, Leg. Analysis).

Available at <http://www.aclu.org/congress/l110101a.html> (last visited January 17, 2002).

84 Letter from Assistant Director John Collingwood to Members of Congress (August 16, 2000). Available at <http://www.fbi.gov/congress/congress00/collingwood081600.htm> (last visited January 29, 2002).

85 Illinois Institute of Technology Research Institute (IITRI), Independent Review of Carnivore System – Final Report (2000). Available at <http://www.epic.org/privacy/carnivore/carniv_final.pdf> (last visited January 29, 2002), pp. 3.4.4.1.1, 3.4.4.1.3, 3.4.4.1.4, 3.4.4.1.6. (Hereinafter IITRI Report.)

86 Statement of Donald M. Kerr, Assistant Dir. Lab. Div. FBI, "Fourth Amendment Issues Raised by FBI's 'Carnivore' Program: Hearing Before the House Subcommittee on the Constitution of the House Committee on the Judiciary," 106th Cong. 1 (2001).

87 Statement of Donald M. Kerr, Assistant Dir. Lab. Div. FBI, "The 'Carnivore' Controversy: Electronic Surveillance and Privacy in the Digital Age: Hearing before the Senate Committee on the Judiciary," 106th Cong. 3 (2000).

88 Kerr statement, "Fourth Amendment Issues."

89 Affidavit of Randall S. Murch, United States District Court District of New Jersey, *United States* v. *Scarfo* (October 4, 2001). Available at <http://www.epic.org/crypto/scarfo/murch_aff.pdf> (last visited January 29, 2001).

90 Ibid. In his affidavit, Murch explains that the public encryption key is usually a long string of computer data that the user cannot simply memorize. Instead, the user has a pass phrase that enables him to decrypt his files. When the pass phrase is entered into a dialog box, the program decrypts the key and then uses it to decrypt the file.

91 "Judge Orders Government to Explain How 'Key Logger' System Works," *Computer and Online Industry Litigation Reporter*, August 14, 2001, p. 3.

92 Order to search Merchant Services of Essex County, filed May 8, 1999. United States Court District, District of New Jersey. Available at <http://www2.epic.org/crypto/scarfo/order_5_99.pdf> (last visited January 29, 2001). (Hereinafter Scarfo warrant.)

93 The component that records the keystrokes can be set to evaluate each keystroke individually before recording it. When a keystroke is entered, KLS checks the status of the computer's communication ports. The component will only record a keystroke if all the communications ports are inactive. See affidavit of Randall S. Murch.

94 Michael Froomkin, "The Metaphor is the Key: Cryptography, the Clipper Chip, and the Constitution," 143 *University of Pennsylvania Law Review* 709 (January 1995).

95 Hiawatha Bray, "Military-Tech Complex," *Boston Globe*, November 29, 2001, p. C1.

96 Ted Bridis, "FBI Develops New Tools to Ensure Government can Eavesdrop on High-tech Messages," *Associated Press*, October 21, 2001.

97 Bob Port, "Spy Software Helps FBI Crack Encrypted Mail," *Daily News*, December 9, 2001, p. 8.

98 Lou Doliner, "With New Tools, Authorities Can Target Suspects' Computers with Accuracy," *Newsday*, December 12, 2001, p. C08.

99 Statement of Jerry Berman, Executive Director, Center for Democracy and Technology, "Hearing on Protecting Constitutional Freedoms from Infringement by Counter-terrorism Efforts Before the Subcommittee on the Constitution, Federalism, and Property Rights of the Senate Committee on the Judiciary Committee," 107th Cong. (2001). (Hereinafter Berman statement.)

100 See ACLU, "Urge Congress to Stop the FBI's Use of Privacy-Invading Software" (2000). Available at <http://www.aclu.org/action/carnivore107.html> (last visited January 10, 2002). See also Aaron Kendal, "Carnivore: Does the Sweeping Sniff Violate the Fourth Amendment?" 18 *Thomas M. Cooley Law Review* 183 (Trinity Term 2001).

101 See ACLU, "Urge Congress to Stop the FBI's Use of Privacy-Invading Software."

102 "FBI Eavesdrops on e-mail, Crashed Privacy Barriers," *USA Today*, July 24, 2000, p. 16A.

103 Cited in Tom Bridis, "Congressional Panel Debates Carnivore as FBI Moves to Mollify Privacy Worries," *Wall Street Journal*, July 25, 2000, p. A28.

104 IITRI Report, pp. ES.5–E.S.6, xi, xiv, ix, xiii.

105 John Schwartz, "Wiretapping System Works On Internet, Review Finds," *New York Times*, November 22, 2000, p. A19.

106 IITRI Report, p. 3.4.4.1.

107 For an example of the Neo-Luddite position, see Chellis Glendinning, "Notes Toward a Neo-Luddite Manifesto," *Utne Reader* (March/April 1990). For an historical discussion of Luddism, see Kirkpatrick Sale, *Rebels Against the Future* (Reading, MA: Addison-Wesley, 1995).

108 Brief of the United States in Opposition to Defendant's Pretrial Motions, *United States* v. *Scarfo* (July 2001). Available at <http://www2.epic.org/crypto/scarfo/gov_brief.pdf> (last visited January 29, 2002). (Hereinafter Scarfo brief.)

109 Motion to Suppress Evidence Seized by the Government Through the Use of a Keystroke Logger, *United States* v. *Scarfo* (June 2001). Available at <http://www2.epic.org/crypto/scarfo/def_supp_mot.pdf> (last visited January 29, 2002).

110 Scarfo warrant.

111 Richard Willing, "FBI Technology Raises Privacy Issues," *USA Today*, July 31, 2001, p. 3A.

112 Scarfo brief, p. 38.
113 Opinion and Order in the case of *United States* v. *Scarfo*, issued December 26, 2001. Available at <http://lawlibrary.rutgers.edu/fed/html/scarfo2.html-1.html> (last visited January 29, 2002).
114 Etzioni, *The Spirit of Community*, ch. 6; *The New Golden Rule*, chs. 1 and 2.
115 *The Economist* reports that the anti-terrorism bill released by the United Kingdom's home secretary David Blunkett on November 13, 2001 includes a provision that would give public authorities the power to force protestors to remove disguises (*The Economist*, November 17, 2001, p. 54).
116 Statement of Louis J. Freeh, Director, Federal Bureau of Investigation, before the House Appropriations Committee, Subcommittee on Commerce, Justice, State, Judiciary and Related Agencies, 105th Cong. (1998). Available at <http://www.fbi.gov/congress/congress98/hac35.htm> (last visited January 29, 2002).
117 Alan Cullison and Andrew Higgins, "How al Qaeda Agent Scouted Attack Sites In Israel and Egypt," *Wall Street Journal*, January 16, 2002, p. 1.
118 Levy, *Crypto: How the Code Rebels Beat the Government*, ch. 7.
119 18 USC 1518 (5).
120 18 USC 2518 (5) (Supp. IV 1986).
121 See, e.g., *United States* v. *Clerkley*, 556 F.2nd 709, 717 (4th Cir. 1977); *United States* v. *Costello*, 610 F. Supp. 1450, 1477 (N.D. Ill. 1985); *United States* v. *Clemente*, 482 F. Supp. 102. 108–10 (S.D.N.Y. 1979).
122 *Scott* v. *United States*, 436 US 128 (1978), pp. 137–9, 142.
123 The Honorable Bob Barr, "A Tyrant's Toolbox: Technology and Privacy in America," 26 *Journal of Legislation* 71 (2000).
124 IITRI Report, pp. 3.4.4.1.6, ES.5, 3.4.4.1.3.
125 Dan Eggen and Brook Masters, "US Indicts Suspect in September 11 Attack," *Washington Post*, December 12, 2001, p. A01.
126 Berman statement.
127 William Carlson, "Secretive US Court May Add to Power," *San Francisco Chronicle*, October 6, 2001, p. A3.
128 Berman statement.
129 Private communication with Orin Kerr, Washington DC, December 14, 2001.
130 Toensing remarks.
131 50 USC 1804(a).
132 "Law enforcement, rather than a Court, will decide what is 'content' and systems like Carnivore will be used without any real judicial supervision." ACLU, "More on ACLU Objections to Select Provisions of Proposed Anti-Terrorism Legislation" (2001). Available at <http://www.aclu.org/congress/Patriot_Links.html> (last visited January 17 2002).

133 *United States* v. *Rodriguez*, 968 F. 2d 130, 135 (2d Cir. 1992).
134 *Boyd* v. *United States*, 116 US 616 (1886). *Weeks* v. *United States*, 232 US 383 (1914).
135 See e.g. *United States* v. *Leon*, 468 US 897 (1984), which established a "good faith" exception to the exclusionary rule; *Nix* v. *Williams*, 467 US 431, 444 (1984), which created the "inevitable discovery" exception to the exclusionary rule; *Massachusetts* v. *Sheppard*, 468 US 981 (1984), upholding the "good faith" exception; *United States* v. *Calandra*, 414 US 338, 348 (1974), which establishes that the exclusionary rule does not proscribe use of all illegally obtained evidence. For further discussion, see Leslie-Ann Marshall and Shelby Webb, Jr., "Constitutional Law – The Burger Court's Warm Embrace Of An Impermissibly Designed Interference With The Sixth Amendment Right To The Assistance of Counsel – The Adoption Of The Inevitable Discovery Exception To The Exclusionary Rule: Nix v. Williams," n1, 28 *Howard University Law Journal* 945 (1985); Christopher A. Harkins, "The Pinocchio Defense Witness Impeachment Exception to the Exclusionary Rule: Combating a Defendant's Right to Use With Impunity the Perjurious Testimony of Defense Witnesses," *University of Illinois Law Review* 375 (1990): 389–411.
136 "The process that brought you this bill is terribly flawed. After by-passing a Judiciary Committee mark-up, a few Senators and their staffs met behind closed doors, on October 12, 2001 to craft a bill. The full Senate was presented with anti-terrorism legislation in a take-it-or-leave-it fashion with little opportunity for input or review. No conference committee met to reconcile the differences between the House and Senate versions of the bill. We find it deeply disturbing that once again the full Senate will be forced to vote on legislation that it has not had the opportunity to read. Senate offices are closed and staff cannot even access their papers to fully prepare you for this important vote. Regular order is being rejected and it is an offense to the thoughtful legislative procedures necessary to protect the Constitution and Bill of Rights at a time when the rights of so many Americans are being jeopardized." Letter from Laura Murphy, Director ACLU, Washington Office to Senate, "Urging Rejection on Final Version of USA Patriot Act," October 23, 2001. Available at <http://www.aclu.org/congress/1102301k.html> (last visited January 17, 2002).
137 Senator Orin Hatch said before Congress: "We can never know whether these tools would have prevented the attack on America, but, as the Attorney-General has said, it is certain that without these tools we did not stop the vicious acts of last month. I personally believe that if these tools had been in law – and we have been trying to get them there for years – we would have caught those terrorists. If these tools could help us now to track down the perpetrators – if they will help us in our continued pursuit of terrorists – then we should not

hesitate to enact these measures into law. God willing, the legislation we pass today will enhance our abilities to protect and prevent the American people from ever again being violated as we were on September 11." Cong. Rec. S11015 (2001).

138 The House Judiciary Committee held a hearing on the Fourth Amendment issues raised by the FBI's Carnivore Program on July 24, 2000. Testimonies are available at <http://www.house.gov/judiciary/con07241.htm> (last visited January 22, 2002). The Senate Judiciary Committee held a hearing on Carnivore on September 6, 2000. Testimonies are available at <http://www.senate.gov/~judiciary/wl96200f.htm> (last visited January 22, 2002).

139 Press Release, ACLU, "In Unique Tactic, ACLU Seeks FBI Computer Code on 'Carnivore' and Other Cybersnoop Program," July 14, 2000. Available at <http://www.aclu.org/news/2000/n071400a.html> (last visited January 29, 2002).

140 Press Release, EPIC, "Lawsuit Seeks Immediate Release of FBI Carnivore Documents," August 2, 2000. Available at <http://www.epic.org/privacy/carnivore/8_02_release.html> (last visited January 29, 2002).

141 Nick Wingfield and Don Clark, "Internet Companies Decry FBI's E-mail Wiretap Plan," *The Wall Street Journal*, July 12, 2000, p. B11A.

142 Opinion and Order requiring submission of report "detailing how the key logger device function," United States District Court, District of New Jersey, *United States* v. *Scarfo* (August 2001). Available at <http://www2.epic.org/crypto/scarfo/order_8_7_01.pdf> (last visited January 29, 2002).

143 John Schwartz, "US Refuses to Disclose PC Tracking," *New York Times*, August 25, 2001, p. C1.

144 Krim, "High-tech RBI Tactics Raise Privacy Questions."

145 See 114 Cong. Rec. 14, 750 (1968).

146 Official report of the Senate Select Committee on Intelligence, headed by Senator Frank Church, as published in *US News and World Report*, December 15, 1975, p. 61.

147 Jim McGee, "The Rise of the FBI," *Washington Post Magazine*, July 20, 1997, p. W10.

148 50 USC 1803.

149 See Robert O. Keohane, "Governance in a Partially Globalized World," *American Political Science Review* 95/1 (2001): 1–13.

150 See Martin Edmonds, Review of Peter J. Rowe and Christopher J. Whelan (eds.), *Military Intervention in Democratic Societies*, in *International Affairs* 62/ 2 (1986): 290–1; Jeffrey Simpson, "What Happens when Society's Guardians Need Guardians Themselves?" *Globe and Mail*, September 11, 1996.

151 Seymour Martin Lipset and William Schneider, *The Confidence Gap: Business, Labor, and Government in the Public Mind* (Baltimore, MD: Johns Hopkins University Press, 1987).

CHAPTER 5   DNA TESTING AND INDIVIDUAL RIGHTS

1   Barry Steinhardt, "Testimony Before the House Judiciary Committee, Subcommittee on Crime," March 23, 2000. Available at <http://www.aclu.org/congress/1033200a.html>
2   Quoted in ibid.
3   For more discussion, see Amitai Etzioni, *The Limits of Privacy* (New York: Basic Books, 1999).
4   See *The Responsive Communitarian Platform: Rights and Responsibilities* (Washington DC: The Communitarian Network, 1991), and Amitai Etzioni, *The New Golden Rule: Community and Morality in a Democratic Society* (New York: Basic Books, 1996), chs. 1 and 2.
5   For further discussion of notching principles, see Amitai Etzioni, *The Spirit of Community: The Reinvention of American Society* (New York: Touchstone, 1993), pp. 177–90.
6   Brooke A. Masters, "DNA Testing in Old Cases Is Disputed: Lack of National Policy Raises Fairness Issue," *Washington Post*, September 10, 2000, p. A1.
7   Quoted in Manuel Roig-Franzia, "DNA Tests Help Find Moving Suspects," *Washington Post*, November 26, 2000, p. C8.
8   Quoted in *CQ Researcher*, special issue on forensic DNA testing, May 28, 1999, p. 2.
9   Ibid.
10 Kevin Flynn, "Fighting Crime with Ingenuity, 007 Style; Gee-Whiz Police Gadgets Get a Trial Run in New York," *New York Times*, March 7, 2000, p. B1.
11 Interview: "Dr. Paul Ferrara, Director of Virginia Division of Forensic Science, Discusses Gathering of DNA Evidence," *All Things Considered*, National Public Radio, July 27, 2000.
12 There have been some isolated reports that rapists have used condoms and left other semen behind. See Richard Willing, "Criminals Try to Outwit DNA," *USA Today*, August 28, 2000, p. 1A.
13 As Justice Brennan wrote in his opinion in *United States* v. *Wade*: "The vagaries of eyewitness identification are well known; the annals of criminal law are rife with instances of mistaken identification." It has been widely documented that eyewitness accounts are unreliable. Gary L. Wells and Eric P. Seelau summarize findings regarding eyewitness identification: "Although there is no way to estimate the frequency of mistaken identification in actual cases, numerous analyses over several decades have consistently shown that mistaken eyewitness identification is the single largest source of wrongful convictions" ("Eyewitness Identification: Psychological Research and Legal Policy on Lineups," *Psychology, Public Policy and Law* 1 (December 1995): 765). See also Edward J. Imwinkelried's comments, reported below (p. 214).

14 One mismatch that did not involve laboratory error has been reported in Britain (Richard Willing, "Mismatch Calls DNA Tests into Question; Case in Britain Was 'To Be Expected' as Databases Include More Samples," *USA Today*, February 8, 2000, p. 3A). A mismatch that resulted from accidental sample contamination occurred in New Zealand ("Reports Show DNA Crime Errors," *Evening Post* (Wellington), March 10, 2000, National News section, 2). An article in *USA Today* reported numerous cases in which criminals have become DNA savvy. Some criminals have begun wearing condoms during rapes, and some have tried to fool law enforcement by planting other people's DNA at crime scenes (see Willing, "Criminals Try To Outwit DNA," p. 2A).

15 Forensic Science Service home page: <http://www.forensic.gov.uk/forensic/entry.htm>

16 Dr. Dwight E. Adams, Deputy Assistant Director, Forensic Analysis Branch, Federal Bureau of Investigation, "Statement for the Record on Forensic DNA Analysis, before the Subcommittee on Crime of the House Judiciary Committee." Available at <http://www.fbi.gov/pressrm/congress/congress00/dadams.htm>

17 More than 600,000 convicted offender samples to be inputted into the CODIS database are still being analyzed, compared to the roughly 300,000 that are being analyzed for STRs (short tandem repeats). (National Commission on the Future of DNA Evidence, *The Future of Forensic DNA Testing: Predictions of the Research and Development Working Group*, November 20, 2000.)

18 "Commentary by Edward J. Imwinkelried," in *Convicted by Juries, Exonerated by Science: Case Studies in the Use of DNA Evidence to Establish Innocence After Trial* (US Department of Justice, 1996), p. xiv.

19 Barry Scheck, Statement before the Senate Judiciary Committee, June 13, 2000.

20 See, for instance, Philip L. Bereano, "The Impact of DNA-based Identification Systems on Civil Liberties," in Paul R. Billings (ed.), *DNA on Trial: Genetic Identification and Criminal Justice* (New York: Cold Spring Harbor Laboratory Press, 1992). Peter Neufeld and Barry Steinhardt made similar statements at the conference "DNA and the Criminal Justice System," as did Troy Duster. (See David Lazer (ed.), *The Technology of Justice: DNA and the Criminal Justice System* (Cambridge, MA: MIT Press, 2005).)

21 John Kifner, "Police Propose DNA Testing for Every Person Arrested," *New York Times*, December 13, 1998, section 1, p. 52.

22 Dorothy Nelkin and Lori Andrews, "DNA Identification and Surveillance Creep," *Sociology of Health and Illness* 21 (September 1999): 695.

23 For a more detailed discussion of the reasonableness inquiry, see D. H. Kaye, "The Constitutionality of DNA Sampling on Arrest," 10 *Cornell Journal of Law and Public Policy* 455 (2001).

24 Richard Willing, "DNA Links Burglars to Harder Crime," *USA Today*, December 7, 1998, p. 1A.

25 Ibid.

26 See ibid. David Coffman reported that "52 percent of the offenders linked to sexual assaults and homicides by DNA Database matches have had prior burglaries" (Florida Dept. of Law enforcement, "DNA Investigative Support Database: An Overview," paper presented at conference "DNA and the Criminal Justice System").

27 Editorial, "DNA Key to Fighting Crime: Privacy Fears about this Law-Enforcement Tool Are Overblown," *USA Today*, August 21, 2000, p. 16A.

28 Editorial, "Balancing DNA Use," *St. Petersburg Times*, March 29, 2000, p. 14A. Also, see Coffman, "DNA Investigative Support Database."

29 Ibid.

30 See Lazer (ed.), *The Technology of Justice*.

31 Note that some of these matters are covered by state laws, and hence there are some differences in these matters among states.

32 See, for example, Fred Drobner, "DNA Dragnets: Constitutional Aspects of Mass DNA Identification Testing," *Capital University Law Review* 28 (2000): 505–7.

33 Quoted in Richard Willing, "Privacy Issue is the Catch for Police DNA 'Dragnets,' " *USA Today*, September 16, 1998, p. 1A.

34 Quoted in ibid.

35 Eric T. Juengst, "I-DNA-fication, Personal Privacy, and Social Justice," *Chicago-Kent Law Review* 75 (1991): 62.

36 Nelkin and Andrews, "DNA Identification and Surveillance Creep," p. 696.

37 Juengst, "I-DNA-fication, Personal Privacy, and Social Justice," p. 63.

38 See Michael J. Markett, "Genetic Diaries: An Analysis of Privacy Protection in DNA Data Banks," *Suffolk University Law Review* 30 (1996): 203–4.

39 See National Commission on the Future of DNA Evidence, "What Every Law Enforcement Officer Should Know about DNA Evidence," National Institute of Justice, September 1999.

40 Juengst, "I-DNA-fication, Personal Privacy, and Social Justice," p. 64.

41 Nelkin and Andrews, "DNA Identification and Surveillance Creep," p. 698; quote cited from Carey Goldberg, "DNA Databanks Giving Police a Powerful Weapon, and Critics," *New York Times*, February 19, 1998, pp. A1, A12.

42 Paul E. Tracy and Vincent Morgan, "Criminology: Big Brother and His Science Kit: DNA Databases for 21st Century Crime Control?" *Journal of Criminal Law and Criminology* 90 (Winter 2000): 672. See also Timothy Lynch, "Databases Ripe for Abuse: Further Expansion a

Mistake. Soon They'll Want All Citizens' DNA," *USA Today*, August 21, 2000, p. 16A.

43 Presentations at conference, "DNA and the Criminal Justice System," John F. Kennedy School of Government, Harvard University, November 19–21, 2000.

44 On notching, see Etzioni, *The Spirit of Community*, pp. 177–91.

45 Charles W. Petit, "DNA Tests: Suspects and Maybe Newborns," *US News and World Report*, December 28, 1998, p. 10.

46 Reg Whitaker, *The End of Privacy: How Total Surveillance Is Becoming a Reality* (New York: The New Press, 1999), p. 4.

47 "Biometric Identifiers: Privacy Opportunities and Problems," *Privacy & American Business* 4 (1997/98): 20.

48 Ellen C. Greenblatt, "Massachusetts Uses Unisys to Track Criminals," *Datamation* (December 1996): 14; Aileen Crowley, "Me, Myself, and Eye," *PC Week*, May 22, 1995, p. E12; "Biometrics: The Measure of Man," *The Economist*, September 19, 1992, pp. 102–3. Once it is more fully developed, as Ann Cavoukian, Information and Privacy Commissioner of Ontario, Canada, puts it, biometrics will link "the individual irrefutably to his or her identity" ("Biometric Identifiers: Privacy Opportunities and Problems," *Privacy and American Business* 4 (1997/98): 20.

49 Federal Trade Commission, "Personal Information Collection from Children," in *Privacy Online: A Report to Congress* (Washington, DC: FTC, June 1998). Available at <http://www.ftc.gov/reports/privacy3/toc.htm>

50 Suzanne E. Stripe, "Genetic Testing Battle Pits Insurers Against Consumers," *Best's Review – Life/Health Insurance Edition* (August 1996): 38; National Academy of Sciences, *For the Record: Protecting Electronic Health Information* (Washington, DC: National Academy Press, 1997), p. 77.

51 Richard Sobel and Harold Bursztain, "Ban Genetic Discrimination," *Boston Globe*, August 7, 2000, p. A15.

52 See Dorothy Nelkin and Lori B. Andrews, "Whose Genes Are They, Anyway?" *The Chronicle of Higher Education*, May 21, 1999, p. B6.

53 Ibid.

54 See Simson Garfinkel, *Database Nation: The Death of Privacy in the 21st Century* (Beijing: O'Reilly, 2000); Jeffrey Rosen, *The Unwanted Gaze: The Destruction of Privacy in America* (New York: Random House, 2000); Whitaker, *The End of Privacy*; Charles Jonscher, *The Evolution of Wired Life: From the Alphabet to the Soul-Catcher Chip – How Information Technologies Change Our World* (New York: John Wiley & Sons, 1999).

55 Quoted in Edward C. Baig, Marcia Stepanek, and Neil Gross, "Privacy: The Internet Wants Your Personal Info. What's in It for You?" *Business Week*, April 5, 1999, p. 84.

56 Presentations at conference, "DNA and the Criminal Justice System." See also Juengst, "I-DNA-fication, Personal Privacy, and Social Justice," pp. 64–7.

57 Dwight E. Adams, Deputy Assistant Director of the Forensic Analysis Branch of the FBI, "Statement for the Record on Forensic DNA Analysis before the Subcommittee on Crime of the House Judiciary Committee," March 23, 2000.

58 Constance Holden, "DNA fingerprinting comes of age," *Science* 278 (November 21, 1997): 1407 (my emphasis).

59 In recent years, for example, STRs (short tandem repeats) have increasingly replaced VNTRs (variable number of tandem repeats) in testing because they allow more accurate analysis of smaller samples. CODIS uses 13 core STR loci in its analysis (*The Future of Forensic DNA Testing*, pp. 1–2.)

60 Presentation at conference, "DNA and the Criminal Justice System." Also reported in Tim O'Brien, "DNA Tests Are Worth Doing If Innocence Can Be Proved," *Milwaukee Journal Sentinel*, September 11, 2000, p. 11A.

61 See Jim Dwyer, Peter Neufeld, and Barry Scheck, *Actual Innocence: Five Days to Execution and Other Dispatches from the Wrongly Convicted* (New York: Doubleday, 2000), p. 247. See also Brooke A. Masters, "Virginia May Drop Deadline for Death Row Retrials; High Court Has Questioned Several Cases," *Washington Post*, October 14, 2000, p. A1.

62 Barry Scheck, "Statement before the Senate Judiciary Committee," June 13, 2000.

63 For fine additional discussion and recommendations, see *Postconviction DNA Testing: Recommendations for Handling Requests* (Washington, DC: US Department of Justice, 1999).

CHAPTER 6   WHAT IS POLITICAL?

1 Aristotle, *The Politics*, trans. Carnes Lord (Chicago: University of Chicago Press, 1984), 488a7–14. For an overview of some of the competing theories on Aristotle's thesis, see Larry Arnhart, "The Darwinian Biology of Aristotle's Political Animals," *American Journal of Political Science* 38/2: 464–85; John M. Cooper, "Political Animals and Civic Friendship," in *Friendship: A Philosophical Reader* (Ithaca, NY: Cornell University Press, 1993).

2 See, for example, George F. Will, *The Pursuit of Happiness, and Other Sobering Thoughts* (New York: Harper and Row, 1978).

3 See David Brooks and William Kristol, "What Ails Conservatism," *Wall Street Journal* 15 (September 1997).

4   See Amitai Etzioni, "Virtue and the State: A Dialogue between a Communitarian and a Social Conservative," Robert George, *The Monochrome Society* (Princeton, NJ: Princeton University Press, 2001), pp. 207–20.

5   Bruce Ackerman, "Why Dialogue?" *Journal of Philosophy* 86/1 (1989): 5–22.

6   For instance, see Amy Gutmann, *Democratic Education* (Princeton, NJ: Princeton University Press, 1987).

7   See Thomas Lickona, *Educating for Character: How Our Schools Can Teach Respect and Responsibility* (New York: Bantam, 1992).

8   See Dennis Wrong, *The Problem of Order: What Unites and Divides Society* (New York: Free Press, 1994).

9   John Stuart Mill, *On Liberty*, ed. David Spitz (New York: W. W. Norton, 1975), p. 71.

10   Alexis de Tocqueville, *Democracy in America*, trans. Henry Reeve, ed. Phillips Bradley (New York: Alfred A. Knopf, 1991), vol. 2, p. 261.

11   See Alan Wolfe, *Moral Freedom: The Search for Virtue in a World of Choice* (New York: W. W. Norton & Company, 2001).

12   For further discussion, see Amitai Etzioni, *The New Golden Rule* (New York: Basic Books, 1996), pp. 85–159.

13   Ibid.

14   For a particularly cogent discussion of the role of reason in deliberations of ends and not just means, see Philip Selznick, *The Moral Commonwealth: Social Theory and the Promise of Community* (Berkeley, CA: University of California Press, 1992), pp. 524–6. Dennis Wrong illustrates the tendency toward reason in stating: "Many sociologists confine themselves, implicitly at least, to the cognitive rather than the motivational or emotional aspects of interaction, often making tacit assumptions about the latter or simply taking them for granted. Berger and Luckmann explicitly call their vivid account of how actors construct an objective social world that then confronts and constrains them a contribution to the 'society of knowledge'" (*Problem of Order*, p. 60). Although Wrong speaks directly of sociology, the affinity for the rational applies to many disciplines.

15   Miriam Galston, "Taking Aristotle Seriously: Republican-Oriented Legal Theory and the Moral Foundation of Deliberative Democracy," *California Law Review* 82/329 (1994): 355.

16   Jack Knight and James Johnson, "Aggregation and Deliberation," *Political Theory* 22/2 (May 1994): 277–96; 285. Furthermore, Knight and Johnson stress the importance of reason: "Deliberation involves reasoned argument. Proposals must be defended or criticized with reasons.... The crucial point is that parties to deliberation rely only on what Habermas calls the 'force of the better argument;' other forms of influence are explicitly excluded so that interlocutors are free to remain

unconvinced so long as they withhold agreement with reasons" (p. 286, italics omitted).

17 James H. Kuklinski, Ellen D. Riggle, Victor Ottati, Norbert Schwarz, and Robert S. Wyer, Jr., "The Cognitive and Affective Bases of Political Tolerance Judgments," *American Journal of Political Science* 35 (1991): 1–27; 1. See also, James Q. Wilson, "Interests and Deliberation in the American Republic, or Why James Madison Would Have Never Received the James Madison Award," *PS: Political Science and Politics* (December 1990): 559; James H. Kuklinski, et al., "Thinking about Political Tolerance, More or Less, with More or Less Information," in Russell Hanson and George E. Marcus (eds.), *Reconsidering the Democratic Public* (University Park: The Pennsylvania State University Press, 1993), p. 227; Benjamin R. Barber, "An American Civic Forum: Civil Society between Market Individuals and the Political Community," *Social Philosophy & Policy* 13/1 (Winter 1996): 275, 276; James S. Fishkin, *Democracy and Deliberation* (New Haven, CT: Yale University Press, 1991).

18 "[It] would probably not be difficult to reach agreement, even among persons of diverse value orientation, that the following values are conspicuous parts of American culture." The list follows: monogamous marriage, freedom, acquisitiveness, democracy, education, monotheistic religion, freedom and science. Robin M. Williams, Jr., *American Society: A Sociological Interpretation* (New York: Alfred A. Knopf, 1952), p. 389.

19 Marc Mowery and Tim Redmond, *Not in Our Backyard* (New York: William Morrow and Company, Inc., 1993).

20 Claiming to be following the War Department's directives against discrimination, Colonel Noel Parrish desegregated the Tuskegee Army Air Field in 1943. Stanley Sandler, *Segregated Skies: All-Black Squadrons of WWII* (Washington: Smithsonian Institution Press, 1992), pp. 38–9.

CHAPTER 7   ON ENDING NATIONALISM

1 Jessica T. Mathews, "Power Shift," *Foreign Affairs* (January/February 1997): 50ff. See also Saskia Sassen, *Losing Control: Sovereignty in an Age of Globalization* (New York: Columbia University Press, 1996).

2 The term "supranational" is used here to refer to bodies that have the authority to act directly on corporations or individuals in participant nations without having to deal with their government. They differ from international bodies whose legitimacy is derived from the consent of the representative of the participating nations for each and every significant measure – the way, for instance, the United Nations works.

3 Cf. Anne-Marie Slaughter, "The Real New World Order," *Foreign Affairs* (September/October 1997): 183ff.

4   For a discussion of Germany's attitudes toward nationalism in the post-war period, see Mary Fulbrook, *German National Identity after the Holocaust* (Cambridge: Polity, 1999); Michael Mertes, Steven Muller, and Heinrich August Winkler, (eds.), *In Search of Germany* (New Brunswick, NJ: Transaction Publishers, 1996).

5   On the importance of identity for the reconstitution of the international order, see Alexander Wendt, "Collective Identity Formation and the International State," *American Political Science Review* 88/2 (1994): 384–96. See also Anthony D. Smith, *National Identity* (Reno, NV: University of Nevada Press, 1991).

6   Charles Tilly (ed.), *The Formation of National States in Western Europe* (Princeton, NJ: Princeton University Press, 1975).

7   Cf. Slaughter, "The Real New World Order."

8   Lester M. Salamon, *Partners in Public Service: Government: Nonprofit Relations in the Modern Welfare State* (Baltimore: Johns Hopkins University Press, 1995), p. 243.

9   See Nina Eliasoph, *Avoiding Politics: How Americans Produce Apathy in Everyday Life* (Cambridge: Cambridge University Press, 1998).

10 For more discussion, see Amy Sherman, "Should We Put Faith in Charitable Choice?" *The Responsive Community* 10/4 (2000): 22–30.

11 T. R. Reid, "Church of Sweden Is Thriving on Its Own," *Washington Post*, December 29, 2000, p. A24.

12 Robert Putnam, *Bowling Alone: The Collapse and Revival of American Community* (New York: Simon and Schuster, 2000); see also Francis Fukuyama, *The Great Disruption: Human Nature and the Reconstitution of Social Order* (New York: Simon and Schuster, 1999).

13 For a discussion of culture wars in America, see James Davison Hunter, *Culture Wars: The Struggle to Define America* (New York: Basic Books, 1991).

14 Arthur M. Schlesinger, Jr., *The Disuniting of America* (New York: W.W. Norton & Co., 1992).

15 See Sanford Levinson, *Constitutional Faith* (Princeton, NJ: Princeton University Press, 1988).

16 For discussion of the development of the European Union, see Simon Serfaty, *Europe 2007: From Nation-States to Member States* (Washington, DC: Center for Strategic and International Studies, 2000); William James Adams (ed.), *Singular Europe: Economy and Polity of the European Community after 1992* (Ann Arbor: University of Michigan Press, 1992); Robert Keohane and Stanley Hoffman (eds.), *The New European Community: Decision-making and Institutional Change* (Boulder, CO: Westview Press, 1991); Alberta Sbragia (ed.), *Euro-Politics: Institutions and Policymaking in the "New" European Community* (Washington, DC: Brookings Institution, 1992); Dennis Swann (ed.), *The Single European Market and Beyond: A Study of the Wider Implications of the Single European Act* (New York: Routledge, 1992).

17 For discussions of sovereignty and the contemporary world, see Stephen D. Krasner, *Sovereignty: Organized Hypocrisy* (Princeton, NJ: Princeton University Press, 1999); David J. Elkins, *Beyond Sovereignty: Territory and Political Economy in the Twenty-First Century* (Toronto: University of Toronto Press, 1995); Maryann K. Cusimano (ed.), *Beyond Sovereignty: Issues for a Global Agenda* (Boston: Bedford/St. Martin's, 2000); Gene M. Lyons and Michael Mastanduno (eds.), *Beyond Westphalia? State Sovereignty and International Intervention* (Baltimore: Johns Hopkins University Press, 1995).

18 See Harvey B. Feigenbaum, *Global Culture vs. Protectionism: The French and Korean Cases in Comparative Perspective*, prepared for the panel "Hollywood and the World: Site of Power, Sites of Resistance?" American Political Science Association Annual Meeting, Atlanta, September 2–5, 1999.

19 See Mark Imber, "Geo-Governance Without Democracy? Reforming the UN System," in Anthony McGrew (ed.), *The Transformation of Democracy* (Cambridge: Polity, 1997).

20 Robert Michels, *Political Parties* (Glencoe: Free Press, 1949).

21 For discussion on the changing political landscape of a globalized world, see James N. Rosenau and Ernst-Otto Czempiel (eds.), *Governance Without Government: Order and Change in World Politics* (Cambridge: Cambridge University Press, 1992).

CHAPTER 8   CYBERSPACE AND DEMOCRACY

1 See Elizabeth Frazer, *The Problems of Communitarian Politics: Unity and Conflict* (Oxford: Oxford University Press, 1999); Robert Booth Fowler, *The Dance with Community: The Contemporary Debate in American Political Thought* (Lawrence, KS: University Press of Kansas, 1991).

2 Amitai Etzioni, *The New Golden Rule* (New York: Basic Books, 1996), p. 127.

3 Benjamin D. Zablocki, "What Can the Study of Communities Teach Us About Community?" forthcoming in Edward W. Lehman (ed.), *Autonomy and Order: A Communication Anthology* (Lanham, MD: Rowman & Littlefield Publishers, Inc., 2000).

4 For more discussion, see Amitai Etzioni and Oren Etzioni, "Face-to-Face and Computer-Mediated Communities: A Comparative Analysis," *The Information Society* 15/4 (1999): 241–8. A revised version of the article is included in Amitai Etzioni, *The Monochrome Society* (Princeton, NJ: Princeton University Press, 2001).

5 Pew Center for the People and the Press: Technology and Online Use Survey 1998, November 1998, cited in Pippa Norris, "Who Surfs?" in Elaine Ciulla Kamarck and Joseph S. Nye, Jr. (eds.), *Democracy.com:*

Governance in a Networked World (Hollis, NH: Hollis Publishing Company, 1999), p. 81.

6   Gallup Poll, conducted February 20–1, 2000, reported in David W. Moore, "Americans Say Internet Makes Their Lives Better," Gallup News Service, February 23, 2000, Gallup Organization home page, <http://www.gallup.com/index.html>

7   Sherry Turkle, *Life on the Screen: Identity in the Age of the Internet* (New York: Touchstone Books, 1995).

8   For a contrary view, see Jerry Kang, "Cyber-Race," *Harvard Law Review* 113 /5 (2000): 1130–208.

9   For a discussion of MediaMOO, see Amy Bruckman and Mitchel Resnick, "The MediaMOO Project: Constructionism and Professional Community," *Convergence* 1 (Spring 1995); available at <http://www.cc.gatech.edu/~asb/papers/index.html>

10   Howard Rheingold, *The Virtual Community: Homesteading on the Electronic Frontier* (Reading, MA: HarperPerennial, 1993), p. 239.

11   Rob Kaiser, "Internet Has Neighborly Side as Users Build Virtual Communities," *Knight-Ridder Tribune Business News: Chicago Tribune*, Illinois, December 20, 1999. For a discussion of the digital divide between Blacksburg and a neighboring town, see Marcia Stepanek, "A Small Town Reveals America's Digital Divide: Equality has yet to reach the net," *Business Week*, November 4, 1999, pp. 188ff.

12   Norman H. Nie and Lutz Erbring, *Internet and Society: A Preliminary Report* (Stanford Institute for the Quantitative Study of Society, February 17, 2000); available at http://www.stanford.edu/group/siqss/

13   Ibid.

14   Press Release, Stanford Institute for the Qualitative Study of Society, February 16, 2000; available at <http://www.stanford.edu/group/siqss>

15   Nie and Erbring, *Internet and Society*.

16   "Survey Shows Widespread Enthusiasm for High Technology," report from the Kaiser Family Foundation, National Public Radio, and Harvard University's Kennedy School of Government, February 29, 2000; available at <http://www.kff.org>

17   "Email: the Isolation Antidote," in *Tracking Online Life: How Women Use the Internet to Cultivate Relationships with Family and Friends*, a Pew Internet Project Report, released May 10, 2000. Available at <http://www.pewinternet.org/reports>

18   Humphrey Taylor, "The Harris Poll #17: The Impact of Being Online at Home," New York: Harris Interactive Inc., March 22, 2000.

19   See Bruce Bimber, "The Internet and Political Transformation: Populism, Community, and Accelerated Pluralism," *Polity* 31/1 (1998): 133–60. Citing Walter Lippmann, Bimber argues that any problems with a democracy are not the result of a lack of information, and that providing citizens with extensive information will not radically change their political behavior. See also David M. Anderson, "The False

Assumption about the Internet," *Computers and Society*, March 2000, pp. 8–9. Anderson argues that the internet can and does do much more than merely provide information.

20   See "Ross Perot, One-Way Wizard," *The New York Times*, April 24, 1992, sec. A, p. 34 (editorial).

21   For more about this experiment, see Amitai Etzioni, "Teledemocracy," *The Atlantic* 270/4 (1992): 36–9 and "Minerva: An Electronic Town Hall," *Policy Sciences* 3/4 (1972): 457–74.

Index

CPSIA information can be obtained
at www.ICGtesting.com
Printed in the USA
BVHW040410240421
605749BV00010B/58